COMING CLEAN

COMING CLEAN

The Rise of Critical Theory and the Future of the Left

ERIC HEINZE

The MIT Press
Cambridge, Massachusetts
London, England

The MIT Press
Massachusetts Institute of Technology
77 Massachusetts Avenue, Cambridge, MA 02139
mitpress.mit.edu

The MIT Press would like to thank the anonymous peer reviewers who provided comments on drafts of this book. The generous work of academic experts is essential for establishing the authority and quality of our publications. We acknowledge with gratitude the contributions of these otherwise uncredited readers.

This book was set in Adobe Garamond Pro by New Best-set Typesetters Ltd. Printed and bound in the United States of America.

Library of Congress Cataloging-in-Publication Data is available.

ISBN: 978-0-262-04958-0

10   9   8   7   6   5   4   3   2   1

EU product safety and compliance information contact is: mitp-eu-gpsr@mit.edu

To George—and to Ivan

We have to own even the darkest parts of our past, understand them and vow never to repeat them. We must not shield our eyes. We must not shrink away lest we lose it all.

—Ketanji Brown Jackson, speech commemorating the sixtieth anniversary of the 16th Street Baptist Church bombing

Contents

1 INTRODUCTION

"This was the right thing to do," sighed Karl Frisch, the first openly LGBTQ+ member of the Fairfax, Virginia, school board. "But it will not sweep away the pain and hurt transgender and other gender-expansive students have experienced for years at the hands of careless peers or adults." It was a sizzling day in the summer of 2021, and by a unanimous vote the board had just adopted rights for trans kids. Frisch felt relieved after school boards in neighboring counties had "descended into chaos" caused by "extremists" who wanted "to deny these students their very existence."[1] From that day onward, teachers and staff would be expected to call children by their preferred names and pronouns—if a trans pupil in the past had been clothed and spoken to as a girl, the child could now decide to be called "he" and "him." The children were also free to use bathrooms and locker rooms matching their chosen identities.

Not everyone celebrated. Traditionally minded parents, both white and nonwhite, had already marched against the new rules. Why did their race matter? They were also demonstrating against their children being taught critical race theory, a set of ideas about how racism has driven US history and society. That protest in turn sparked a counterprotest from liberal parents, including Michelle Leete, who snapped at her conservative rivals: "Let them die."

Leete was a member of the local Parent-Teacher Association and local vice president of the National Association for the Advancement of Colored People (NAACP), one of the leading civil rights organizations in the United

States. She branded the right-wing backlash as "anti-education, anti-teacher, anti-equity, anti-history, anti-racial reckoning, anti-opportunities, anti–help people, anti-diversity, anti-platform, anti-science, anti-change agent, anti–social justice, anti–health care, anti-worker, anti-LGBTQ+, anti-children, anti-environment, anti–admissions policy change, anti-inclusion, anti-live-and-let live."[2] Leete immediately apologized for her outburst, but it was too late. Conservatives were already tarring her online as a "hard" leftist who spouts "hateful, incendiary rhetoric."[3]

"TEACHING PEOPLE TO HATE OUR COUNTRY"

A year earlier Donald Trump was still president. Rallying for a second term, Trump blasted a federal diversity training program, charging that course leaders were "teaching people to hate our country." On the campaign trail, he threatened to slash the program's funding.[4] A few weeks later Trump was snarling that his reelection had been stolen, and from that moment onward right-wing assaults on racial and gender politics swung into high gear. Trump's disciple, then rival, then disciple again Governor Ron DeSantis of Florida echoed: "Teaching kids to hate their country and to hate each other is not worth one red cent of taxpayer money." Eyeing his own White House bid, DeSantis growled: "There's no room in our classrooms for things like critical race theory."[5]

The term *critical race theory*, already circulating for decades on college campuses, now spread like wildfire, and people across the globe were googling it. Trump called for a nationwide ban on promoting these ideas in schools and government programs. Steve Bannon, the one-time Trump confidante who was later convicted for contempt of Congress in conjunction with the attacks on the US Capitol on January 6, 2021, boasted that the people scorning race and gender theory were not fanatics but "mainstream suburban moms." He winked at one interviewer: "This is how we are going to win."[6]

But going back to Michelle Leete, what jumps out from her impromptu list is the mix of causes she fused together. Consider the two that sparked the protests, trans rights and racial justice. Where some people would see two very different issues, many on the left see a shared history of social exclusion.

Of course, several items on Leete's list do not belong only to the left. We all want children to learn history, but whose history? How much time should schools spend on the accomplishments of straight, white men and how much on slaves, women, colonized peoples, and ethnic, national, or gender and sexual minorities?

What also jumps out from these battles is an arsenal of new vocabularies. For decades, conservatives had ignored critical race theory, so how did figures such as Trump, DeSantis, and Bannon suddenly become captivated by it? Before January 2020, the term had been heard on the right-wing Fox News network all of three times, then suddenly it was uttered 537 times in May 2021 and more than 900 times the following month.[7] Meanwhile, *transsexual* became *transgender*, then *trans person*, which is the opposite of *cis person*, while *gender* in many contexts replaced *sex* for reasons many people still struggle to grasp. When a bill was introduced in Congress in early 2021 to ban discrimination against LGBTQ+ people, unlikely feminists such as the hard-right Ted Cruz, Josh Hawley, and Tom Cotton suddenly turned incandescent that trans rights were sparking a "war on women."[8]

The mass media soon realized that they needed to bring the public up to speed. For example, the *Healthline* website observed: "Despite their similar definitions, many transgender people don't identify with the term transsexual."[9] Meanwhile, as to critical race theory, one Associated Press article explained that it "examines the way race and racism influences politics, culture and the law."[10] Yet that definition doesn't help much, given that the media have talked about these problems for ages. Surely critical race theory must stand for something more or something different. In another article, *Time* quoted Priscilla Ocen, a Los Angeles academic who describes critical race theory as "calling for a society that is egalitarian, a society that is just, and a society that is inclusive."[11] This gets us closer, chiming with Leete's idea that values such as equality, justice, and inclusion are about more than just race. Also at stake are conflicts around class, sex, gender, religion, poverty, nationality, and any number of intersections of these and other traits.

In fact, *intersectionality* is another term being newly bandied about. It means that histories of oppression include subgroups that divide and interact in complex ways, so we cannot generalize about any single group. For example, in Western societies the higher status of whites over nonwhites has in some ways overlapped with, but in other ways differed from, the higher status of men over women. Black women are situated neither like white women nor like Black men.[12] Given the range of combinations, it will come as no surprise that the policies in Fairfax concerning critical race theory and LGBTQ+ politics form only a subset that we can place under a broader tent known as *critical theory*, which examines a variety of interrelated histories of violence, exploitation, and discrimination.[13]

MEMORY POLITICS

Today we find critical theorists—or "crits," as they are often called—around the world, hatching many of the ideas that propel the left. This is why I usually refer to leftist, progressive, and critical theory interchangeably in this book, even though distinctions could be drawn between them.[14] Crits write in fields as varied as economics, law, politics, war, media, education, art, and climate change, and it can be hard to find much unity among them, yet many crits accept some version of the following point: *it is crucial to educate the public about patterns of oppression waged by and within Western societies over hundreds of years.*[15]

Some people dismiss this trend as "grievance studies," serving, as Trump and DeSantis would have it, to make people "hate" Western liberal democracies. It can also be described in more neutral terms as *memory politics* because we can remedy current social controversies only by grasping their historical roots.[16] If you wonder whether dwelling on the past is time well spent, then try telling a group of leftists that you're a pragmatist—that you refuse to brood about history because you want to tackle problems in the here and now. The longer you persist, the more you will end up talking about history because only in history do patterns of longstanding injustice emerge. Race, colonialism, gender, sex, war, and economic exploitation involve problems of historical knowledge, so there is no such thing as *no* memory politics. State-orchestrated amnesia itself is a form of memory politics—indeed, the most sinister kind. It is the history taught in Putin's Russia and Xi's China. It is the history favored by school boards in the United States that want to replace the words *slave trade* in children's textbooks with euphemisms like *involuntary relocation* or to describe nineteenth-century plantation slavery as an opportunity for slaves to learn "skills" that "could be applied for their personal benefit."[17]

Memory politics unfold in two steps. *Memory* forms the first step, where we gather evidence about past injustices. But, for crits, *politics* forms the second and decisive step because harms caused by racism, colonialism, sexism, heteronormativity, or militarism have never stopped. These evils have continued into the present and can never be overcome until the public understands them. Recall William Faulkner's quip: "The past is never dead. It's not even past."[18] Memory politics demands that we connect the dots from past wrongs to present crises. We will end cycles of injustice only by publicly and proactively communicating the West's bleak histories to future generations.[19]

Memory politics can be called the left's most powerful contribution to today's world, as a quick comparison makes clear. A few centuries ago, our disputes about justice often involved questions about who held the rightful claim to a throne, or how powers should divide between the church and the state, or what kind of authority a monarch could legitimately wield over other members of the aristocracy. But nowadays, when you find yourself locked into a war of words around the dinner table, I doubt you are debating those types of questions. More likely, you are arguing about issues such as race, class, sex, or gender. Here are a few examples. Typical social problems today involve topics as different as earning power, street crime, illegal immigration, health care, environmental protection, child protection, abortion rights, weapons possession, substance abuse, criminal justice, or access to education. At first glance, these issues seem to have little in common, yet in all of them discussions about unfair impacts based on race, class, sex, or gender often end up playing a crucial role.

Progressive stances do not always triumph in debates on these issues, yet the left's single greatest achievement in today's society consists in having defined the very terms we use to discuss justice, regardless of the positions each of us may take on any given controversy. People like Trump and DeSantis may holler right-wing stances in debates about race, class, sex, or gender, but what leftists pioneered long ago was a culture in which *these* are the issues that define the arguments we are all having and the ways in which we are all thinking about justice. Leftists often claim to speak from an underdog position, yet when it comes to the single most powerful idea in ethics, law, and politics—the idea of justice—it is the left that has defined our conversations. To shape culture in such a pervasive way is to wield power indeed.

Once justice is defined in terms of race, class, sex, or gender, our debates swiftly become debates about history. We saw this in Fairfax's culture wars, which involved plenty of memory politics. Again, recall school board member Frisch lamenting the "pain and hurt . . . experienced for years" by trans kids. Today, battles about memory are raging around the world. In 2020, more than 250,000 people signed a petition to the British Parliament entitled "Teach Britain's Colonial Past as Part of the UK's Compulsory Curriculum." The document insisted that by educating children about "the events of the past, we can forge a better future." How would this education work? The petition stated: "Colonial powers must own up to their pasts by raising awareness of the forced labour of Black people, past and present mistreatment of BAME [Black, Asian, and Middle Eastern] people, and most importantly, how this contributes to the unfair systems of power at the foundation of our modern society."[20] At that time, Britain's government was headed by Prime Minister Boris Johnson of the Conservative Party, whose minister for education dismissed the campaign, announcing that he did not want to "pile on" more topics in schools.[21] Yet the petition authors fired back: "Vital information has been withheld from the people by institutions meant to educate them."[22] One of them recalled that she had read Charlotte Brontë's *Jane Eyre* and Jane Austin's *Sense and Sensibility* in school but "never got to read a book with a person of colour in it."[23]

COMING CLEAN

In this book, I discuss some topics that might at first seem unrelated, such as the Ukraine war, LGBTQ+ people in Cuba, the concept of "hatred" in international relations, and the problem of left-wing antisemitism. I also discuss plenty of history, yet this is not a history book. Most of my focus is not on what I have just described as step 1 of memory politics but on step 2—not on recording facts but on how facts are then spread into public awareness.

For more than a century, critical theorists have revolutionized what it means to discuss history. Today, crits can be found around the world, but in this book I focus on voices active in western Europe and North America. These voices rightly reject efforts to whitewash history through tales of national grandeur. They rightly demand that we must come clean about Western violence and exploitation at home and abroad. At step 2 of memory politics, they also rightly exhort us to push history beyond the seminar rooms and meeting halls. They argue that we must teach the public how to scrutinize centuries of Western wrongdoing, and any crit will tell you that the task is far from complete.

But this leads to my main question: How have crits taught the public about the left's *own* histories? A defining feature of critical theory is the left's ethos of collective self-examination, sometimes called "autocritique."[24] What this means is that leftists feel entitled to insist that we must all take a critical view of Western history because they have always reflected on the left's own histories, openly and candidly confessing leftist failures. For example, today's leftists usually distance themselves from atrocities committed in Stalin's Soviet Union, Mao's China, Pol Pot's Cambodia, and the North Korea of the Kim dynasty. In other words, when it comes to a memory politics *of the left,* most leftists today do take step 1. The problem is that they never take step 2. They never carry knowledge of leftist atrocities out of the seminar room and onto the streets. The left pushes the widest possible public education about Western wrongdoing, yet engages in no public education about leftist wrongdoing.

But surely this is how politics always works? Doesn't everyone in politics talk more about their rivals' evil than about evil on their own side? Perhaps. But then what do leftists mean when they insist that they engage in collective self-scrutiny? Why do they even bother making that claim? What light does it shed on the positions they advocate? As I argue in this book, to name just two examples for now, no tradition of leftist self-scrutiny can explain how a leading public intellectual such as Noam Chomsky, arguably the best-known American progressive of his generation, could have told the

Ukrainian people in 2022 that they ought to bear Russia's onslaught as if it were a "hurricane."[25] Nor can any such tradition explain how Jeremy Corbyn, leader of Britain's opposition Labour Party from 2015 to 2020, could oversee repeated episodes of antisemitism within his ranks while standing on the sidelines, clueless about how to respond.

Depending on definitions, all and sundry people have been described as leftist, from Olympe de Gouges to Karl Marx, Vladimir Lenin, Kwame Nkrumah, Martin Luther King Jr., Simone de Beauvoir, Malcom X, Fidel Castro, Angela Davis, Michel Foucault, Jürgen Habermas, and Ruth Bader Ginsberg. We could add many more, only to discover that it would be futile to try unifying them under any single set of ideas, not least because they have waged battles against each other. In this book I do not attempt to define leftism but focus only on a few ideas that have exerted influence in recent years. Clearly, figures such as Chomsky and Corbyn do not represent the entire left, yet they raise questions about whether today's leftists are practicing the kind of self-scrutiny that they rightly demand from the rest of us.

This book puts some challenges to the left but not in the usual right-versus-left way. Nowadays the most predictable way to bash the left is through attacks on "wokeness," yet I am not antiwoke. I am pro-woke, but pro a very different kind of woke.[26] Another way to bash leftists would be to recite long lists of their hypocrisies, yet that tactic, too, would get us nowhere because hypocrisies arise everywhere in politics. Just to compare, conservatives today rail endlessly about free speech, yet in recent years we have seen them crack down on peaceful protesters and limit educators' choices to teach even an author such as Toni Morrison.[27] So for all my criticisms of the left, I shall have no warmer words for the right. Yes, conservatives—the clue lies in their name—may sooner or later be willing enough to concede their classist, racist, colonial, sexist, heteronormative, militarist, and other such histories. Indeed, in some countries conservatives have come up from behind to promote women and minorities within their parties and movements more successfully than their leftwing rivals.[28] Yet for the most part, conservatives have come late to the table of historical responsibility, and many still can't find the door.[29] At various points in this book, I certainly mention conservatives, but my aim is not to match every criticism of leftist injustice with a comparison to injustice on the right. I do not attempt to balance every rebuke of socialism with a comparison to capitalism or every objection to the Soviet Union with a comparison to some Western nation at the same period.

Rather, the achievement of having conquered the very terms of our debates about justice comes with more responsibility than many leftists have been willing to acknowledge. If the left is to maintain any integrity in our public conversations, it must start to do what it has taught the rest of us to do. It is time for the left's memory politics *of the left* to progress from step 1 to step 2—to proceed from merely confessing leftist injustices to actively teaching the widest possible public about them. After all, if leftists do not think that mass education about *leftist* injustices is vital, then it becomes a mystery as to why they think that education about *Western* injustices should merit any attention at all. When leftists fail to take charge of their own histories, the right inevitably sweeps in to do it for them, often in mischievous ways. Of course, there are more forms of injustice between heaven and earth than only "Western" ones and "leftist" ones. Yet Western leftists have drawn repeatedly on this binarism without seriously considering both sides of it, so this book is not about all forms of injustice but focuses instead on leftist attitudes toward the left's own injustices. The reason democracy exists is so that we can review the past and debate solutions for the future, but leftists must change their attitudes toward history if they are to contribute credibly to that future.

I BASICS

So makest thou faith an enemy to faith,
And like a civil war settest oath to oath,
Thy tongue against thy tongue. O, let thy vow
First made to heaven, first be to heaven performed.
. . . .
What since thou sworest is sworn against thyself
And may not be performèd by thyself.
. . . .
It is religion that doth make vows kept,
But thou hast sworn against religion,
By what thou swearest against the thing thou swearest,
And makest an oath the surety for thy truth
Against an oath! The truth thou art unsure
To swear, swears only not to be forsworn—
Else what a mockery should it be to swear!
But thou dost swear only to be forsworn,
And most forsworn to keep what thou dost swear.
Therefore thy later vows, against thy first,
Is in thyself rebellion to thyself;
And better conquest never canst thou make
Than arm thy constant and thy nobler parts
Against these giddy loose suggestions.
—William Shakespeare, *King John*

Critical theory traces largely back to the nineteenth century, when industrialization was widening the gaps between elites and working people. In 1845 the German publicist Friedrich Engels witnessed crushing exploitation in Britain, where workers "were not human beings" at all. Not only men and women but even children had been reduced to "machines toiling for a few aristocrats."[1] Workers faced grueling hours with few protections, often suffering injuries and illnesses with no safety net provided by employers or the state. At the end of the workday they returned to crowded, unsanitary neighborhoods, and still languished in poverty after decades of toil. Industrialization brought capitalism to its "logical conclusion" by "turning workers into machines pure and simple."[2] For Engels, capitalism would be the final stage in a progression of social hierarchies that had structured human societies from time immemorial.[3] Workers everywhere had to throw off their parasitic employers and repressive governments.

FROM MARX TO CRITICAL THEORY

Engels's collaborator, Karl Marx, would soon be toiling away at the British Library to write the anticapitalist bible *Das Kapital*, which was later published in three volumes in 1861, 1886, and 1894. Marx saw private property becoming ever more concentrated in the hands of elites. Classical economics had promised that through hard work people at the bottom could improve their circumstances, yet all around him he witnessed their quality of life plummeting. Marx saw capitalism on a collision course with itself, fueling ever-accelerating cycles of consumption and competition that would become unsustainable, and predicted that this would in turn push economies worldwide to collapse.

In Marx's vision, an age of socialism would follow in which workers would more efficiently and more fairly meet people's needs. Workers would take on active roles in a self-governing society without the big property owners and overweening governments that had kept exploitative practices in place. At first, collectivization of property would unfold in a postcapitalist state, yet in a further future the very apparatus of the state, founded on the age-old hierarchies of rulers and ruled, would become superfluous. This "withering away" of the state would usher in the transition from socialism to communism, the final stage of human history.[4]

Marx and Engels were far from alone in challenging capitalism, which was reviled on both the traditionalist right and the progressive left. At the same time, the left had long been fragmented, often pitting revolutionaries against reformists.[5] By the early twentieth century, global capitalism had indeed swung from one crisis to the next, yet it had not crumbled. History had failed to follow the path that Marx and Engels predicted, while reports of Soviet brutality following the Bolshevik Revolution of 1917 spurred further rifts on the left.[6] In 1930s Germany, a philosopher named Max Horkheimer coined the term *critical theory* to seek new ways of scrutinizing industrial societies without being bound to the letter of Marx's writings.[7] Horkheimer joined his colleagues at the Institute for Social Research in Frankfurt, later known as the Frankfurt School, studying society by drawing eclectically on politics, philosophy, economics, sociology, psychology, literature, and the arts.[8]

These thinkers reshaped the concept of history in ways that may no longer be apparent to people in the West today. After all, many of us have grown up in cultures where challenges to authority are familiar, so we may underestimate the shift sought by a figure such as Horkheimer, born in 1895. In a tradition dating back to antiquity, intellectuals had always peered into history to contemplate the social problems they observed around them, yet by the nineteenth century this study was still an elite pastime. For the most part, schoolrooms were still molding citizens to conform with established values. In one 1889 edict, Kaiser Wilhelm II declared that German primary education needed to cultivate "the fear of God and love for the fatherland." He even took a step further, calling on schools to "convince young people that the teachings of social democracy not only contradict the divine commandments and Christian moral teaching, but are in reality impossible to implement and their consequences are equally destructive for the individual and the whole."[9]

Similarly, an 1897 English schoolbook projected Victorian ideals of the middle-class family backward as a constant over time, teaching that in the Middle Ages "the head of the household, who made the final decision in all things, was of course the man. The housewife reigned as mistress of kitchen and pantry, and took special care in devoting her efforts to childrearing."[10] So it comes as no surprise that Horkheimer and his colleagues wondered whether our ways of understanding the past needed to be overhauled. Over the next hundred years, progressives reconceptualized the study of history to make it a public exercise in collective self-scrutiny. In the decades after World War II, Western education increasingly emphasized that citizens should think independently about the world around them, without blindly obeying institutions that root their authority in their past or present social status.

Of course, workers' exploitation had long preoccupied leftists, but this was never their sole concern. Alongside economics, tensions caused by racial, ethnic, colonial, gender, and other hierarchies had long lurked on the radar and after World War II took center stage.[11] Marxist assumptions about a single oppressed class—"Workers of all nations, unite!"—shifted toward a focus on multiple forms of oppression, meaning that leftism no longer translated into a single set of ideas.[12] Even figures such as the German philosophers Martin Heidegger and Carl Schmitt and the French novelist Louis-Ferdinand Céline, who deeply influenced leftist critiques of capitalism, detested socialism in equal measure—although their own fascist leanings would later leave them with plenty to answer for.[13]

In the latter half of the twentieth century, leftism often looked less like a united movement and more like targeted responses to local conflicts. In much of Latin America, progressive movements were driven by poverty, corruption, workers' exploitation, and US domination.[14] In Africa, they were often inspired by anticolonial struggles and economic forces operating beyond local control.[15] In the United States, the left frequently focused on race, ethnicity, gender, sexuality, and other identitarian struggles.[16] In western Europe, differences in, for example, Dutch, Swedish, French, German, Italian, Greek, and Portuguese leftism confirmed that progressives were often responding more to immediate demands than to global aspirations. The range of schools drawing from and feeding into each other became dizzying—Marxism, critical race theory, critical legal studies, postcolonial studies, feminism, queer theory, and others.

THE RADICAL CRITIQUE OF WESTERN LIBERAL DEMOCRACY

Words such as *leftist, crit, progressive,* and *radical* overlap in complex ways. Some who bear these labels would wholly overthrow or thoroughly overhaul Western institutions. Others by no means reject mainstream liberal or democratic values but believe the West must change course if these values are to serve all citizens. So we cannot view the left as a monolith. In this book, I am interested not in what *all* leftists think, or what *only* leftists think, but in what I shall call "the Radical Critique of Western Liberal Democracy," particularly as embraced by Western leftists. It can be summarized as follows: *Over several centuries, Western societies have damaged millions of lives through militarism, economic exploitation, colonialism, racism, patriarchy, heteronormativity, and other forms of injustice on a global scale. Yes, such evils have also arisen outside Western societies, yet their Western versions have proved to be extensive, systemic (or "structural"), and exceptionally destructive.*[17]

Of course, any visitor to cities such as Beijing and Mumbai will know that nowadays no clear lines separate "Western" from "non-Western." In some countries it is conservatives who voice ideas contained in the Radical Critique. For example, in Russia and Iran it is largely the religious traditionalists who believe that Western politics and economics have undermined their culture.[18] Yet for Western crits the crucial point is that the West's power has long ruled the globe with grievous consequences. Marx and Engels had hoped for a unified left, claiming that by eliminating economic classes we would eliminate other inequalities, but in the nineteenth century writers such as the antislavery activist Frederick Douglass and the women's rights activist Susan B. Anthony were already creating an identity-conscious politics.[19] By the mid-twentieth century, the shift seemed irreversible as yesterday's worldwide proletariat morphed into today's patchwork of identity groups.

In 1955 the Martinican writer and statesman Aimé Césaire published *Discourse on Colonialism* after the Caribbean Island had traversed plantation slavery and colonial repression. Césaire abhorred that millions of people had been "torn from their gods, from their land, from their customs, from their lives." World War II and the Holocaust were still recent memories when Césaire deplored: "It would be worthwhile to study, clinically and in detail, the methods of Hitler and Hitlerism—to lay bare to the oh-so distinguished, oh-so humanist, oh-so Christian bourgeois of the twentieth century that deep down inside he is carrying a Hitler that is unaware of itself, a Hitler that *inhabits* him, a Hitler that is his *demon*."[20] Around the same time, the philosopher Jean-Paul Sartre lashed out at European elites: "You have pushed your love of culture to the point of self-indulgence, as if you were oblivious to the massacres being waged in your name." He admonished that populations exploited by Western powers were still talking about Western humanism, "but only to chastise us for our inhumanity."[21]

Of course, placing one class above another is no Western invention, nor are evils such as slavery, militarism, economic exploitation, and patriarchy. Yet crits respond that Westerners cannot legitimately condemn other societies when we have failed to come clean about our own pasts. However much some crits might be branded as Stalinists, most of them have no problem with democratic values and indeed accuse the West of abandoning its own proclaimed values, undermining opportunities for mass political participation at home and abroad.[22] Another illustrious Martinican, Frantz Fanon, diagnosed the resentments that Western domination had bred: "The emergence of violence amid a colonized people will be proportionate to the violence inflicted by the contested colonial regime."[23] For crits, concepts such as "free" markets, "whiteness," "masculinity," "heterosexuality," and, indeed, "the West" never exist outside of politics. We can understand "white" only by asking how it emerged in power-political contrast to "nonwhite," "man" in contrast to "woman," and so forth.[24] The West has long claimed to champion values such as individual freedom, equal citizenship, economic opportunity, advancement through merit, self-government, and the rule of law, yet crits argue that these values have been betrayed through networks of privilege and exclusion.[25]

One important idea in the Radical Critique is the problem of *systemic* injustice, which means that injustice equals more than the sum of its parts. When a Minneapolis police officer brutally killed the African American George Floyd in 2020, no leftist viewed the event as a fluke but rather as part of a centuries-old chronicle of white racism. Crits argue that economic, racial, ethnic, colonial, patriarchal, and heteronormative injustices do not occur by chance.[26] These injustices encompass more than a few odd killings, a few incidental police beatings, a few haphazard episodes of school or work-place discrimination. Incidents such as Floyd's murder might at first look like dots randomly splashed on a page, but there are many such dots and they link up.[27] What makes it possible for us to identify economic, racial, ethnic, patriarchal, and heteronormative hierarchies is precisely their systemic character.[28] This is why I speak not just about a critique of liberal democracy but about a *radical* critique. In the words of the postcolonial scholar Uday Singh Mehta, racial, ethnic, and other forms of exclusion amount to more than "a mere occasional happenstance."[29] Instead of viewing injustices as separate or discrete, crits talk about patterns born in the past and persisting still into our own time.

When crits talk about "systemic" or "structural" injustice, they are talking about something more than occasional deviations from a background normality of equality and fairness. Their point is that the default normality itself is unjust. Mehta speaks of a "liberal exclusion" that is "intrinsic" to the West.[30] Incidentally, he does not use *liberal* here in the way English speakers often use that word today, as a synonym for *leftist* or *progressive*. He means the opposite, an earlier or "classical" liberal philosophy dating back to the eighteenth century. That older liberalism had proliferated high-minded ideals of universal human dignity, individual freedom, and civic equality, yet in practice the benefits were bestowed mostly on property-owning white males.[31]

For crits, histories of repression rarely evaporate through on-paper changes in law and policy because ingrained attitudes take time to change. Prejudices may seem to vanish, yet they reemerge in new guises. Crits describe these patterns as part of the normalization of injustice—that is, domination works best by convincing subordinates of the rightness of their own lower status.[32]

In 1949 Simone de Beauvoir, another leading twentieth-century philosopher and Sartre's longtime companion, pioneered contemporary feminism in her groundbreaking tome *The Second Sex*. De Beauvoir witnessed parallels to racial domination through women's socialization into subordinate roles. The "young man's entrance into life" entailed no clashes between his dual callings "as a male and as a human being." From his earliest years, "his easier destiny was announced." This privileged status contrasted with that of a girl, who would grow up to face "a divorce between her human condition and her identity as a woman."[33] A decade later, in 1957, the Tunisian writer Albert Memmi observed processes by which colonized peoples' inferior status became internalized. Memmi compared "the negrophobia of the Negro" to "the antisemitism of the Jew."[34] These problems identified under the Radical Critique do not coincide in all respects, yet nor do crits see them as wholly unrelated.

I should note that I refer in this book mostly to "systemic" injustice because "structural" sounds as if oppression follows fixed patterns, while crits teach about oppression as enduring through time even while mutating in its outward forms. In America's pre–Civil War South, racism had taken the form of lawful slavery, but then after the war it transformed into other types of discrimination and violence. After the civil rights reforms of the 1950s and 1960s racism often became more subtle and informal. Official pronouncements that slavery had ended, or that segregation had ended, often told us little about how racism was reconfiguring. Similar observations have been made about women and LGBTQ+ people, who have steadily achieved greater equality in Western nations yet still often face violence and discrimination.[35]

Systemic injustice links in turn to *unconscious bias* and *institutional discrimination*. These terms remind us that supremacist conduct continues even where members of a historically privileged group believe they harbor no hostilities toward other groups.[36] In Britain in the 1990s, one high-profile incident catapulted both of these ideas into public awareness. The teenager Stephen Lawrence, from an African Caribbean background, was ambushed and murdered by white thugs. The police launched an investigation but later dropped all charges against the perpetrators and even bugged and followed members of Lawrence's family.[37] A government committee later found that the police had bungled the case compared to how they would have treated white victims, even though the officials involved sincerely believed they held no racist views.[38] This finding underscored how ordinary people become complicit in racism even when they have no intention of doing so and believe they hold no racist attitudes. We become racists despite our good intentions. A few decades after the assault on Lawrence, the killing of George Floyd rekindled concerns about institutional racism in the United States, a society that some people had hoped to see as "postracial" after Barack Obama's two-term presidency.[39] Floyd's death underscored that police were excessively targeting people of African backgrounds and readily subjecting them to violence.[40]

Also relevant here is the problem of *microaggressions*, which denote ways in which we provoke people inadvertently, perpetuating systemic exclusion even when our words or deeds seem harmless. In 2022 an aide to Britain's royal family repeatedly asked the African Caribbean charity director Ngozi Fulani, who had been born and raised in London, "Where are you *really* from?"[41] Or consider online chats in which we read the recurring meme "Trans women are con men." Such asides may be spoken offhand but can hit hard at a trans person or someone with a trans child or family member, regardless of our views on controversies around, say, the restrooms trans people should use or the competitive sports they should play.[42]

Opposite to these types of "micro" remarks, we find exclusion at a "macro" level where whole populations can participate in oppressive practices without knowing it and without feeling any ill will toward the victims. You could call these acts *macroaggressions* insofar as ordinary practices intend no harm but can have oppressive effects.[43] After all, many of us prosper within global economies that rely on exploitative means of production and trade. To acquire coffee, tea, cocoa, clothing, electronics, and countless other goods, we become complicit in systemic oppression. Even closer to home, we may enjoy a night out at a good restaurant, unaware that kitchen staff are migrants who lack the means to achieve decent working conditions.[44] We become perpetrators regardless of the private moral codes that, we would like to think, guide our everyday lives.

In chapter 1, I noted that the left has largely defined our controversies about injustice regardless of the positions we individually take. This means that our debates about injustice involve the Radical Critique of Western Liberal Democracy even when we are not examining it in any rigorous or comprehensive way. And this is why some of the voices I discuss in this book, although seemingly marginal, often stake out influential viewpoints on important issues of the day. For crits, the Radical Critique stands not merely as a point of view but as a precondition for any legitimate point of view. Crits accept that we may disagree about the best policies to promote and the best politicians to elect, but they will not accept that any of us should state a view about, say, class, race, gender, sexuality, economics, diplomacy, or warfare without some prior grounding in the Radical Critique. For example, we may differ about LGBTQ+ rights, but we will not be taken seriously without basic grounding in the histories of heteronormativity. We may differ about abortion rights, but we will not be taken seriously without basic grounding in the histories of control over women's bodies. We may differ about affirmative action, but we will not be taken seriously without some basic grounding in histories of racial discrimination.

3 HISTORIES TEACHING

Museums dedicated to memory politics have multiplied over the years to educate the public about histories of Western injustice. The Holocaust Memorial Museum was launched in Washington, DC, in 1993, followed less than a decade later by a museum in Berlin honoring the history of Jews in Germany. The National Women's History Museum went online as a virtual resource in 1996, and a London venue entitled Queer Britain welcomed its first visitors in 2018. In 2007, the British city of Liverpool inaugurated the International Slavery Museum, and in 2023 the International African American Museum opened in Charleston, South Carolina.[1]

These museums are examples of step 2 in memory politics, where history moves out of seminar rooms and meeting halls and into public consciousness. Such initiatives do not always aim to topple traditional historical narratives. Often their goal is more to fill in the gaps, expanding and deepening public knowledge by connecting dots from past discrimination to injustices occurring in our own time. These initiatives emerge not only in museums but in our everyday lives, where we find public and private organizations hosting programs, workshops, and training sessions to promote ethnic, religious, gender, and LGBTQ+ diversity.[2] These programs' efficacy has been questioned, but for the foreseeable future they show how ideas from critical theory have moved into the mainstream via schools, workplaces, the mass media, and other channels. It is worth taking a few moments to consider this step 2, where history talks to society.

VERGANGENHEITSBEWÄLTIGUNG AND
ERINNERUNGSKULTUR

Recall that in the term *memory politics*, both components are crucial: the *memory* component (step 1) means recording and preserving historical knowledge, and the *politics* component (step 2) refers to campaigns aimed at informing the public about past injustices and their links to ongoing social problems.[3] This second step hearkens back to Karl Marx's famous quip: "Philosophers have only ever *interpreted* the world in various ways; the point, however, is to *change* it."[4] Ideas might bounce around in textbooks and classrooms, but if they are to spur change then they must find their way into broad public awareness. There can be no wall between theory and practice: memory politics is never just about private commemoration but also about acting in the world.

Marx's call to arms has continued to echo in leftist slogans such as "Silence is complicity" and Sartre's "Not to choose is still to choose."[5] Sartre largely created the contemporary French image of the *intellectuel* in contrast to its English cognate. Sartre's term translates better as "public intellectual" as opposed to what he called the *savant* or technocratic expert. The *savant* aims to recite impartial facts and judgments as if hovering above the political fray, while *les intellectuels* place their careers on the line by taking positions on the great struggles of the day.[6]

These two steps, "memory" and "politics," recording history and then spreading knowledge about it, have proliferated in Germany for decades as responses to World War II and the Holocaust. One prominent concept is *Vergangenheitsbewältigung*, "confronting the past." It includes archives and history books but also demands a public reckoning in politics, education, media, and culture. An alternative translation might be "managing the past," but I dislike that phrasing because it sounds too much like "crisis management," which often means spinning and downplaying embarrassments in the hope that people will forget them.[7]

Public explorations of historical memory became prominent in the second half of the twentieth century, as witnessed by novels such as Günter Grass's *Die Blechtrommel* (*The Tin Drum*) and Heinrich Böll's *Billard um halb zehn* (*Billiards at Half-Past Nine*). Both were published in 1959 and counted among the first major confrontations with the Nazi past, as parallel trends emerged beyond German borders. In 1963 the French filmmaker Alain Resnais released *Muriel, ou le Temps d'un retour* (*Muriel, or The Time of Return*). As the film opens, the main character's stepson, Bernard, has just completed his military service in Algeria, where he participated in torturing a young woman, perhaps a political dissident. Bernard's sense of guilt derails his life and relationships, egging him on to suicide. In several films, most famously the seemingly unpolitical *L'année dernière à Marienbad* (*Last Year at Marienbad*, 1961), Resnais asks how fragmented pasts construct and reconstruct us, in turn summoning and recomposing those pasts. A few years earlier in *Nuit et brouillard* (*Night and Fog*, 1956), Resnais had counted among the first directors to explore the methods and technologies that were used to carry out the Holocaust. That project was later carried forward in films such as Claude Lanzmann's *Shoah* (1985), Louis Malle's *Au revoir les enfants* (*Goodbye, Children*, 1987), and, more recently, László Nemes's *Saul fia* (*Son of Saul*, 2015). In yet another film, *Mon oncle d'Amérique* (*My American Uncle*, 1980), Resnais recorded the biologist and philosopher Henri Laborit defining the living organism as "memory in motion."[8] Yet amnesia always forms part of memory, and I would wager that humans are better described as amnesia in motion, a trait highlighted in such Rainer Werner Fassbinder films as *Die Ehe der Maria Braun* (*The Marriage of Maria Braun*, 1978) and *Die Sehnsucht der Veronika Voss* (*Veronika Voss*, 1982).

In 1968, just prior to the Romanian dictator Nicolae Ceaușescu's "Cultural Rectification" of the early 1970s, Lucian Pintilie's film *Reconstituirea* (*The Reenactment*) showed how the officially re-created memory of a teenager's entirely trivial breach of law entailed heavier consequences in the hands of low-level functionaries than his original breach, ultimately culminating in his death. In 1974, Carlos Saura's *La prima Angélica* (*Cousin Angelica*) probed a character whose life ends up destroyed under Spanish fascism, followed in 1976 by Bernardo Bertolucci's portrayal of fascist violence in *Novocento* (*1900*). In 1977 the American series *Roots* was the first mass broadcast television epic to trace Black Americans' historical memory back to the African continent, through slavery and Jim Crow.[9]

Related to *Vergangenheitsbewältigung* is *Erinnerungskultur*, which refers to a "culture of memory" and stresses remembrance not only as a private experience but as a project for all government and society. Long heard among Holocaust survivors was the lament, "We can forgive, but we must never forget."[10] It placed knowledge above blame and retribution. Prosecuting perpetrators or compensating victims has often been impossible, nor can such responses ever suffice because there can be no remedy for mass atrocities. The only remaining option has been to call for educating later generations. Next worst to the actual crimes would be amnesia around them. A failure to take step 2 of memory politics, the step of proactive dissemination of history, would nullify step 1, the step of recording history. Skeptics inevitably roll their eyes at such efforts, grumbling that we cannot undo the past and should stop obsessing about it. In May 2023, Suella Braverman, the Conservative British home secretary, of Asian background, railed that white people bear no "collective guilt" over their role in slavery and should not be "blamed for things that happened before they were born." According to Braverman, "The defining feature of [Britain's] relationship with slavery is not that we practised it, but that we led the way in abolishing it. We should be proud of who we are."[11] Yet, again, there can be no such thing as *no* memory politics because we cannot grasp today's injustices without recognizing their roots in the past.

Memory politics in itself is neither left-wing nor right-wing. Germany promotes Holocaust education in a progressive vein of national *self-inculpation* by promoting mass education about the nation's historical wrongdoings. Yet neo-Nazis have their own memory politics of denying or mocking the Shoah, propagating myths of national *self-exculpation*, as I further explore in chapter 8. When Vladimir Putin's Russia and Xi Jinping's China promote official histories through public education and mass media, they propagate national self-exculpation, omitting or sanitizing historical injustices by propagating one-sided myths of collective virtue and benevolence.[12] The notion of studying the past as an exercise in national self-inculpation still remains highly unusual, and carries forward the tradition of critical theory first promoted by Max Horkheimer and the Frankfurt School. As any crit will acknowledge, public awareness campaigns such as media initiatives, diversity and equality programs, and other initiatives do not emerge independently of politics. They are political responses to political histories.

GAPS IN HISTORY

"We hold these truths to be self-evident," the American Declaration of Independence proclaimed in 1776, "that all men are created equal, that they are endowed by their Creator with certain unalienable Rights." In the late eighteenth century, this passage captured an idealism borne of the European Enlightenment. In 1791 similar ideals followed in the US Bill of Rights. The First Amendment to the US Constitution proclaims that "Congress shall make no law respecting an establishment of religion, or prohibiting the free exercise thereof; or abridging the freedom of speech, or of the press; or the right of the people peaceably to assemble, and to petition the Government for a redress of grievances." The Fourth Amendment protects citizens from "unreasonable searches and seizures." The Eighth Amendment bans "cruel and unusual punishments," and so forth. The Virginia Declaration of Rights of 1776 had provided a template for the Bill of Rights, and in France the Declaration of Human and Civic Rights proclaimed similar rights and freedoms in 1789.[13]

Before this time, European monarchies had often scorned such protections, so making these pledges seemed like a giant step forward.[14] Yet within a few decades after the French and American Revolutions, it became clear that such rights and freedoms rarely if ever applied to African slaves, Native Americans, colonized peoples, women, and other nonwhite, nonmale populations. The problem for progressives was no longer monarchs laying claim to divine supremacy but nominally representative governments promulgating rules that purported to grant citizen equality. After all, in the 1857 case *Dred Scott v. Sandford*, the US Supreme Court recited values of individual liberty not to strike down slavery but to uphold slaveholders' rights to keep their slaves.[15] In the 1873 case *Bradwell v. Illinois*, the Court held that the Fourteenth Amendment to the Constitution, which requires states to guarantee to all citizens equal protection of the laws, was consistent with women's exclusion from professional legal practice.[16] In the 1896 case *Plessy v. Ferguson*, the Court recited values of equal protection for all citizens under law—not to abolish racial segregation but to uphold it.[17] Many more examples can be cited.[18] Similarly, according to Marx, systems of individual rights, above all private-property rights, were serving not to promote greater opportunity for ordinary workers but merely to entrench and to justify existing class hierarchies. Marx by no means rejected Enlightenment values such as individual freedom and a vibrant press, both of which were essential to his career.[19] However, he argued that classical individual rights served not to overthrow privilege but to reconfigure it, all the while stamping it with the imprimatur of rights and freedoms for all.[20]

Despite these criticisms, plenty of more centrist intellectuals have maintained an allegiance to the institutions of liberal democracy. In the twentieth century, one leading writer to do so was the philosopher Karl Popper, who published *The Open Society and Its Enemies* in 1945. While the embers of Nazism smoldered, Popper defended liberal democracy against totalitarian encroachments. He condemned socialist dictatorships in an era when admiration even for Stalin's Soviet Union was still common on the left.[21] In 1971, another leading exponent of liberal democracy, the Harvard political philosopher John Rawls, followed up with *A Theory of Justice*. Rawls formulated a detailed model for liberal democracy as a framework for pursuing the greatest level of justice that a modern society could realistically expect. Then in 1977 the legal theorist Ronald Dworkin published *Taking Rights Seriously*, another contribution toward explaining the burdens placed on any legal system that is adopted to safeguard individual rights.

These writers explicitly or implicitly rejected Marxist currents by affirming the value and function of individual-rights regimes. Writing in the mid-twentieth century, they had experienced a post World War II era very different from the Europe that Marx and Engels had known, including middle-class expansions and rising educational and working conditions for manual workers. For these new advocates of liberal democracy, systems of individual rights, admittedly far from perfect, offered guarantees for women and minorities who had long been excluded from equal legal protections.[22] To be sure, Popper, Rawls, and Dworkin never undertook minute surveys of past wrongs committed by Western nations. They left that task to historians, surely assuming that readers would grasp how their models inherently rejected slavery, colonialism, segregation, sexism, and other such wrongs.

Yet for crits these efforts were not enough, given that such books barely skimmed step 1 of memory politics and never performed any step 2 at all. Admittedly, these men did not deny histories of Western brutality, yet from a crit standpoint their models scarcely progressed beyond tacit acknowledgments of the West's bleak pasts. For crits, then, it was not enough to stop at step 1, merely acknowledging textbook histories or tacitly weaving them into their analyses. The decisive moment could come only with step 2, when we proactively teach these histories to the public. This is how crits ended up at odds with mainstream liberal democracy. Most crits did not object to core democratic values, yet they viewed figures such as Popper, Rawls, Dworkin, and their fellow travelers as striking compromises with the status quo, neglecting the essential step 2 of memory politics even while acknowledging step 1.

COSTS AND BENEFITS

Edward Colston was an eighteenth-century merchant and philanthropist from Bristol in the southwest of England. His wealth derived in part from the slave trade, which prompted several activists to tear down a statue of him at a Black Lives Matter demonstration in 2020. Today there is no single view on the left about how to deal with public monuments that honor figures linked to past injustices.[23] Yet crits surely would agree on a more basic point: it would never be legitimate to assert that Colston's charitable donations can ethically offset the slave trading from which he profited. For crits, it would be outrageous to claim, "Certainly, Colston's wealth derived from slavery, but look at how well he spent it!" Or to take another example, for crits the millions of lives damaged or destroyed during the 1947 partition of India can never be counterbalanced by recalling whatever benefits British colonial rule may have brought to India.[24]

In other words, no crit accepts a cost–benefit computation that would justify a past atrocity by reciting offsetting benefits. Far from praising

Colston's philanthropy as a tactic to diminish the evils of the slavery, crits would cite that kind of rhetoric as grounds for amplifying their condemnation and prompting them to investigate how the notion of a valid utilitarian trade-off could even surface in anyone's mind. Of course, a question arises about whether leftists themselves indulge in such calculations when countering engineered famines and mass murders in the Soviet Union with claims such as, "At least everyone had a home," or "At least everyone had a job," or "At least everyone had health care." Be that as it may, after the Bristol marches, the *Guardian* columnist Nesrine Malik connected a few historical dots. She recalled the "deep inequalities that run, like cracks, from the past to the present." Malik portrayed British history as a "legacy of supremacy, both racial and national," arguing that this legacy lives on "not just in our streets and squares but in our politics, our education and our economy." She accused Britain of being "as delusional about the moral integrity of its colonial heroes as it is about the health of its race and ethnic relations."[25]

Of course, no one rejects weighing up costs and benefits under all circumstances. Finite resources mean that lawmakers must constantly make unsatisfying trade-offs—for example, reducing the budget for public parks to increase the budget for health care. However, if we care about memory politics, then the central point remains: straightforward profit-maximizing calculations cannot lead to just outcomes when the price paid involves mass brutality. Indeed, not only crits reason this way. Mainstream defenders of Enlightenment liberal values reached that conclusion long ago.[26] Weighing costs against benefits can certainly be ethical (or is at any rate unavoidable) under some circumstances, yet it is widely regarded as inadmissible under others.

Taking a step further, let's assume for now that Western societies have made some progress on social justice over the past century. For example, consider the rising numbers of successful members of ethnic-minority groups, women, and LGBTQ+ persons. For crits, these improvements by no means license us to downplay abuses that members of these groups have faced in the past and continue to face. For example, Barack Obama's presidency may well have launched a postracial era in America—though, again, plenty of people doubt it—yet crits would still argue that the successes of Obama and other prominent African Americans do not diminish centuries of racism that preceded them or the ongoing problems of racism in our own time.

Rivals sometimes accuse the left of indulging in anachronisms. They argue that we cannot judge people and events from the past according to today's ethical standards. After all, some whites in earlier times sincerely believed they were acting in the best interests of slaves and colonized peoples. Some men sincerely believed they were acting in the best interests of their wives and daughters through sexist practices. Some therapists inflicted coercive treatments on LGBTQ+ persons, sincerely believing that they were curing mental illness. Some industrialists inflicted economic exploitation because they sincerely believed that hard work and sacrifice would keep society from degenerating. Along the same lines, let's assume that Edward Colston sincerely believed that his philanthropy outweighed any evils linked to his involvement in the slave trade. The strategy behind all these defenses is obvious: we cannot hold past perpetrators responsible if they acted with benevolent motives.[27]

Yet no crit accepts these apologetics. Here, too, far from diminishing past injustices, references to benign aspirations only fuel crits' questions about how such worldviews have served to justify oppressive hierarchies. For crits, concrete outcomes must trump virtuous motives. The good intentions of perpetrators and of their supporters and collaborators cannot diminish the harms caused by mass injustices. If a crit were to argue that we must spread knowledge about slavery, segregation, classism, colonialism, sexism, and LGBTQ+ oppression, it would not suffice to respond: "But today's values are different from those of earlier eras" or "But not everyone in earlier times approved of these practices."

What matters for crits is not to blame individual actors but to teach about how entire societies could have rationalized mass injustice by framing it in the language of justice, as in the legal cases *Dred Scott, Bradwell, Plessy v. Ferguson*, and others. No one expresses this idea better than the twentieth-century French historian Michel Foucault, who dissects sciences such as psychology and criminology, which, he observes, emerged in the nineteenth century with all the seeming benevolence of Western humanism. These new disciplines promised breaks from benighted methods of earlier times, yet in practice they served to construct entire classes of people as deviants, thereby prescribing social and psychological normality so as, in turn, to coerce conformity either overtly or subtly. Foucault did not blame scientists or clinicians individually and indeed spent little if any time asking about their motives, except perhaps anecdotally. Above all, he promoted public awareness about how policies presented in good faith as civilized and compassionate can function as tools of repression.[28]

II AMNESIA

Yes, the liberal west is hypocritical, applying its high standards very selectively. But hypocrisy means you violate the standards you proclaim, and in this way you open yourself up to inherent criticism—when we criticize the liberal west, we use *its own standards*.
—Slavoj Žižek, "We Must Stop Letting Russia Define the Terms of the Ukraine Crisis" (emphasis added)

4 HURRICANES RAGING

In 1994, Moscow unleashed forces in Chechnya, following up with attacks on Georgia in 2008, Ukraine in 2014, Syria in 2015, and again Ukraine in 2022. All the while, the Kremlin threatened other former Soviet and satellite nations, yet Western responses were mixed. Some prominent figures wanted appeasement while others demanded a hard line, and these schisms never split across a tidy left–right divide.[1]

Shortly after Russia's incursion into Ukraine in February 2022, the veteran activist Lindsey German published a *Guardian* op-ed denouncing any response by the British government that would fuel hostilities.[2] German was not quite a household name though she had come to prominence two decades earlier after founding the Stop the War Coalition, a group that spearheaded a million-strong march against participation in George W. Bush's Iraq War in 2003, becoming one of the largest political demonstrations in UK history.[3] Stop the War subsequently turned its efforts toward "preventing and ending the wars in Afghanistan, Iraq, Libya and elsewhere."[4] Can German's response to the Ukraine war teach us anything about today's left?

CONTEXT AND HISTORY

Many factors drive armed conflicts. Sometimes nations fight just to survive, yet clashes can also be driven by economic interest, diplomatic maneuvering, military pragmatics, news cycles, popular sentiment, and electoral tactics. Governments wage war sometimes directly and sometimes indirectly by supporting foreign regimes or factions.[5] Whether you view any given government involvement as direct or indirect will depend as much on your political leanings as on facts and figures. Indeed, what even counts as reliable facts and figures is often part of the dispute.[6] From the start of the Ukraine conflict, worries amplified about whether Western aid risked crossing the line from indirect engagement to a direct attack on a major nuclear power.[7]

These intricacies mean that people can legitimately oppose war without being in league with their country's—real or fabricated—enemies.[8] This was German's first claim, and she was right to make it. She spurned charges of treachery that are often hurled at antiwar movements. Dissidents opposing interventions in Afghanistan and Iraq were not necessarily "fifth columnists," "traitors," "friends of the Taliban," or "allies of Saddam."[9] German needed to rebuff the same accusations when Stop the War warned against escalating hostilities in Ukraine. She blasted any suggestion that Stop the War was cozying up to Putin. She insisted that the organization viewed the invasion with "horror and sickness" and openly supported Russia's antiwar protesters.[10]

German also chided pundits for playing guessing games about Putin's mental states. Certainly, Western governments needed to anticipate Kremlin movements, yet crits rightly reject the armchair psychologizing that would portray mass brutality as nothing more than the whims of political honchos. In taking this view, German echoed a long tradition of progressive thinkers who have diagnosed modern violence, reminding us about the mighty machines chugging away behind rulers' words and deeds. The cogs and wheels include aspiring cadres, yes-man bureaucrats, opportunist legislators, compliant lawyers and judges, obedient media, co-opted intellectuals, self-serving religious leaders, complacent businesspeople, and oftentimes millions of ordinary citizens. These forces fuel the engines of atrocities, even while individuals scarcely grasp the roles they are playing and believe they are acting honorably.

In the aftermath of World War II and the Holocaust, the political theorist Hannah Arendt described this gliding of everyday routine into mass injustice, dubbing it "the banality of evil."[11] Arendt coined the phrase to explain how networks of violence emerge through something greater than the quirks of individual officials.[12] Her ideas have often been misread to suggest that she was dismissing injustice as banal, or was absolving collaborators of ethical responsibility. Yet her point was that the horrors committed through the machineries of modern, industrial states could no longer be explained via the old "great men of history" narratives, which would reduce mass atrocities to so much horse-trading among cigar-chomping grandees. At first it might have felt comforting to dismiss Nazis as monsters, opposite to ordinary humans, yet the real question was about ordinary humans and how they could commit industrial-scale murder, exterminating millions in a modern world that combined conveyor-belt precision with moral indifference.[13]

Chiming with Arendt, German shifted our attention away from individual politicians toward underlying forces and processes. She reminded us that the West does not approach Russia with clean hands, and recalled the thousands of civilians killed by Western interventions in Serbia in 1999, Afghanistan in 2001, Iraq in 2003, and Libya in 2011. German's j'accuse still rattles nerves today: "There was no referral to the international criminal court for the US following its use of depleted uranium in the Iraqi city of Falluja; no sanctions when Trump ordered the dropping of the 'mother of all bombs' on Afghanistan"—the latter charge particularly prickly at a time when some were praising Trump's supposed pacifism.[14] German rebuffed Western outrage toward Moscow, insisting that "the features now so widely and correctly condemned in Russia's invasion of Ukraine—from cluster bombs to targeting of civilians to besieging cities—have all been part of western wars." She objected that there has been "no outcry at Britain's continuing support for Saudi Arabia's brutal bombing of Yemen."[15]

These points recall long traditions of leftist memory politics. In the key paragraph of her *Guardian* op-ed, German exhorted us to take stock of the West's record before condemning Moscow: "We cannot accept a narrative that ignores *context and history*. . . . The *roots* of this conflict lie in *what has happened since the end of the cold war and the collapse of the Soviet Union*. . . . NATO expanded ever closer towards the Russian border, incorporating 14 new member states, mainly in eastern Europe. It has also expanded into 'out of area operations,' including central involvement in Afghanistan and Libya. It now plans further expansion into the Indo-Pacific as part of an increased military presence against China."[16]

German focuses here on military and power-political factors, yet other commentators have long expanded these criticisms beyond the sphere of military power. Many observers have claimed that Western domination of global commerce, finance, and media have wrought havoc on traditional ways of life around the globe, eroding them through market forces over which whole populations have no control.[17] These critics slam the West for sanctifying values of unlimited choice—for example, the "freedom" to own or not own a car, which becomes no real choice at all and, indeed, is a subtle form of coercion when an economy increasingly renders cars indispensable, or the "freedom" to purchase either domestic or imported goods, even while local goods end up uncompetitive and ultimately driven out of the market by multinational interests. My task for now is not to weigh up these arguments but only to recall what it means for many places to perceive the West as more of a threat than a boon.

WHEN THE TIMELINE BEGINS

Given these inconvenient truths, must we join in German's conclusion that the West was to blame for provoking Moscow? She was certainly right to claim that "context and history" must lie at the heart of our reply. Curiously, however, when she went on to recite the war's context and history, she deleted any mention of her own political home—the left itself. This omission is glaring when we bear in mind that once we plunge into history, a good deal depends on our starting point. Again, German began her timeline by referencing "the end of the cold war and the collapse of the Soviet Union," but why would she think that the "roots of this conflict" stretch back only so recently? After all, when leftists probe injustices committed by Western societies, they rightly place them within timeframes spanning centuries. So having insisted that we look at context and history, why did German proceed to leap over the lion's share of it?

Russia's journey from czarist despotism to Soviet dictatorship to post-Soviet autocracy might at first seem to unfold through those three respective stages as if each was distinct, yet historians increasingly grasp them as just so many incarnations of the same behemoth.[18] By beginning her story only after the end of the Cold War, German stopped short of the Soviet era, and the reason seems all too obvious. If we were to extend her chronicle further back, then we would have to ask about a regime that throughout the course of its 70-plus years had damaged and destroyed millions of lives while enjoying continuous and often hefty leftist support.[19] In fact, we could stretch the timeline back even further to include Russia's longer history of imperial expansion, but if Western leftists are to critically engage with their own histories, then we must start at the very latest with the Bolshevik Revolution of 1917, which placed Moscow front and center of decades of political commitments that followed, even if Western leftists never spoke about Russia, or about socialism, with a single voice.

Many on the left might well roll their eyes at this point, thinking, "Yes, we know that we wrongly supported the Kremlin in earlier days. We have constantly conceded it and we have moved on. So what's the point of endlessly rehashing that story?" Yet in chapters 2 and 3, we saw that it is above all leftists who rightly demand that sinister histories of the West be retold anew. This makes German's omission incongruous if the left genuinely claims to practice self-scrutiny. Indeed, these notions of pro-Moscow "support" and "commitment" are decisive. On crits' own readings of history, it makes no difference that in hindsight some might insist that the Soviet Union did not embody *real* socialism or that leftists of earlier generations hoped they were supporting something better. As we have seen, the decisive point for crits is concrete effects, not high-minded aspirations. This is why militarism, classism, colonialism, racism, sexism, and heteronormativity do not lose their gravity simply because their perpetrators might have acted with benign motives. On crits' own readings of history and despite some dissenting voices among progressives, once various degrees of pro-Kremlin support were in place, nitpicking as to whether a given dictatorship was genuinely, partially, or only nominally leftist became irrelevant.

I should also note that in my phrase "damaged and destroyed" I follow critical theory by including not only killings but also coerced mass obedience and conformity, which stifled professional, cultural, and interpersonal opportunities of the types that leftists have rightly deemed to be crucial when we study Western oppression.[20] Even cautious estimates run into tens of millions of lives extinguished under socialist dictatorships worldwide, yet when we add persons brutalized or otherwise deprived of professional, cultural, and interpersonal life chances, not to mention broader damage to families and communities, these numbers skyrocket.[21] The repression of any civic education that would have allowed citizens to publicly discuss their grievances and hold their governments to account has bequeathed doleful legacies—writers who never were, composers who never were, poets who never were, painters who never were, philosophers who never were, and, above all, political and social activists who never were.[22]

A long line of scholars, focused mostly on Western power, have shown how violence takes subtle, indirect, and "slow" forms beyond cops wielding batons, and by these same analyses, regimes long supported on the left were nothing *but* regimes of slow violence.[23] In 2018 the Hungarian psychologist Noémi Orvos-Tóth published *Inherited Fate* (*Örökölt sors*), showing from an ex-Soviet-bloc perspective how unacknowledged trauma transmits from one generation to the next. Whatever analysis various experts might offer to explain these psychological phenomena, the book became a bestseller among masses of readers long deprived of a vocabulary for articulating the grief and loss engendered within societies of mass repression. In addition to murders, tortures, imprisonments, and ubiquitous surveillance, less notable features of everyday life had equally pervasive effects.

A friend of mine cannot bear to hear some of the more majestic works of Mozart, Beethoven, and Mendelssohn that were endlessly used to soundtrack the propaganda footage that pervaded his youth, in which the Romanian dictator Nicolae Ceaușescu waved to adoring street crowds and visited factories bursting with grateful workers. This same friend recalls that scarcely a household in his home village lacked a battered wife, one of countless taboos in a country where he spent his schoolroom hours learning about human dignity and social progress under socialism. It is no coincidence that, in the same year as *Inherited Fate*, Orvos-Tóth also published *In the Grip of a Narcissist—Healing from an Emotionally Abusive Relationship* (*Egy nárcisztikus hálójában—Felépülés egy érzelmileg bántalmazó kapcsolatból*). Under socialist dictatorships, parallel structures of state patriarchy and household patriarchy, state repression and household repression did not exist on separate planes. They maintained an ongoing symbiosis as two sides of the same coin.

Meanwhile, my friend and his classmates often had to choose between denouncing others to the authorities or being denounced themselves. By their early twenties, anyone not wholly conforming, anyone who carelessly let slip a trace of originality or creativity, let alone dissent, could count on a thick secret police file and limited educational and career prospects—and no, this was not because Romania was so much more oppressive than the nations more securely under Moscow's thumb. Critical theory teaches that slavery and discrimination were not the opposite of Western liberalism. They followed directly from liberalism's own premises, as witnessed by judicial decisions such as *Dred Scott, Bradwell,* and *Plessy,* as I mentioned in chapter 3, which invoked norms of equality as grounds for upholding such invidious practices. Accordingly, on crits' own assumptions, mass murder and repression followed directly from socialists' own premises. Did leftist values subsequently evolve? No more or less than values of liberal democracy have evolved, depending on how we measure evolution, yet crits still view education about Western atrocities as vital. Writers like German deceive us about the left's supposed traditions of self-scrutiny when they push for mass education about histories of Western injustice while subtracting their own political home from that same ("step 2") ethos of public awareness.

Some people may imagine figures such as Vladimir Putin and Viktor Orbán of Hungary to be arch-opposites to early Bolsheviks, and superficially they are. Clearly, countries such as Croatia, Czechia, Estonia, Hungary, Latvia, Lithuania, Poland, Romania, Russia, Serbia, and other central and eastern European nations have their own histories and do not fit into a single template. Yet from the hour of the Soviet Union's demise, far-right nationalisms throughout central and eastern Europe flowed directly from societies in which active civic participation had been impossible—or, rather, exceptionally dangerous for oneself, one's family, and one's acquaintances—outside state-orchestrated parliaments, ceremonies, and other puppet shows. No, the link from earlier socialist autocracies to today's nationalist ones is neither straightforward nor everywhere identical, but nor is it coincidental.[24] The point is not that today's leftists must be held responsible for every evil in socialist and postsocialist societies—no more than crits would blame white populations today for every detail of the trans-Atlantic slave trade, European colonialism, or Jim Crow. Moreover, Western-directed cowboy capitalism exported to postsocialist nations in the 1990s did little to succor millions of ordinary citizens in mid- or late career who often faced hefty losses in their professional and civilian lives.[25] Nevertheless, the absence of civic education and civil society in the Soviet sphere, a sphere that enjoyed considerable legitimacy and support among Western leftists, left fertile ground for today's autocrats to supplant the old socialist ones.[26]

MASS INJUSTICE: INCIDENTAL OR SYSTEMIC?

My question in this book is not "Who was worse?" My aim is not to toss historical injustices onto the scales to weigh up which regimes or ideologies caused the most or the worst injustices. The gravity of one atrocity cannot diminish the gravity of another.[27] In the 1980s, what was then West Germany witnessed a "historians' dispute," the *Historikerstreit*, about whether or how the Holocaust could be compared to other mass injustices. Even the experts who insisted on its uniqueness in no way sought to downplay other atrocities. Their point was that the Holocaust was unprecedented in how government, technology, private industry, and ordinary citizens had been mobilized to execute it, as Arendt explained, but they never sought to rank atrocities on a scoreboard.[28] When asked about how to compare, say, the Holocaust, the trans-Atlantic slave trade, Stalin's Holodomor, Mao's Cultural Revolution, America's treatment of Indigenous populations, Harry Truman's bombing of Hiroshima and Nagasaki, and Pol Pot's killing fields, the answer cannot be that one was "worse" than another. Even body counts tell only part of the story because counting survivors and assessing wider social and psychological impacts on individuals, families, and communities can never be done in tidily measurable terms.[29]

This is why I am proposing no definitions for terms such as *atrocities*, *horrors*, *mass injustice*, and *mass wrongdoing*.[30] Once any nation has overseen widespread damage and destruction of human lives, then such acts demand accountability regardless of whether other nations have also done hideous things. Diplomatic, military, and economic support for repressive regimes has crossed the spectrum, including Western governments cooperating with repressive regimes such as those of Francisco Franco in Spain, António Salazar in Portugal, Mohammad Reza Pahlavi in Iran, Fulgencio Batista in Cuba, Suharto in Indonesia, Augusto Pinochet in Chile, Anastasio Somoza in Nicaragua, Alfredo Stroessner in Paraguay, P. W. Botha in South Africa, the Saud dynasty on the Arabian Peninsula, and others.[31] So if, for example, we are to confront Western wrongdoing during the Cold War, it is no defense to point to atrocities committed by socialist regimes. By the same token, if we are to confront socialist atrocities, it is no defense to point to Western evils. Incidentally, some people might question this East–West division, arguing that Russia forms part of Europe through long-standing political and cultural ties. Yet the concept of "the West" has always fluctuated, and the Cold War demarcated spheres of influence in ways that continue to drive Kremlin policy.[32]

Some might argue that the grossest atrocities under Stalin, Mao, Pol Pot, and others took place within brief time spans and that these regimes later settled into a normality that was perhaps no better yet not necessarily worse than much Western normality under which plenty of brutality continued over longer periods. (In chapter 8, I will describe such an objection as a "*Vogelschiss* claim.") For now, I will not debate this premise but will assume its truth for argument's sake. What follows? *If* leftists had practiced self-scrutiny on a par with the scrutiny they demand of societies committed to liberal democracy, and *if* we assume that the Cold War power blocs persisted in this kind of overall parity, *then* we would have expected the left's public and proactive memory politics to have split more or less evenly across liberal-democratic and socialist nations, yet we have seen no such balance.

Incidentally, the reason I have launched my criticisms by citing Lindsey German is not because she is signally culpable or highly influential but because, as we will see, she set out a template that often recurs on the left. Crits rightly insist on the systemic character of mass injustice and that dots must be connected from the West's past outrages to today's wrongs, yet while willing enough to concede leftist injustices, crits have too rarely treated them as systemic or structural on the left. Hence this book's central question:

Outside the meeting halls and seminar rooms, what does leftist self-scrutiny mean? What does it look like and how does it work? When German alluded to leftist histories, it was only by recalling positions that were heroic or benign, which, of course, is not autocritique at all. Certainly, Stop the War does not speak for all leftists, nor have crits been the only people to blame the West for Putin's assault.[33] This is why I am asking not about what all leftists think or what only leftists think.

Note that I am taking no position on whether or how Western nations should act in Ukraine, since that is a separate discussion. My immediate aim is not to resolve the conflict but to challenge the credibility of some figures who have taken leftist positions. Crits rightly teach that no one floats above politics trumpeting objective truth from neutral vantage points. Yet German shows how a leftist standpoint falls into that trap when she teaches about historical responsibility but then subtracts leftist pasts from the histories she recites. Yes, few leftists today openly praise Stalin, Mao, Pol Pot, or the Kim dynasty, yet by the same logic few leading defenders of mainstream liberal democracy today openly praise histories of, say, colonialism, slavery, or racial segregation. Among the writers and activists who defend liberal democracy—in the preceding chapter I cited Popper, Rawls, and Dworkin as examples—we would be hard-pressed to find many who hold up 1950s Alabama or British colonial India or French colonial Algeria as the *real* liberal democracy.

Nor, then, can crits explain leftist wrongs as random dots, as errors and aberrations safely consigned to the past, as if Leninist, Stalinist, Maoist, and other dictatorial regimes had been mere deviations from the *real* socialism, a tactic that I will describe in chapter 8 as a *purity narrative*. For crits, shifts in attitudes within liberal democracies were never a reason to stop teaching bleak Western histories or to cease all related memory politics. After all, what would happen if a politician today were to condemn equality and diversity programs by arguing that Alabama under segregationist Jim Crow laws or colonial Britain or France never represented *real* democracy or that they are no longer supported by mainstream defenders of liberal democracy today? For crits, this condemnation would be a reason *not* to discontinue these programs but to augment them. I, too, am asking not for less critical theory but for more. For crits, it would be illegitimate if defenders of Western liberal democracy dodged self-scrutiny by declaring, "We have learned from our mistakes and no longer support racist, patriarchal, heteronormative, or other oppressive institutions." But then it would also be illegitimate on the left to avoid self-scrutiny by declaring, "We have learned from our mistakes and no longer support Stalinism or Maoism."

German's silence about leftist pasts shrouds her assumptions about both time and causation. Her problem lies not only with her timeline but with her ideas about how trends and events converge. Crits' core insights stem from the view that culture, politics, economics, and law are deeply linked. None of these spheres exists in isolation, yet nor do they act on each other via fixed chains of cause and effect.[34] So the origins and effects of racism and colonialism can never be called exclusively cultural, exclusively political, exclusively economic, or exclusively legal. Similarly, to ask how leftist support for repressive regimes might have "caused" those regimes' injustices would be to miss the point that such support always formed part of broader, often worldwide movements and trends.

ZEITENWENDE

After World War II, the French Socialist Party steadily moved from radical to centrist policies, particularly under President François Mitterand from 1981 to 1995 and President François Hollande from 2012 to 2017.[35] That shift sparked a backlash in the form of a new, stridently leftist party called La France insoumise (LFI), founded in 2016 by the firebrand Jean-Luc Mélenchon and emphatically wedded to critical scrutiny of historical and ongoing Western injustices.[36]

The word *insoumise* is teasingly defiant, translatable as "untamed," "untrammeled," "unvanquished," "refusing to submit," or "refusing to obey." For members, the term denotes all these things, and since the party's founding Mélenchon has rarely failed to make waves. Today, he speaks or is quoted daily in Francophone media, so we're not talking about a more fringe voice like German's.[37] He has twice run as a presidential candidate, scoring almost 20 percent of the popular vote in 2017 and a little more than 20 percent in

2022.[38] By 2024 the party held several dozen seats in the French National Assembly.[39] Like Stop the War, Mélenchon duly condemned Russia's invasion, yet once it came time to discuss context and history, he, too, heaped all blame on the West. He spoke not a word about the French left's own historical commitments, instead proclaiming that the United States had "never wanted the Cold War to end."[40]

A different picture emerged in Germany. Like the French Socialists, Germany's once radical Social Democratic Party (SPD) had drifted to the center in recent decades. Yet unlike center-left parties in other countries, top members of the German SPD reacted to Russia's 2022 onslaught by openly denouncing the party's past policies of appeasing Kremlin autocracy and calling for a *Zeitenwende*—a sea change or "change of the times."[41] That more confessional response was spurred in part by the embarrassment of Gerhard Schröder, who had served as SPD party leader from 1999 to 2004 and as German chancellor from 1998 to 2005. Schröder continued his open and long-standing friendship with Putin even after the 2022 invasion, when he was invited to join the board of directors for the Russian state oil company Gazprom, a role he stepped away from only after a fierce public outcry. At the same time, leading members of Germany's Green Party, stemming from a long pacifist tradition, abandoned their former insistence on unilateral limits to defense spending.[42]

But then in stark contrast to the SPD and the Greens, a party called Die Linke (The Left), originating from an East German past and embracing an earlier brand of leftism, resembled Stop the War and La France insoumise in sidestepping its own histories. On its website, Die Linke tossed in the expected off-the-shelf condemnation of Putin while excising any mention of Soviet history or the left's records of support for the Soviet regime. According to Die Linke's website, "After the end of the Cold War, NATO [North Atlantic Treaty Organization] *opted for confrontation* instead of negotiating a new security system for Europe."[43] Die Linke has rightly acknowledged the Holocaust as well as genocides committed with German complicity in Armenia and Namibia.[44] Of course, these positions were easy to take since leftists have always defined their politics by condemning the right. Die Linke even conceded that the Holodomor, the Soviet mass-starvation efforts in the

Ukraine and other Soviet-ruled territories from 1932 to 1933, were wrong, but then rejected designations of this policy as a crime against humanity, claiming that it would be unfair to compare Stalin's crimes with Hitler's.[45] In the same spirit, the party has defended the former East German tyranny as a *Rechtsstaat*, a state that, in its view, had respected individual rights under the rule of law.[46]

Perhaps Stop the War, La France insoumise, and Die Linke believe that the left has already taken enough flak for siding with dictators? Perhaps they want to balance the scales by reminding us that the West does not come to the Ukraine table with clean hands? Yet once again the problem is that they do no such balancing at all. As with Mélenchon's broadside, let's assume for argument's sake that Die Linke's postulated "new security system" was possible and feasible. The logical conclusion would be that NATO governments had knowingly disregarded it, thereby opting "for confrontation" with Russia.[47] From this standpoint, the party's website further claims that Western nations "wasted a historical opportunity" because "NATO's eastward expansion, troop positioning and maneuvering, and missile defenses decisively eroded relationships with Russia."[48] Sahra Wagenknecht, one of Die Linke's prominent figures until a later falling out, took the further step of organizing demonstrations to halt Germany's support for Ukraine's defense. Like Mélenchon, Wagenknecht is anything but a marginal voice, has enjoyed constant attention in German mass media, and has formed a political party bearing her name and garnering considerable success on the left. She claimed that after the invasion in February 2022, the US and UK governments obstructed Putin's efforts at "compromise."[49] Such accusations went too far for many in Die Linke, yet a question remains about whether such ideas would have gained traction in a climate where leftists had pursued a public and proactive memory politics *of the left*.[50]

CONNECTING THE DOTS

In July 2022, the American public intellectual Noam Chomsky granted an interview to Ramzy Baroud, editor of the *Palestine Chronicle*. Baroud summarized their discussions in articles published in the online periodicals

Common Dreams and *Counterpunch*. Chomsky launched his attack with trademark hyperbole: "Everybody who knows anything has been warning Washington that it is reckless and provocative to ignore Russia's very clear and explicit red lines."[51] Chomsky rehearsed ideas he had espoused for decades, explaining the conflict as the result of Western neo-imperialism. Like German, Mélenchon, and Wagenknecht, Chomsky began with the predictable pro forma condemnation of Moscow, conceding "that the invasion of Ukraine has no (moral) justification," only to devote the rest of his analysis to NATO expansionism:

> Starting in 2014, after the Maidan uprising, the United States began openly, not secretly, moving to integrate Ukraine into the NATO military command, sending heavy armaments and joining military exercises, military training and it was not a secret. They boasted about it. . . . Just before the invasion . . . Biden . . . produced a joint statement . . . calling for expanding these efforts of integration. That's part of what was called an "enhanced program" leading to the mission of NATO. In November, it was moved forward to a charter, signed by the Secretary of State. . . . [T]he United States Department [of State] acknowledged that they had not taken Russian security concerns into consideration in any discussions with Russia. The question of NATO, they would not discuss.[52]

Citing these and other factors, Chomsky then turned to the question of blame: "All of that is provocation. Not a justification but a provocation and it's quite interesting that in American discourse, it is almost obligatory to refer to the invasion as the 'unprovoked invasion of Ukraine.' Look it up on Google, you will find hundreds of thousands of hits. . . . Of course, it was provoked. Otherwise, they wouldn't refer to it all the time as an unprovoked invasion."[53] But then why has the West failed to take these concerns more seriously? For Chomsky, it seems there are no essential differences between Russian and Western state pressures on the mass media or on opportunities for citizens to dissent from official pronouncements:

> By now, censorship in the United States has reached such a level beyond anything in my lifetime. Such a level that you are not permitted to read the Russian position. Literally. Americans are not allowed to know what the Russians

are saying. Except, selected things. So, if Putin makes a speech to Russians with all kinds of outlandish claims about Peter the Great and so on, then, you see it on the front pages. If the Russians make an offer for a negotiation, you can't find it. That's suppressed. You're not allowed to know what they are saying. I have never seen a level of censorship like this.[54]

Of course, from the moment Western nations imposed sanctions on Russian state media, and even before then, the Kremlin was proliferating its messages far and wide, throughout the West and around the world, so it is unclear which of Putin's opinions, in Chomsky's view, the West was missing.[55] Some might praise Chomsky for waging a counterhegemonic position. In ancient Greek, the term *hegemon* referred to someone in a commanding role, and the Italian Marxist Antonio Gramsci coined the terms *hegemony* and *hegemonic* to show how classically liberal-capitalist ideologies of individual freedom, civic equality, and advancement through merit colonized and commanded the minds of workers who drew no benefit from them. Gramsci called these ideals hegemonic because they were propagated as universal so that underclasses would commit to values that benefited only the upper classes.[56] Internationally these terms signify the ways in which Western norms and institutions have been presented as necessary and benevolent even when they place non-Western populations at disadvantages.[57] Be that as it may, in our age of rival poles of influence, particularly as reflected in the soft power transmitted via information technologies, the notion of one solely omnipotent hegemon in a context like the Ukraine war becomes tenable only when we sideline vast swaths of history, as Chomsky and his fellow travelers so conspicuously do.[58]

A few weeks earlier Chomsky had given an interview to the *New States-man*'s Europe correspondent Ido Vock, who wondered whether Chomsky's ideological commitments had led him "to overlook facts that might contradict his narrative." Was it true that Chomsky knows better than Swedes and Finns themselves why they were now recording high levels of support for NATO membership? In Vock's words,

> Sweden and Finland, which had been officially non-aligned for 210 and 73 years, respectively, both applied to join Nato in May 2022. To most observers,

the end of their decades of neutrality might seem at least tangentially related to the invasion of Ukraine three months earlier. However, Chomsky says that both countries seeking to join Nato had "nothing to do with fear of a Russian attack, which has never been even conceived." Claims that Russia could threaten either country amount to "Western propaganda," he adds. Instead, Chomsky argues that joining Nato gives the military industries of both Nordic countries "great new market opportunities [and] new access to advanced equipment."[59]

This style of closed-circuit reasoning has a long vintage on the far right and the far left. When a majority's views line up with those of the speaker, it means that the people have woken up to reality. This proves that the speaker stands on the side of truth. But when the majority's views contradict those of the speaker, it shows the people have been brainwashed by sinister powers, which equally proves that the speaker stands on the side of truth. The parallel to religious fundamentalism could hardly be clearer: each of our victories proves that God is on our side, yet each of our defeats proves that God is only testing us, which in turn proves that God is on our side. It is the very model of closed-circuit dogma that such diametrically opposite results serve equally to prove that any given theory is correct. For dogmatic Marxists, capitalists are the exploitative class. So if you bring evidence of workers' conditions improving, this merely shows how you have been brainwashed by capitalism, which proves that capitalists are the exploitative class. By the same token, for dogmatic capitalists, programs for redistributing wealth are wasteful and dictatorial. So if you bring evidence of citizens' lives having improved under some redistributive schemes, this merely shows that you are blind to waste and dictatorialism, which proves that programs for redistributing wealth are wasteful and dictatorial. For white nationalists, nonwhites threaten to exterminate white culture, so if you bring evidence that majority white culture has benefited from nonwhite contributions, this proves that people like you are in the grip of the enemy, which proves that nonwhites threaten to exterminate white culture, and so on.

Here, too, some might argue that people like Chomsky do not represent all leftists. Or that exponents of unpopular views must take stark positions to be heard. Or that leftist activism does not always enjoy the luxury of nuanced analyses and must play a gadfly role. Yet few voices have had so many public platforms at their beck and call or have taken better advantage of them. Conspicuous in many of Chomsky's broadcast interviews on Ukraine are the vast stretches of time handed to him to promenade through every detail at his leisure. Yet as in the case of Swedes and Finns, Chomsky purported to know better than the Ukrainians what they wanted. As Vock observed:

> Chomsky's world-view does not leave space for Ukrainian agency. It is the "US and Britain" who have "refused" peace negotiations in Ukraine, Chomsky tells me, in order to further their own national interests, even as the country is being "battered, devastated." That negotiations with Russia would mean de facto abandoning millions of Ukrainians to the whims of an aggressor that has shown itself capable of extraordinary brutality, such as in Bucha and Izyum, is dismissed. "Ukraine is not a free actor; they're dependent on what the US determines," he says, adding that the US is supplying Kyiv with weapons simply to weaken Russia. "For the US, this is a bargain. For a fraction of the colossal military budget, the US is able to severely degrade the military forces of its only real military adversary."[60]

Certainly, much has happened since Putin's invasion in 2022. As I type these words, ethnic Armenians have fled from a clannish autocracy in Azerbaijan, a pro-Kremlin populist has taken power in Slovakia to join Viktor Orbán among Putin's men in central Europe, and Serbian forces commanded by the right-wing president Aleksandar Vučić are continuing to destabilize Kosovo.[61] Each of these situations has a strong local aspect, yet leftists have done little by way of educating the public about how their own past commitments supported earlier autocracies that paved the way for these regimes, still leaving an open question about what, exactly, leftist autocritique is supposed to be.

In the heyday of European colonialism, Eurocentric worldviews imagined the West as mature and enlightened and non-Westerners as backward and barbaric, as if it were the West's prerogative to dictate values for the whole world.[62] Of course, the *Euro* in *Eurocentric* was only ever loosely defined. It does not refer solely to the European landmass. For example, white American racism is often described as Eurocentric as it presupposes the superiority of populations descended from the European continent.[63] In this sense, a Muscovite could certainly be Eurocentric—on the right this might take the form of standard racism, while on the left we can recall that early Soviet ideology placed Bolsheviks as the pioneers of global history.[64] And then to complicate matters further, we must bear in mind that internalized Eurocentrism has been documented in colonial and postcolonial societies where Indigenous peoples have been taught to blame their individual and collective crises on their own failures to act and think in European ways.[65]

Regardless of how we might define Eurocentrism, in our discussion of Ukraine the term might seem irrelevant given that (Western) Russia and Ukraine are European nations fighting a European war. However, in practice the concept of "Eurocentrism" has mostly been used to denote political and cultural supremacism among powers such as Britain, France, and the United States. Certainly, this is how crits commonly use words like *Western* and *Eurocentric*. But then, ironically, German, Mélenchon, Wagenknecht, and Chomsky end up taking strikingly Eurocentric positions. They do this in part, as we have seen, by excising the histories of Soviet rulers who—if we wish to combat prejudices about Westerners being history's only rational actors—were perfectly competent to reach ethical decisions, indeed during the Cold War, when leftists widely insisted that the West must show due respect for Soviet influence and policies.

Leftists' anti-Eurocentrism has manifested through their efforts to dismantle myths about superior Western rationality, yet they have ended up adopting the same Eurocentric biases. When there is weighty power on two or more sides of a conflict situation, to assign all essential blame to just one side is to treat it as rational and mature, and therefore bearing the onus of ethical reason, while treating the others as incompetent. In chapter 10, I describe that anomaly as *Eurocentric anti-Eurocentrism*. Admittedly, the West needed to display respect for Soviet power as a practical matter because nations need to promote good mutual relations even with rivals. This need for diplomatic stability was widely recognized, its compromise character commonly diffused through foreign circumlocutions—*détente, entente cordiale, modus vivendi*, and the like. By contrast, on the more ideological left, respect for Moscow was never only a question of pragmatics.[66] Even assuming that there was no leftist consensus in championing the Soviet Union, many took the relativist view that both East and West had their pros and cons and therefore deserved equal respect. Yet this never seriously translated as ascribing heavy ethical responsibility for repressive policies to the Kremlin, an omission that has carried over into our own time.[67]

Akin to Eurocentrism is orientalism, a concept made famous in 1978 by the Columbia University literature professor Edward Said in his book bearing that word as its title. The West had nurtured orientalist mindsets for centuries, often characterized by depictions of non-Westerners hovering between savagery and mystique. Orientalism, too, meant that Westerners had to make ethical choices that non-Westerners lacked the capacity to make.[68] With apologies for overloading my "isms" here, orientalism in turn represents a form of paternalism. Orientalism casts the superior decision-maker in the role of a providential father and colonial subjects in the role of dependents, while inflating racist myths used to justify mass subordination. In the words of the Princeton University historian Gyan Prakash, European colonialism "instituted enduring hierarchies" consisting of "the colonizer and the colonized, the Occidental and the Oriental, the civilized and the primitive, the scientific and the superstitious, the developed and the under-developed."[69] Compare this posture with the point I have just observed: that figures such as German, Wagenknecht, Mélenchon, and Chomsky invariably dismiss both Russian and Ukrainian agency—the choices for self-determination expressed by Ukrainians and the choices for flaunting raw power made in Moscow, particularly after the 2013 Maidan protests and 2014 Crimean annexation.[70]

In an interview by *Current Affairs* in 2022, Chomsky argued that to prevent bloodshed and avoid nuclear war NATO must stop arming Ukrainians, who should surrender to Russia and make substantial territorial concessions.[71] Plenty of experts have rejected this view, wagering that NATO could help Ukraine without risking nuclear war, but my task for now is not to weigh up military strategies.[72] Rather, what leaps out from Chomsky's remarks is that he urged Ukrainians to surrender in the same way they would capitulate to a "hurricane."[73] This was no silly goof-up from a world-class linguist whose word choices are ordinarily meticulous. We have seen that crits often view wrongheaded policies and practices of liberal democracies as systemic or structural, and in that sense inherent to liberal democracy. By contrast, I shall have further occasion to note in this book crits' opposite tendencies in the face of wrongheaded leftist commitments, namely to dismiss them as errors and accidents—not the *real* leftism. With this statement of Chomsky's we witness speech that flows with utter consistency. His view yields no other interpretation, regardless of how he might otherwise have phrased it. Once Chomsky had peripheralized Moscow's ethical responsibility, just as a hurricane cannot exercise ethical reason, and dismissed Ukrainians as autonomous actors, the only conclusion that could follow was that Ukrainians had to acquiesce to whatever the Kremlin was doling out to them.

Some might argue that the aim of crits is to move beyond a binary "West versus the rest" way of thinking. Yet as this book will continue to show, to rail tirelessly against wrongdoing by the West with little to say about wrongdoing in the history of the left is to push a one-sided history that does more to entrench simplistic binaries than to overcome them. The pattern is clear. After pat and fleeting condemnations of Putin's aggression, German, Mélenchon, Wagenknecht, Chomsky, and their fellow travelers end up taking positions entirely in line with Kremlin policy. No, this trend does not define the entire Western left, but it has been prominent on the left for more than a century, and nor is the Ukraine war the only embarrassment, given that Western leftists long supported autocratic governments in places such as Cuba, Nicaragua, and Venezuela. They rightly criticized unequal conditions in the histories of those nations, and have rightly connected those dots to US policies and practices, yet they rarely linked their stances to the left's own decades of support for dictatorial regimes, as if suddenly there were no dots to connect.

5 EDUCATION RESPONDING

In the late nineteenth century the Prussian parliamentarian Rudolf Virchow warned that a "culture war" (*Kulturkampf*) was haunting Europe, pitting religious conservatives against cosmopolitan liberals.[1] More than a century later, with Cold War divisions crumbling, the binary of "capitalism versus socialism" steadily came to be supplemented by multiple and intersectional classifications defining us by nation, ethnicity, language, sex, gender, and other identity-based categories. Soon after the Berlin Wall fell in 1989, the American sociologist James Davison Hunter revived Virchow's warning in a book entitled *Culture Wars: The Struggle to Define America*. Then in 1995 the sociologist, novelist, and activist Todd Gitlin published *The Twilight of Common Dreams: Why America Is Wracked by Culture Wars*. Lamenting what he feared to be a narrow and parochial drift on the left, Gitlin quipped: "While the Right has been busy taking the White House, the Left has been marching on the English department."[2] Today, university campuses in Western nations continue to incubate step 1 of the Radical Critique of Western Liberal Democracy through comprehensive critiques of historical Western wrongdoing, and also promote step 2 through artistic and cultural events, diversity and equality programs, campus protests, mass and social media, and other means of public education. But is something missing from these campaigns?

MEMORY POLITICS *ON* THE LEFT

Imagine Braynington University, a liberal arts institution located in a prosperous Western nation and boasting an impressive international profile.

Upon its founding in the seventeenth century the university enrolled only white males but in 1930 opened admissions to nonwhites and women.

One day a group of staff and students formed the Campus Historical Network, or CHN. They drew up plans to run projects such as an annual Black History Weekend and an annual Women's History Weekend to educate their campus and community about the university's pre-1930 past along with broader problems of racism and sexism in society. These events would be open to the public and would feature exhibits, readings, artistic performances, guest speakers, and panel discussions. CHN began by submitting an application to the university's senior administration to obtain recognized status as a campus organization. That status would allow the group to book campus facilities and apply for event funding. A few days later, a university vice president replied to CHN with the following message:

> Dear Members of the Campus Historical Network—Thank you for your application. We in university administration have now read and discussed it, and we regret to inform you that we will not be approving it. We certainly understand the painful pasts of ethnic minorities and women, and do not wish to give the impression that the university's pre-1930s policies were justified. However, those policies changed long ago, and our country has changed, too. Just to be clear, we resolutely approve of our academic departments researching and teaching about the histories of racism and sexism, although we would underscore our belief that those discriminatory practices never represented anything that what we would recognize today as real democracy. Be that as it may, now is the time for our nation and our institution to move forward and not to dwell on the past.

The CHN members felt outraged, yet we must note that the administrators in no way denied histories of racist, sexist, or other forms of exclusion. In their message, they gladly embraced step 1 of memory politics through campus research and through curriculums that would cover racism and sexism in the classroom. But they stopped short of step 2, which would have facilitated the CHN's plans to promote public awareness. For CHN, there was only one conclusion they could draw. Without step 2, step 1 would forever remain idle chatter, diminishing to hollow words without committed action. So CHN persisted by sending another message, this time explaining that histories of discrimination must not be relegated to the past in the way the administrators seemed to do. The CHN argued that when the university abolished its discriminatory policies in the 1930s, it still did not wash away a longer history, particularly since malicious attitudes persisted in the broader society. The CHN members added that they were not "dwelling" on the past but aiming to wake up the public to the ongoing realities of social division.

Periodic exchanges between CHN and senior administration bounced back and forth over several years. During that time, some people left the university, new people joined, and after a new set of administrators took charge, the CHN finally succeeded. The new administrators approved the CHN application, perhaps spurred by renewed incidents of racism and sexism in the country that had drawn great media coverage. In fact, the administrators went even further by designating CHN as the authorized campus committee to oversee proposals for future events dedicated to commemorating historical injustices. In a spirit of renewed confidence, the CHN celebrated these gains by adding a third annual event called Queer History Weekend to promote acceptance of LGBTQ+ identities.

Then one day another group of students—some descended from ancestors who had fled from left-leaning dictatorships in eastern Europe, Asia, Africa, and Latin America—felt disgruntled after attending an extracurricular students' meeting entitled "The Ukraine War: How Should the Left Respond?" Very few speakers praised Russia, and those who did were mostly disregarded, yet the students felt surprised that so many speakers who identified as progressives were talking only about Western failures. The students wondered whether there was too little awareness about the history of the Kremlin and of leftist support for it, so they formed a group of their own called "Braynington-Memorial."

They chose this name in tribute to the highly praised Russian organization Мемориал (Memorial), founded in 1988 during the final days of the Soviet Union to investigate injustices hidden from the public throughout Soviet history.[3] For several years, Мемориал had contributed to Russian civil society by breaking taboos about the Soviet past but witnessed ever tighter surveillance under Putin and in 2021 was shut down and forced out of the country.[4] Мемориал won the Nobel Peace Prize in 2022 along with the Belarusian human rights activist Ales Bialiatski and the Ukrainian Center for Civil Liberties.[5] It has since continued online but without easy access to data and archives that would be vital for further research.

The difference for Braynington-Memorial was that they would focus not only on Russia and the Soviet Union but also on China and other nations with socialist histories that continue to wield influence in the world. The students submitted to the CHN in its new official role the standard university application for formal status as a campus organization, including a request for funding to launch an annual Socialist History Weekend. They felt inspired by the university's Black History, Women's History, and Queer History Weekends and thought that something like a Socialist History Weekend would move beyond the high-minded ideals that often attracted students, focusing instead on the concrete realities of dozens of movements and regimes that had been set up in the name of socialism over more than a century.

Many of the Braynington-Memorial group's members came from the humanities and social sciences, where they had often been taught by left-leaning instructors who explained how to study Western politics, economics, law, society, literature, and art through not only representations of, but also silences about, long-standing patterns of Western violence and oppression. A widespread idea was that leading philosophers such as Aristotle, Locke, Hume, Kant, or Hegel should still be read, but "against the grain"—not taken at face value but instead grasping the ways in which seemingly universalist and humanist values had correlated to practices of racism, colonialism, patriarchy, and heteronormativity. The feminist poet Adrienne Rich had urged this strategy in 1972: "We need to know the writing of the past, and know it differently than we have ever known it; not to pass on a tradition but to break its hold over us."[6] The Braynington-Memorial members believed that progressive thought had always known practices of internal scrutiny, associated with figures such as Adorno, Arendt, Sartre, De Beauvoir, Althusser, Habermas, and others. However, without wanting to draw up scorecards of atrocities, they felt that problems such as race, colonialism, gender, and sexuality were now steeped in highly nuanced concepts and vocabularies of a type that the left had scarcely disseminated when discussing millions of victims of socialist regimes. The members believed that when the left's public silences consigned these millions of victims to namelessness it made such victims easy to sideline in political discussions. This looming silence had always facilitated the censorship practices that pervaded totalitarian regimes, still carried on by their autocratic successors today, which in turn perpetuated intergenerational trauma and suppression. The members agreed that critical theory had played a valuable role in challenging unilateral readings of history but doubted that much was to be gained when one set of unilateral readings was merely replacing another.

The students realized that socialist regimes, too, had vaunted on-paper promises of rewarding merit, fair political representation, and equal treatment of all citizens yet had imposed mass repression in the name of these ideals. The aim of a Socialist History Weekend would not be to bash leftist ideals but to teach about how they had been deployed to bring about the opposite of what leftists had preached, propping up dictatorships in ways that would later pave the way for the autocracies we still witness today. Such an event would teach about how these devastating effects have continued into our own time, and why many Western leftists had supported these regimes. But a few days after Braynington-Memorial submitted its application, the CHN responded:

> Dear Members of Braynington-Memorial—Thank you for your application. We on the CHN have now read and discussed it, and we regret to inform you that we will not be approving it. We certainly understand the painful pasts of persons persecuted under socialist regimes and do not wish to give the impression that leftist support for such regimes was justified. However, many of those regimes changed long ago, and leftism has changed, too. Just to be clear, we resolutely approve of our academic departments researching and teaching about these histories, although we would note our belief that those oppressive practices never represented real socialism. Be that as it may, now is the time for our nation and our institution to move forward and not to dwell on the past.

The Braynington-Memorial members felt outraged, yet we must note that the CHN's response in no way denied histories of socialist repression. CHN cheerfully endorsed academic departments teaching those histories in the classroom but stopped short of a proactive program for spreading public awareness about those pasts. In sum, CHN had taken valuable initiatives in establishing Black, Women's, and Queer History Weekends yet hesitated when leftist histories were at stake.

Yes, Braynington is imaginary. In a real-life counterpart, would a committee such as CHN truly reject a proposal like this one for Socialist History Weekend? Have universities in the West ever blocked efforts by staff or students to commemorate histories of socialist oppression? I doubt it. The parable of Braynington University illustrates not what has happened in intent but what has happened in effect. If we are to judge by actual outcomes, there might as well have been a university authority blocking such events in more or less every university in the Western world. The question is not whether a real-life university body would reject a request for a Socialist History Weekend. Rather, the question is why people who believe in leftist autocritique would wait for others to initiate such requests.

Some people might fear that events like a Socialist History Weekend would sow divisions, whereas racial, sexual, or gender identity apply to all people and have nothing to do with right versus left. They might argue that any Black people, any women, and any LGBTQ+ people can face discrimination, so events such as Black, Women's, and Queer History Weekends serve the university's immediate need to promote inclusion. This would mean that struggles against racism, sexism, and heteronormativity are universal, transcending politics, while disputes about socialist histories are purely political. Yet that account would flatly contradict crits' insistence that there is no objective and neutral politics hovering above all politics; at Braynington the politics rightly driving Black, Women's, and Queer History Weekends draws largely from a critical approach to histories of Western injustice. But if it is true that Black people, women, or LGBTQ+ people have faced repression in the West, it remains equally true that millions of citizens have faced repression under regimes long and widely supported on the left, and to omit them is to entrench hierarchies of atrocities that create the most noninclusive world of all.

Imagine Volodymyr, a young, straight, blond-haired, and blue-eyed man from Ukraine who witnessed his parents killed, siblings tortured, and children deported to Russia. What kind of social status would Volodymyr's biography bring him if a charitable foundation were to award him cost-free tuition and residence at Braynington? Of course, if there were enough other Ukrainians, they might join together for mutual support and perhaps for political action. If not, then under Braynington's tacit hierarchies, Volodymyr would count as nothing but a straight, white male, an obvious beneficiary of privilege. He might officially benefit from some form of refugee status, but his status as the bearer of a repressive history engineered from the Kremlin several generations before the Ukraine war would be far less recognized than the status of students associated with more typically Western identity-based groups.

Or imagine Joo Kyung, an escapee from a North Korean prison camp, whose family members had been starved, raped, and beaten to death in the same camp. After the dangerous journey through China, she traveled to Seoul, then a few years later won an award to attend Braynington. The only generally acknowledged social status that would apply to her would be as a woman or a member of an ethnic minority, yet neither of these classifications would explain the grief she had endured, and which still plagued millions of her compatriots back home.

Many on the left might well sympathize with Volodymyr and Joo Kyung, arguing that their attention to problems of identitarian inequalities does not render them insensitive to other forms of oppression. Yet if leftists fail to address forms of oppression in which the left has been historically implicated with the same energy they have poured into conventionally recognized forms of Western oppression, then, in practice, such lip service amounts to little more than a shrug. Of course, as a practical matter, some might object that it is unfair to expect leftists to spread their energies so thin, since even the noblest activists cannot agitate for all causes at once. Yet when CHN adopted Women's History Weekend, no one argued that it would spread the efforts of Black History Weekend too thin. When they adopted LGBTQ+ History Weekend, no one argued that it would spread the efforts of the Black History and Women's History Weekends too thin. It seems implausible that suddenly energy and resources would be too scarce when it comes time for leftists to confront their own histories.

But perhaps we find no events like Socialist History Weekend because there has never been a demand for them. Yet surely this would be an example of how it is supply that stimulates demand. Some leftists might argue that we must focus on abuses in our own backyard. They might express sympathy for Ivan Denisovich, Aleksandr Solzhenitsyn's symbol of countless victims of socialist brutality, but would argue that we must focus our energies on George Floyd.[7] Yet this argument, too, would merely default to hierarchies of atrocities. Progressives have constantly underscored foreign crises when they saw links to actual or alleged perpetrators or allies in the West—in places like Cuba, Guatemala, Chile, El Salvador, Nicaragua, South Africa, Palestine, or Venezuela—so it would seem far-fetched to argue that the abuses of socialist regimes are too far removed in time or space.

I recall from my student days a student cinema series that included D. W. Griffith's 1920 film *Way Down East*. Some students protested, condemning Griffith due to his earlier, racist film *Birth of a Nation* (1915), which vilified Blacks and glorified the Ku Klux Klan. I opposed a cancellation of the screening but agreed with those who argued that introductory announcements and leaflets for viewers would offer a more legitimate and effective response. But a few years later, as a young academic, I was surprised to attend a number of crit events in which writers like the Nazi-party members Carl Schmitt and Martin Heidegger—not to mention figures like Vladimir Lenin or Evgeny Pashukanis, some of whose writings had been penned in the very midst of mass exterminations—were cited as authoritative without the sense that such writings needed to be framed by any serious reference to the regimes they had served ("We already know this," seemed to be the tacit assumption), let alone any calls for cancellations. As with the Griffith incident, I would not censor these events given the importance and influence of such authors, whose works certainly should be studied, but would advocate for context to be included. Again, crits exhort us to read the standard canon of Western classics "against the grain" by educating people about how their ideas have emerged within projects of mass violence, repression, and dehumanization. Yet they apply this method so selectively that it serves more to parody critical theory than to advance it.

Does this all mean that I am pushing "whataboutery" or "whataboutism"?[8] Am I diverting attention from valid critiques of the West by pointing a finger back at leftists, arguing, "You on the left accuse the West of wrongdoing, but what about Russia, China, and others?" The political commentator Ben Burgis explains whataboutism: "There even was a special phrase used during the Cold War to describe the Soviets' response to criticism. That phrase wasn't 'whataboutism.' It was 'And You Are Lynching Negroes'—since that was the Soviets' go-to example." Burgis adds that "every use of the phrase would remind listeners that the Soviets had a point." Yet he also notes that whataboutery is not always diversionary. It asks whether we practice what we preach, so it "can be a test of whether we are serious about our principles."[9] Burgis's more constructive approach to whataboutery is what we have always known as calling out hypocrisy, yet, again, hypocrisy crosses the political spectrum because all political outlooks are expressed in general terms that can break down in complex situations. By contrast, autocritique is a promise to undertake the kind of public self-scrutiny that leftists have always accused other political homes of failing to do.

MISSED OPPORTUNITIES

I began this book with a glance at a Virginia school district that adopted rights for trans kids. Angry parents protested, insisting they wanted to maintain control over their children's education on matters relevant to gender and sexuality. It would be wrong, and it would be shortsighted, to dismiss their concerns. Yet it would be just as wrong to ignore anti-LGBTQ+ violence and aggression in schools and society—particularly in view of the damage that is often caused to LGBTQ+ youth, who perennially have high rates of suicide and self-harm.[10] Clearly, thoughtful balances need to be struck on such complex questions. Yet thoughtful balancing was nowhere to be found in March 2022, when a conservative majority in the Florida legislature passed the sweeping Parental Rights in Education (PRE) Act, widely branded the "Don't Say Gay" law, to which Governor Ron DeSantis promptly added his signature. PRE makes it impossible for schools to discuss anti-LGBTQ+ discrimination because even a mild encouragement to respect LGBTQ+ people creates a risk of steep litigation costs for already-strapped schools.[11]

A few weeks later, PRE was followed up by the so-called Individual Freedom Act, which covers schools as well as workplaces, yet also rides roughshod over what needs to be a more adult weighing of interests. Dubbed the "antiwoke" law, the Individual Freedom act bans training or instruction programs that depict any individual as being "inherently racist, sexist, or oppressive, whether consciously or unconsciously," or as being either privileged or oppressed based on "race, color, sex, or national origin." It also prohibits schools from teaching that any "individual . . . bears responsibility for, or should be discriminated against or receive adverse treatment because of, actions committed in the past by other members of the same race, color, sex, or national origin."[12] Ironically, Karl Marx, Friedrich Engels, Rosa Luxemburg, and Vladimir Lenin would have agreed. For them, racism and sexism were not "inherent" forms of oppression since repressive social hierarchies derived from capitalism. I will not rehearse old debates among leftists because my point here is a simple one: Florida used a sledgehammer to crack a nut. The legislature raised valid concerns but resolved them in censorious and vindictive ways.

It may take years before we have a clear sense of how courts will interpret these laws. Clearly, writers such as Frederick Douglass, Martin Luther King Jr., or Lorraine Hansberry were probing racial privilege and oppression long before critical race theory emerged, yet under the antiwoke law teaching even these authors could land a school in court. In 2022, one Florida county removed 176 books originally written to promote tolerance among children, with no indication of whether or when any of the titles would be restored. It was especially alarming that the confiscated books included a biography of civil rights activist Rosa Parks, and another about the Nobel Peace Prize–winner and girls' rights activist Malala Yousafzai.[13] Teachers and school boards will ordinarily welcome constructive parental feedback, and parents should certainly raise concerns about programs that would inflict feelings of personalized guilt on school-age children. However, a problem with these laws is that they treat histories of race, gender, and sexuality as matters that can be cleanly separated from the rest of the curriculum. We must not forget that a core task of public education is to develop civically aware citizens by teaching what democracy is and how it works. This can be done only when students can study and discuss how democracy has succeeded and failed in past.

Be that as it may, the Florida lawmakers were now on a roll. In May 2022 the state legislature adopted a law designating November 7 of each year as "a day honoring the 100 million people who have fallen victim to communist regimes across the world."[14] The figure of 100 million deaths under socialism has been disputed, although as I mentioned in chapter 4, in addition to individuals who were killed, the word "victim" should be read to include people, and their families and friends, who were harmed in other ways, with effects rolling out over generations.[15] This memory law also requires that, on or around that date each year, all students enrolled in the state's compulsory United States Government class "must receive at least 45 minutes of instruction [on] topics such as Mao Zedong and the Cultural Revolution, Joseph Stalin and the Soviet System, Fidel Castro and the Cuban Revolution, Vladimir Lenin and the Russian Revolution, Pol Pot and the Khmer Rouge, and Nicolás Maduro and the Chavismo movement." The instruction must demonstrate "how victims suffered under these regimes through poverty, starvation, migration, systemic lethal violence, and suppression of speech."[16]

Taken on its own, this law is not a big ask. Nor has there been much backlash against it, as teachers have been more stoked by the other two laws. I suspect that many of them would have gladly taught those 45 minutes as part of a rounded curriculum aimed at sharpening students' minds about the ways in which all power can be and has been manipulated. In other words, what is irksome is not that schools must teach about socialist atrocities but that, alongside the other two laws, this one creates a scoreboard of horrors, promoting scrutiny of some while silencing discussion about others. The lawmakers have turned history into a zero-sum game. They have weaponized the victims of socialism, pitting them against victims of violence and discrimination within liberal democracies. Taken as a whole, these three laws swing from one extreme, in which socialist abuses have been neglected, to the opposite extreme, in which they are taught as a way to distract attention from Western injustices. Conservatives are justified in wanting to dedicate 45 minutes per year to millions of victims of socialist regimes, yet they do this in bad faith, weaponizing those victims, when they refuse to allow schools to teach the abusive histories of liberal democracies.

But must the left shoulder some of the blame for this backlash? We cannot know whether Florida's education debacle would have occurred had the left pushed years ago for teaching about injustices committed in the name of leftism alongside entirely justified teaching about racism, sexism, heteronormativity, and the like. Yet it is hard to escape a sense that, for decades, the left has been missing some opportunities. The point is not that we must descend into a tit-for-tat by correlating every event focused on Western injustices to an event about those on the left, no more than every Black History Weekend must be paired with a Women's History Weekend, or a Women's History Weekend paired with an LGBTQ+ History Weekend, and so forth. The point is about balance over the long run, which is not too much to expect.

6 INTERESTS CONVERGING

In 1980 the Harvard law professor Derrick Bell, a pioneer of critical race theory, set out to understand why racist violence and discrimination had persisted in the United States despite decades of law reform. Didn't these reforms prove that the white establishment had learned from the past? Bell replied with what he called an "interest-convergence" theory. He explained that legislatures and courts expanded rights for African Americans only when those concessions converged with white interests.[1] Whites may well have been engaged in self-scrutiny, but it was always bounded by self-interest. Bell made his case persuasively, yet a further question now has to be posed: What about leftists? Have they, too, allowed their collective self-interest to trump their collective self-scrutiny?

AN OLD PROBLEM

In the United States, federal and state efforts to promote everyday equality, beyond on-paper reforms, did not occur until as late as the 1950s, almost a century after the Thirteenth Amendment to the Constitution outlawed slavery. As Bell observed, only following World War II did lawmakers grasp that racial discrimination was harming America's international reputation as a force for liberal democracy. This embarrassment spurred white elites to take bolder steps.

In 1954 the Supreme Court announced its decision in the landmark case *Brown v. Board of Education*, which struck down laws requiring racial segregation in public schools.[2] Bell explained how "the decision helped to provide immediate credibility to America's struggle with Communist countries to win the hearts and minds of emerging third world peoples."[3] He cited the example of *Time* magazine, which instantly celebrated the Court's ruling: "In many countries, where U.S. prestige and leadership have been damaged by the fact of U.S. segregation [the *Brown* result] will come as a timely reassertion of the basic American principle that 'all men are created equal.'"[4] Bell also cited chief justice Earl Warren, who had authored *Brown*. Shortly after retiring in 1972, Warren wrote: "The segregation and extermination of non-Aryans in Hitler's Germany were shocking for Americans, but they also served as a troublesome analogy. While proclaiming themselves inexorably opposed to Hitler's practices, many Americans were tolerating the segregation and humiliation of nonwhites within their own borders. The contradiction between the egalitarian rhetoric employed against the Nazis and the presence of racial segregation in America was a painful one."[5] In Bell's view, the Constitution had not generally been applied to provide "effective racial equality for blacks" in situations that might undermine "the superior societal status of middle and upper class whites."[6]

The problem with Bell's theory is not that he was wrong but that he was too right by half. White power has indeed worked through interest-convergence, not because of anything distinctive about American power arrangements but because power has always worked this way. Throughout history, powerful forces might well have conceded ground when they believed they stood to gain more than they would lose, as observed centuries ago by the Florentine Renaissance writer Niccolò Machiavelli, often regarded as the founder of modern political science. In a world immersed in Christian theology, Machiavelli's *The Prince* (1532) scandalized Europe by presenting successful governments throughout history as pursuing nothing *but* self-interest. As the book warns early on, "there is nothing more difficult to execute, nor more dubious of success, nor more dangerous to administer than to introduce a new order of things; for [the ruler] who introduces it has all those who profit from the old order as his enemies, and he has only lukewarm allies in all those who might profit from the new."[7] It takes little ingenuity to translate such advice to mean: "If you want to keep power, don't act until you're sure that your gains will outweigh your losses."

By Shakespeare's time, these ideas were well known. In *Antony and Cleopatra* (ca. 1607), albeit through post-Elizabethan lenses, Shakespeare takes us back to the era after Roman republican government had been overthrown and Julius Caesar murdered. Rome was then governed by an imperial triumvirate made up of Julius's adopted nephew Octavius along with the generals Marc Antony and Marcus Lepidus. Octavius and Antony cast Lepidus aside but then broke out in mutual enmity, dragging Rome into civil war. This showdown drew in Egypt, whose celebrated queen, Cleopatra, became Antony's mistress. After triumphing over the two lovers, Octavius seemed to stake out his moral high ground by proclaiming that "the time of universal peace is near."[8] Yet all he really meant was that "universal" equated with "Roman," that "Roman" equated with "imperial," and that the emperor was now himself. Octavius granted "peace" to Egypt because that choice converged with Roman dominance. This kind of maneuver became known as Pax Romana, Roman Peace, an empire's self-interested peace secured through calculated subjugation. In fact, in Shakespearean political drama, governing classes rarely fret about the wrongs they inflict on wider populations through their military escapades. Consider *Henry V* (ca. 1599), where the English king captures French territory then commands his troops to treat the locals gently. Henry issues this order prompted not by spasms of empathy but to set up a propaganda machine over his newly won subjects.[9]

We can travel farther back in time to find similar calculations. Ancient Confucianism offers one of humanity's masterpieces of interest-convergence, bursting with insights about how upper classes maintain power by prudently appeasing subordinates.[10] Meanwhile, Plato rails against sophists and orators from the Athens of his time who knew how to pile argument upon argument to prove that in politics self-interest decides all.[11] Anticipating Bell, Socrates responds by insisting that justice must prevail over self-interest, yet Socrates struggles to make his point, and it is far from obvious that Plato allows him to win the argument.[12]

In our own time, not only Western racism but also socialist repression have followed the rule of interest-convergence. From time to time, socialist regimes might have marginally expanded freedoms of political or artistic expression, striving to counter their negative image largely as Bell saw America doing during the Cold War. Throughout those years, Kremlinologists' recourse to meteorological metaphors such as "thawing" and "fresh winds" in lieu of candidly political ones such as "liberation" and "democratization" underscored the doubts hovering over whatever freedom was supposedly being granted, and which rarely amounted to much.[13] Under dictatorships, any supposed "rights" that are granted one day can always be snatched away the next because they are never seriously rights at all.[14] Even as late as Gorbachev, new freedoms were promised via visual metaphors such as "glasnost" (openness, transparency) and "perestroika" (rebuilding, restructuring), as if the climatological ones had become too hackneyed to be believed. No firmer promises could yet be made because it was anyone's guess who was really calling the shots in Moscow.

So Bell was correct if he meant that *any* given sphere of power or influence tends to make concessions only where these fortify its own interests. Just to be clear, my point is not that people only ever act on self-interest. After all, both individual and group motivations can be varied and complex, and can certainly include altruism. Yet there are few moments in world history when the spectacle of elites pursuing self-interest would have caused a shock.

LEFTIST INTEREST-CONVERGENCE

Of course, given that liberal democracy promises equal citizenship, nor can we be surprised that progressives have held it to a standard higher than we might apply to ancient China, classical Athens, imperial Rome, medieval Florence, and Soviet Russia. But then the next question is: What about leftists themselves?

In the early twentieth century, the British philosopher and political activist Bertrand Russell, a progressive on many issues and originally sympathetic to the newborn Soviet power, traveled there shortly after the October Revolution of 1917 and met Vladimir Lenin personally. Yet Russell soon fell out of love with a despotism that seemed wildly disproportionate to whatever internal or external pressures the regime faced. In 1920, aware of Western leftists who still cheered the new Soviet entity, Russell condemned Lenin roundly and publicly.[15] A decade later, the novelist and later Nobel Prize winner André Gide, also socially progressive and at first sympathetic to the revolution, took up an invitation to witness Stalin's early years firsthand. Yet like Russell, after witnessing the regime up close, Gide sought to dissuade his comrades from their romantic illusions.[16] Writers such as Max Horkheimer and Theodor Adorno followed, seeking alternatives to orthodox Marxism and Leninism. By the mid-twentieth century, progressives such as Ruth Fischer, Hannah Arendt, and Claude Lefort had published breathtaking condemnations of socialist oppression. Lefort bluntly scolded his leftist friends, leaving no doubt about their complicity in mass violence and oppression.[17]

These figures exhibited leftist self-scrutiny at its best. Other thinkers have not so minutely unpicked the mechanics of leftist repression but have assimilated these lessons by seeking an antidespotic leftism. They have included writers as varied in their outlooks as Jean-Paul Sartre, Simone de Beauvoir, Franz Fanon, Louis Althusser, Michel Foucault, Gilles Deleuze, Jürgen Habermas, Jacques Rancière, Cornel West, Giorgio Agamben, Alain Badiou, Kimberlé Williams Crenshaw, Antonio Negri, Roberto Unger, Judith Butler, Slavoj Žižek, Simon Critchley, Wendy Brown, Ernst Laclau, Chantal Mouffe, and many more. Admittedly, some of these thinkers have at times taken reprehensible positions of their own, which some of them later renounced. In any event, an ongoing exercise within critical theory has been the continuous rethinking of leftist thought with each new generation.[18] Accordingly, most of these authors acknowledge the mass injustices that were committed by regimes long supported on the left, even when they do not make it a central theme of their work in the manner of writers such as Fischer, Arendt, and Lefort.

Yet, on closer inspection, and particularly in the prosperous decades after World War II, these reevaluations were an easy step for Western progressives to take, given their increasingly obvious self-interest in dissociating from Stalin, Mao, Pol Pot, the Kim dynasty, and other such tyrannies once the chronicles of their horrors had become impossible to deny. Of course at the right and in the center of politics people also tend to confess the wrongs of their past allegiances when these wrongs are already widely known and further links would tarnish their image, so interest-convergence arises no more on the left than anywhere else. Nor am I claiming that these leftists were insincere, no more than Bell felt the US Supreme Court was insincere when it struck down race segregation laws. Clearly, then, step 1 of leftist memory politics *of the left*, meaning candid acknowledgment of leftist atrocities, has long been in place. The problem, as we have seen, is that leftists have stopped short of taking step 2. Why? Because, following Bell, any plans for proactive campaigns to educate a wide public about leftist atrocities have held out too few prospects of gain for the left. For some on the left, any further admissions of error would be a sellout. Few crits want to hear right-wing media shrieking, "Leftists admit that they were cheerleading for mass murder."

That risk almost stopped me from writing this book, as the following story will explain. In 2006, Ferenc Gyurcsány, at the time the center-left prime minister of Hungary, delivered a closed-door speech at a conference of his Democratic Coalition party. Gyurcsány summoned the party to engage in collective self-scrutiny: "We have screwed up. Not a little but a lot. No country in Europe has screwed up as much as we have. It can be explained. We have obviously lied throughout the past 18 to 24 months. It was perfectly clear that what we were saying was not true."[19] So much for well-meaning self-flagellation. After a recording slipped out, Viktor Orbán's right-wing Fidesz party relentlessly repeated these lines with the aid of an opportunist right-wing media, then swept into power with an autocratic government that proved far more mendacious and corrupt.[20]

So at a time when the far right has been mobilizing worldwide, perhaps this is the worst possible moment to invite leftists to undertake public education campaigns about leftist atrocities. Yet even assuming cynical backlashes, no crit has ever suggested that oppressive histories of the West should wait until the timing is better. As Martin Luther King Jr. exhorted in 1963, "Frankly, I have yet to engage in a direct action campaign that was 'well timed' in the view of those who have not suffered unduly from the disease of segregation. For years now I have heard the word 'Wait!' It rings in the ear of every Negro with piercing familiarity. This 'Wait' has almost always meant 'Never.' We must come to see, with one of our distinguished jurists, that 'justice too long delayed is justice denied.'"[21] When Donald Trump and Ron DeSantis twisted ideas in the way Orbán did, the prospect of further backlash in no way spurred leftists to call for less critical theory. This is why I, too, am calling not for less critical theory but for more. It is precisely at a time of right-wing resurgence that leftists need to reconsider the messages they have been sending.

Consider two other contexts, within feminist and LGBTQ+ politics, in which a seeming leftist self-scrutiny has really only reflected the left's self-interest. Western feminism has long formed a pillar of critical theory, yet by the final decades of the twentieth century women from ethnic-minority and non-Western backgrounds were increasingly accusing the movement of perpetuating white, middle-class biases. Many Western feminists took the reproach on board, although not without some ruffled feathers, and opened their doors to ethnic-minority, non-Western, and other perspectives.[22] The same shift occurred in LGBTQ+ politics, which had also been inaugurated in the West largely by middle-class white males but then opened up to include a greater range of voices.[23] In these situations, too, leftists certainly seemed to be practicing collective self-scrutiny, yet they could easily embrace these types of changes because the ethnic-minority and third-world voices they incorporated had already long ago adopted critiques of Western liberal democracy, hence a broadly leftist consensus about histories of Western injustice. Ultimately, these were allies coming together to join forces, not acts of self-scrutiny undertaken regardless of prospective gains. The interest-convergence is so conspicuous in these examples that it becomes doubtful whether serious autocritique was ever being practiced at all. As crits rightly teach us, collective self-scrutiny takes place not because of self-interest but regardless of it.

LIMITS OF COLLECTIVE SELF-INTEREST

Let's return for a moment to Ukraine. Some progressives have compared the war with Russia to the Israel–Palestine conflict. For example, Slavoj Žižek equates Ukrainians with Palestinians and Israel with Russia.[24] Nimbly linking all the dots from past to present, many crits have interpreted Israel as an incarnated continuity of Western racism and colonialism.[25] They ask: How has the West reconciled its declared ideologies of peace and stability with its actual histories of violence, its declared ideologies of freedom and self-government with its actual histories of domination, its declared ideologies of equal citizenship with its actual histories of subjugation? How did these forms of violence, domination, and subjugation become systemic? How have these patterns continued into the present? How has the West acted to downplay these histories in the public mind? To each of these questions, they respond that Israel supplies a disastrous answer.

To be sure, we might well challenge which dots these and other critical theorists do and do not connect for purposes of recounting their histories of the Middle East. Yet for present purposes we have already seen the more telling overlap: the same method of dot connecting from leftist pasts through to crises in our own time wholly vanishes from too many leftist commentaries on Ukraine. This amnesia is striking because any serious autocritique would mean that all the same questions would have to be posed about the left: How has the left reconciled its historical support for violent regimes with its own declared ideologies of peace and stability? Where, exactly, has it connected those dots to crises such as Putin's various invasions? How has the left reconciled its own declared ideologies of freedom and popular self-government with its actual histories of domination, its own declared ideologies of equal citizenship with its actual histories of subjugation? How did such violence, domination, and subjugation become systemic, and how have these patterns continued into the present? And how have leftists acted to downplay these histories in the public mind? To each of these questions, today's leftists deliver disastrous answers, if any at all.

Again, none of this means that all progressives have taken identical views. For example, contrary to German, Chomsky, Mélenchon, and Wagenknecht, authors such as Žižek and Judith Butler have been less inclined to place the crux of blame for Putin's invasion on the West.[26] In particular, I zealously endorse Butler's rejection of official Kremlin heteronormativity as part and parcel of its ethnonationalism. Both she and Žižek—diametrically opposed to these other leftists—rightly recognize Putin's power mongering as a force that operates often obliviously to how the West is acting and responding. So we can certainly spot divergences between, on the one hand,

Butler and Žižek and, on the other hand, German, Chomsky, Mélenchon, and Wagenknecht. These differences might even be cited to prove that we cannot generalize about the left and that not all leftists think alike—that the left is no monolith but encompasses vast and often mutually divergent viewpoints. Yet what all these progressives share is the same failure to cite any leftist memory politics of the left as a factor crucially relevant to the contexts and histories of such global crises. In diagnosing the Ukraine war, Butler and Žižek do not explore long histories of leftist complicity in Soviet Russia any more than their seeming opposites German, Chomsky, Mélenchon, and Wagenknecht. In a word, the differences in these leftists' approaches dwell entirely at the surface.

Žižek grew up under Josip Tito's Yugoslav dictatorship, and Wagenknecht came of age in a Kremlin-controlled East Germany. Both sat with windows onto Soviet-style oppression, which Žižek in particular has long and often comically criticized.[27] But precisely like his supposed rival Chomsky in matters concerning Ukraine, Žižek has always narrated this oppressive chronicle as a past that remains unrelated to the leftism that he espouses. Suddenly there are no dots that would connect the left's past support for despotic regimes to its present positions. With Butler and Žižek no less than with German, Chomsky, Mélenchon, and Wagenknecht, we witness a tidy leftist divorce from history that crits have forbidden to defenders of liberal democracy.

Why has it never occurred to leftists that they owe countless millions of victims of leftist politics, at the very least, some minimal public display of respect or remorse—on par with the public commemorations they have rightly introduced in response to the injustices committed by liberal democracies—be it only for a few minutes from time to time, let alone more concerted public campaigns? Because they have seen no gain in doing so. Yet by avoiding self-scrutiny, crits have kept critical theory from *being* critical. Autocritique wherever and whenever it applies is one thing; autocritique only when it converges with self-interest is not autocritique at all and remains the arch-opposite of critical theory.

Some leftists might respond that when they committed themselves to progressive platforms in earlier times, those platforms were then wrongly hijacked by power mongers and party machines. In this view, the only fair response would be to judge leftists on the basis of their intentions at the times they lent support to such regimes—times when there was often confusion about how new regimes were unfolding. This argument asks us to judge leftists on the basis of their benign motives in earlier times, yet we have already seen that this is the kind of narrative that crits rightly reject when they are scrutinizing histories of Western injustice. It would be an abandonment of critical theory to assume that virtuous ambitions should trump concrete results. Again, people in earlier times often supported militarist, classist, racist, colonialist, patriarchal, heteronormative, and other systems of domination because they believed this was the right thing to do, even if those beliefs appall us today. Therefore, evidence of noble aspirations has given crits reason to do *more* public and proactive memory politics to understand how such good intentions could have served to justify mass injustice. Benevolent impulses cannot excuse the atrocities committed by or within liberal democracies, nor can they excuse the atrocities committed by or within regimes that long enjoyed a leftist imprimatur.

Here is a related objection. Past socialist regimes often had reason to believe that Western military and economic power posed threats, typically branded by those regimes as "counterinsurgency" or "counterrevolution." Only immediate and decisive measures could foil these threats, and the Western left cannot be blamed for atrocities committed under these conditions of urgency. Yet this claim, too, would raise problems for critical theory by assuming a cost–benefit calculation of the kind that crits reject in their scrutiny of the West. It would mean that the benefits of maintaining such regimes outweighed the costs in lost and damaged lives. If someone were to argue that American southern states needed to maintain slavery or segregation to promote stability, or that Britain and France needed to maintain their colonies to keep the peace, or that men needed to maintain dominance over women to preserve the existing social order, leftists would rightly wince at such trade-offs. Along the same lines, it would be bogus to claim, for example, that some populations under socialist regimes witnessed improvements in their lives because this claim, too, rests upon a cost–benefit calculation that crits have never accepted in condemning Western injustices.

7 UNDERDOGS BITING

It is right to stand up for underdogs, and another of Lindsey German's claims about the Ukraine war ran as follows: "I regard Russia as an imperialist power, although considerably lesser economically and militarily than its opponents."[1] Similarly, as we have seen, Noam Chomsky regretted that citizens in the West were being deprived of Putin's opinions about the Ukraine war, which placed Russia at an unfair disadvantage. While perhaps heard by some as balanced assessments, these "lesser power" tropes reinforce the tactic of placing all essential blame on the West. Are these claims about greater and lesser powers as clear-cut as Chomsky and German would have us believe?

UNEQUAL POWER

Let's start with three simple principles. The first should be obvious: *for a party to possess greater power in any given situation is for it to possess greater freedom of action.* This is true of governments, organizations, businesses, and individuals. To have power over a situation is to have choice and control over it, so the more power any given party has, the more choice and control it has. The more choice and control it has, the more freedom of action it has.

The second principle should be equally obvious: *greater freedom of action imposes greater ethical responsibility.* Accordingly, when a government exercises power over a situation, we expect it to minimize unnecessary harms to its citizens and within the wider world. Of course, governments do at times cause unnecessary harms so we widely share this expectation, even if we may differ about what counts as "unnecessary harm" in particular situations.[2] For example, many conservatives believe that a government causes unnecessary harm to others who have not yet been born when it grants abortion rights to women. In response, many leftists believe that a government causes unnecessary harm to women and perhaps to future unwanted children by unduly restricting abortion rights. While these sides disagree about what counts as the greater harm, they do still agree on the principle that a powerful actor, such as the state, should not cause unnecessary harm or allow individuals to cause unnecessary harm.

If these two principles are basically sound, then a third logically follows: *greater power imposes greater ethical responsibility.* Crits have long developed broad understandings of political power based on the premise that power over others creates greater freedom of action for the more powerful actors— for rich over poor, for white over Black, for colonizer over colonized, for male over female, for heteronormative over LGBTQ+. Within those pairings, the more powerful party has traditionally enjoyed the greater range of personal, political, social, economic, and cultural choices, while the less powerful party has faced a narrower range. It is also true that the West has long commanded greater wealth and influence in the world than Russia. If we combine the yearly economic output of the United States, Germany, France, Great Britain, Italy, Canada, Australia, and others in recent years, the Western nations show far greater wealth than Russia.[3] So would it be accurate to insert "the West over Russia" alongside these other pairings? If leftists are to stand up for the underdog, must they indeed place ultimate blame for Russian aggression on the West?

I hope we can agree that such a conclusion would be insane. Some hierarchies—for instance, systems of North American plantation slavery—do indeed correlate to vast freedoms for the more powerful party compared to few freedoms for the less powerful. Yet there are countless power differentials that do not work in this all-or-nothing way. Here's an analogy. In 2022 the McDonald's corporation boasted a net worth of more than $150 billion while its competitor Burger King recorded a little more than $7 billion, a gap that carried over from earlier years.[4] In other words, that year Burger King's market share tallied less than 5 percent of McDonald's.

Yet the discrepancy hardly rendered Burger King a powerless actor bearing only slight social responsibility whenever it had to compete with its rival. So imagine the following scenario. To lower its prices and with full knowledge of the risks, Burger King secretly adds a cheap but allergenic filler to its food, not harming most consumers but killing a few. The victims' families then sue Burger King for causing the deaths. Burger King responds that it had to add the filler because of the company's lesser power in a competitive marketplace. Such a defense would be so ludicrous that, we can only hope, even the most brazen lawyer would never venture it in court.

Yes, power dynamics do at times work in an all-or-nothing way, yet in complex social and political situations they usually do not. Once a nation disposes of enough organizational and material capacity to have mowed down populations in the millions over the course of a century while exercising overwhelming control over education and the mass media, that regime's "lesser" power cannot plausibly shift its ethical responsibility to its rivals, making it unclear why writers like German, Mélenchon, Wagenknecht, and Chomsky would consider the disparity to be relevant to the Ukraine war. Has the left's failure to push for proactive public discussion of its own bleak histories *caused* these figures to commit such a stark historical and ethical reductionism? If we were to take their arguments seriously, and given that Soviet and post-Soviet Russia have historically been less wealthy than the West, it would become questionable whether Moscow would bear responsibility for *any* of its atrocities committed over more than a century whenever some wealthy Western power had played some more than negligible role.

The "lesser power" trope becomes even more reductionist when we toss nuclear arsenals into the mix. For example, NATO's stockpile dwarfs North Korea's, yet even the Kim regime's paltry supply has a—not perfectly yet substantially—equalizing effect. If crits could climb into a time machine and travel back to the Cold War, we can only hope they would not seek to explain to countless millions of victims and survivors of Lenin, Stalin, Mao, Pol Pot, Kim Il-Sung, or other dictators that the ultimate source of their woes could be traced to Western nations holding greater overall power in the world. Yet if crits would say no such thing in those situations, then it becomes hard to see how anyone can put that case to Ukrainians today. Indeed, as nations such as China, Russia, North Korea, Iran, and other autocracies enhance their military, economic, and diplomatic cooperation while far-right autocrats loom in the West, any suggestion that liberal democracy lays an unrivaled claim to global domination remains far from obvious.[5]

THE MATHEMATICS OF INNOCENCE

Crits have widely taken a stance on the problem of unequal power, and it, too, can be summarized in three straightforward principles. First, to repeat, hierarchies such as rich over poor, white over Black, colonizer over colonized, male over female, and heteronormative over LGBTQ+ have witnessed injustices committed by those who hold more power against those who hold less. Second, a time-honored task for leftism has been to stand up for underdogs. But then surely a third principle must run as follows: *If more powerful actors compel less powerful actors to commit unjust acts, then the blame lies with the more powerful actors.*[6]

Here's a bare-bones example. Imagine that Bessie aims a loaded gun at Cassie, then commands Cassie to steal food from Desi, who is weak and poor. Cassie, fearing for her life, carries out the theft. Before this moment, none of these individuals had any knowledge of the other two, nor did Cassie have any reason to suspect such an event would occur. Assuming that Cassie had no safe way of avoiding the command and acted as prudently as possible, then, in my view, the blame for the theft would lie entirely with Bessie. Strictly speaking, Cassie still had a choice to steal or not to steal the food, and is responsible for that choice. However, any blame for the consequences of that choice, such as the theft itself and any other related harm to Desi, such as physical or emotional detriment caused by the theft, must lie with Bessie. I call this the *Principle of Relative Innocence.* Cassie committed an unjust act but must be deemed innocent of any harm it caused relative to the role that Bessie played. I think most mainstream defenders of liberal democracy would endorse this principle, and I also think most crits would endorse it. It seems correct not only as an ethical matter but also in law. Under many legal systems, persons who have acted under duress can be declared innocent or can have their guilt largely mitigated.[7]

Now here's an overtly political example. Many people would argue that laws permitting slavery could never be ethically defensible in contemporary industrial societies. If we were to find a society in which plantation-type slavery is lawful, many of us would pardon a group of slaves for killing their sadistic master, Legree, if that were the only way for the slaves to flee. Strictly speaking, like Cassie, these slaves have a free choice to kill or not to kill the master, and are fully responsible for that choice. However, here, too, I would maintain that any ethical blame for the consequences of that choice, such as Legree's death and any other damage to his family, business affiliates, or anyone else, lies with fully with Legree. We might well view the rebellion as a form of legitimate, collective self-defense. We would also be right to pardon any outside activists who had helped the slaves carry out the killing if no less violent option had been available. So we can refine the Principle of Relative Innocence as follows: *If more powerful actors compel less powerful actors to commit unjust acts, then the blame lies with the more powerful actors and not with the less powerful actors or with their accomplices or allies.*

Yet here, too, not all power hierarchies are so clear cut. Consider the harder example of a brutal dictatorship in which there is widespread yet stifled popular support for democracy. Whether we would approve of citizens murdering senior officials might depend on several factors, such as whether the dictatorship is willing to accept a transition to democracy, with what guarantees and timeframes, and so forth. Even with this information, we might disagree about when or whether we would endorse such killings. Yet despite this type of harder case, the earlier Legree scenario shows that there are situations in which both crits and defenders of liberal democracy would widely approve of violent defensive action committed by those who have less power. In that sense, I believe we would find wide acceptance for the Principle of Relative Innocence.[8]

However, that principle must not be confused with another, which I call the *Principle of Absolute Innocence*, and which, in effect, figures like German, Mélenchon, Wagenknecht, and Chomsky ultimately endorse. It runs like this: *By definition, when less powerful actors commit unjust acts, then they deserve no blame.* What is the difference between the two principles? The former one, the Principle of Relative Innocence, takes context and history into account, such as degrees of relative power and coercion. By contrast, the Principle of Absolute Innocence requires nothing more than a superficial tally of relative wealth and influence, such that any power imbalance shifts the blame for unjust actions to the more powerful party, which, again, if strictly applied, would lead to the absurdity of allowing Burger King to claim that market pressures forced it to resort to dangerous practices. The Principle of Absolute Innocence stakes out an ideologically closed system engineered to confirm a predetermined stance, irrespective of the facts of concrete situations.

I call the confusion of these two principles the *innocence fallacy*. It consists of the assumption that lesser power suffices to exculpate an actor from having committed unjust acts. I hope it is now clear that lesser power may justify violence under some circumstances but not in all circumstances. German, Chomsky, Mélenchon, and Wagenknecht commit this fallacy even if they do not call Russia the victim in so many words. A related concept is that of the *dominant narrative*. What this means is that a range of explanations might well shed light on a given social or political problem, but the messages most widely disseminated are those that are backed by wealthy or powerful interests.[9] A dominant narrative commonly draws on preexisting prejudices or attitudes, which exert pressures on those who hold alternative views to remain silent in important spheres of life such as educational and employment situations.[10] Yet the more complex a controversy becomes, particularly in our era of information wars waged via electronic media along with bots of all and sundry origin, the less obvious it is whose messages carry how much weight.[11] For example, in the run-up to the British referendum on leaving the European Union in 2015, the "dominant narrative" on all accounts favored remaining, which was the choice of leading Western governments and multinational corporations at the time, yet that side lost.[12] In lamenting the Kremlin's muted voice, Chomsky posits the supposedly rigged Western mass media agencies as stewards of a dominant narrative favoring NATO aggression, yet voices such as those of Wagenknecht and Germany's far-right Alternative für Deutschland, along with the prominent US politician J. D. Vance—to name only a few—have scarcely lacked platforms to oppose Western aid to Ukraine.

Here is another familiar claim. Leftists target liberal democracy not because they take a harsher view of it but on pragmatic grounds. It makes sense to channel their energies where they stand the best chance of wielding influence. Changing minds in Russia, China, or Iran seems hard, but in Washington, London, or Brussels there may be chances of success. Of course, plenty of dissidents in those countries would appreciate far more support from the Western left than they have ever mustered, but for now let's assume that it is both justified and expedient to reproach one's own government and those allied to it before chiding other regimes. Even if we make all these assumptions, they still fail to explain the left's lopsided public-awareness campaigns. Recommending concrete steps for immediate policy is one thing and teaching history is another. If leftists view public consciousness about history as intrinsically important, then they can publicly engage about their own past support for repressive regimes while still tactically emphasizing whichever steps they believe Western governments ought to take in any given situation.

A related argument would be that it is fair to hold the West to higher ethical standards. Liberal democracies often proclaim human rights as a universal benchmark, so it seems legitimate to apply human rights standards first and foremost to liberal democracies. Of course, many non-Westerners would dispute the suggestion that their governments should be held to lower standards, adding that the core values of human rights can be found in many cultures and traditions.[13] Yet even if we were to disregard human rights as a benchmark, the fact remains that all governments in today's world proclaim self-justifying ideals, and these ideals are invariably proclaimed in some language of ethical norms.[14]

It is certainly true that Western governments proclaim values of human dignity, civic equality, and the rule of law, and crits rightly hold them to these pledges. Yet to stick with the present example, the post–Cold War Russian Constitution, too, boasts of "human rights and freedoms" and the nation's "democratic basis."[15] To date, Russia has not formally repudiated these passages, even if it did so informally long ago. Similarly, the current Chinese Constitution announces that "exploitation of man by man [has been] abolished" and has been replaced by "the people's democratic dictatorship led by the working class and based on the alliance of workers and peasants."[16] It would be vintage orientalism to assume that we must hold Western societies to their own proclaimed values but must not treat other powerful nations the same way when they wage atrocities at home or abroad. The idea that even the most powerful non-Western governments should be held to a lower standard, a version of the old "racism of low expectations," smacks more of orientalism, more of cross-cultural condescension, than of treating other nations as morally responsible agents or promoting mutual respect across cultures.

In 2016, Slavoj Žižek proclaimed in a tweet to the (Western) world: "You've had your anti-communist fun, and you are pardoned for it—time to get serious once again!"[17] Žižek had recently completed *Trouble in Paradise: From the End of History to the End of Capitalism* (2014). The book was published by Penguin, enabling Žižek to enjoy ample public-speaking and other promotional events in addition to his frequent mass-media publications. Žižek's reputation has drawn in part from his relish for frivolous provocations, and we certainly cannot collapse his voluminous output into an off-hand tweet. His faith in the communist ideal has attracted plenty of debate, but my aim for now is not to weigh up the pros and cons of communism.

When I first read the tweet, I imagined a crit conference devoted to histories of Western racism and colonialism. I pictured in my mind an audience member shouting out, "OK, you've all had your fun," goading participants to "get serious" about liberal democracy. How would the audience respond? With ridicule or disdain, and probably both. Yet the deeper problem lies with Žižek's assumption that leftist pasts can be antiseptically removed from his own ideal of a truer communism. Žižek has penned a wealth of writing to dissect systemic injustice within Western liberal democracy without offering any explanation of mass injustice on the left *as systemic and ongoing*. So he did not just post a playful tweet. *Trouble in Paradise* plunges into all and sundry ills flowing from Western capitalism with no suggestion that the grim histories of his own political home have continued just as destructively.

We are constantly told that whereas liberal democracy remains steeped in its bleakest histories, leftists have transcended their own. The problem is not that Žižek denies atrocities on the left but that he treats them as lying entirely in the past once the time has come for him to advocate his own brand of leftïsm. In his defense, Žižek would presumably argue, as Chomsky does, that he *can* propose a politics that is not bound to its past. Yet this is precisely the response that crits reject in any contemporary defense of liberal democracy. Crits rightly condemn discussions of Western liberal democracies that surgically remove their past injustices from their high-minded ideals and might well cast such a schism as a denial, even a calculated silencing, of the past. Yet, for Žižek, a "communist horizon" shines forth as the political ideal from which the left's past can be antiseptically excised, meaning that past injustices amounted to nothing more than aberrations and deviations from *real* socialism or *real* communism or *real* leftism.[18] Žižek mocks Western opinion for having confused the *real* communism with its own bleak past, yet among crits it would be risible for, say, a free-marketeer to sing the praises of some liberal-capitalist future as if it could be neatly separated from 200-plus years of problems it has sown across the globe. As we have seen, Žižek is far from alone in this tactic.

Two conclusions seem to follow from Žižek's stance. First, we are inept to link some professed leftist ideal to leftism's own bleak histories. Second, we are also inept when we *fail* to link some professed liberal-democratic ideal to liberal democracy's bleak histories. Yet if this second proposition is true—and critical theory has no existence at all if it is not true—then, on critical theory's own account, the first proposition must be false. Crits today are in denial about their responsibility for perpetuating that falsehood.

"Hitler and the Nazis were just some passing bird shit in more than a thousand years of glorious German history." In 2018, Alexander Gauland, leader of the far-right Alternative für Deutschland (AfD), rallied the party's youth wing with these words.[1]

Outrage across the political spectrum was instant. Germany was led at the time by Prime Minister Angela Merkel's center-right Christian Democratic Union (CDU) in coalition with the center-left Social Democratic Party (SPD). The CDU's party head, Annegret Kramp-Karrenbauer, fired back: "For the AfD and Gauland, 50 million victims, the Holocaust, and all-out war merely amount to 'bird shit'! Behind its mainstream mask, this is the AfD's true face." The SPD's party head found it "shameful that such people can sit in the German Parliament." The parliamentary leader for Die Linke (The Left) charged Gauland with "historical amnesia," recalling that Nazi Germany "was responsible for the deaths of more people than in all previous periods of history." The Green Party chair added that such amnesia was "not the exception, but the rule" in the AfD.[2]

What exactly was wrong with Gauland's remark? Just the crude phrasing? Not at all. Had Gauland used a less vulgar word such as *chaos*, he still would have sparked this backlash. Or was it that he denied that Nazi crimes had been committed? Not at all. Not only did he *not* deny them, but he equated Hitler and Nazism with shit. Nor was Gauland's timeline wrong. We can indeed observe a continuous population in German-speaking central Europe stretching back over a thousand years, and praising the "glory" of that long history may sound prosaic but in most countries would hardly trigger such revulsion. No, Gauland's perversion lay not in denying Nazism but in sidelining it.

The German word Gauland used for "bird shit" is *Vogelschiss*, and, as I mentioned in chapter 4, we can use the term "*Vogelschiss* claim" to refer to this strategy of superficially acknowledging a historical atrocity as a way of actually downplaying it. This is a well-worn rhetorical trick, known in classical rhetoric as *paradiastole*, where the speaker dresses up tragedy as trivia. In this chapter I will treat such verbal ploys as examples of what we can call *purity narratives*. In politics we find purity narratives right, left, and center—across governments, religions, movements, and ideologies—but Gauland offers a convenient jump-off because his is so easy to grasp.

FACTUAL DENIALISM AND ETHICAL DENIALISM

Here's another example. At the outbreak of the COVID pandemic in 2020, a Wuhan resident posted an online video of desperate conditions at a local hospital.[3] He was swiftly arrested as authorities hurried to erase all traces of the video. Over the following months, Chinese officials jammed the media with tales of government heroism in fighting the disease.[4] This was a purity narrative being manufactured from the very beginning of the history in question. Suppressing critical coverage wherever possible, the regime drowned the country in pro-government propaganda. Beijing massively suppressed reporting in a country where most people have little or no access to nonstate news, airbrushing the domestic crisis out of history. Another of its standard ploys was to allege that the pandemic had been spread in China by the US government.[5]

If you have seen posters of cheery North Korean supremos painted against baby-blue skies, cotton-white clouds, and trees bearing candy-cane-pink blossoms all surrounded by beaming faces of adoring children, laborers, or soldiers, then you have seen the purest of all purity narratives because they need no words and become all the more hideous when used to paper over a regime that has ravaged its population for generations.[6] A related technique of the purity narrative is *silencing*: historical injustices are neither affirmed nor denied but quietly passed over without a word. A government puts history to sleep to avoid public notice altogether, propagating sunnier images in their place. Today, millions of Chinese scarcely know about Mao's murderous campaigns, about the Tiananmen Square massacre in 1989, or about the oppression of Tibetans and Uyghurs. Any citizen initiatives to commemorate these injustices are suppressed and lead to intimidation, imprisonment, or loss of education or employment for individuals as well as for their friends and families.[7] Essential information is not merely censored but actively eclipsed by stories about national valor and government altruism. At the same time, real or fabricated enemies, internal and external, are portrayed as devious and destructive.

Governments manufacture historical amnesia by immersing citizens in whitewashed stories about their nation's past and, above all, by allowing no room for dissent.[8] Purity narratives flourish wherever it is too dangerous to challenge them. They are propagated not only by governments but also by members of independent movements and belief systems. Nostalgia about a golden age when everything was better is also a purity narrative, as sanitized histories become a tool for casting a nation, religion, movement, or official belief system in the best possible light. This is off-the-shelf interest-convergence, the arch-opposite of collective self-scrutiny.

The crudest purity narrative consists of the *factual* denial of an injustice. In western Europe, Holocaust denial has long stood as a paradigm case, with deniers claiming either that extermination did not take place at all or that it happened only in small numbers.[9] Factual denialism creates an *absolute* purity narrative: a government, group, or movement denies that it or its allies have committed any serious wrongdoing at all. Yet this strategy becomes weak when the historical existence of atrocities is already widely understood and documented, so a handy alternative is *ethical* denialism, whereby injustice is conceded in one breath but then dismissed in the next. This was Gauland's *Vogelschiss* tactic—not denying Nazi crimes but portraying them as a drop in the bucket, a few moments of evil steeped in a millennium of splendor, perhaps unethical in the short term yet secondary to any assessment of German history over time. Decades earlier, the far-right French politician Jean-Marie Le Pen (founder of what was then the country's

National Front party, now rebaptized the National Rally) had paved the way, dismissing the Holocaust as nothing more than a "detail" in the history of World War II. By confessing—or, rather, boasting—that he "hadn't particularly studied the question," Le Pen did not literally deny the Shoah's occurrence but instead parodied liberal open-mindedness, all the while winking and nudging that the Holocaust merited little attention one way or the other, being so insignificant that, far from lamenting his ignorance as a defect, Le Pen could flaunt it as an achievement.[10]

Crits encounter ethical denialism when they speak about wrongs committed by or within the histories of today's Western liberal democracies.[11] Generations of British and French school children were once raised on stories about the grandeur of their empires, with little time spent on the cruelties of slavery and colonialism, just as the American "frontier spirit" was long lionized through legends about white settlers overcoming hardship, with little mention of the harms inflicted on Indigenous peoples. Purity narratives—along with their techniques of denial, silencing, sanitizing, and sidelining—are attempts to orchestrate mass amnesia about painful histories.

For example, North American plantation slavery and the subsequent era of racial segregation cannot be factually denied. Unlike the Holocaust, which was executed quickly and furtively, slavery and racial segregation remained on proud display for centuries, so we do not find "slavery denial" or "Jim Crow denial" taking the same forms as Holocaust denial. Instead, given that factual denial becomes untenable, ethical denial sweeps in to take its place. One Florida school district tried to push a purity narrative that would replace the term *slavery* in textbooks with periphrases such as *involuntary relocation* or *Black immigration* while Florida mandated its schools to teach that slavery offered the means by which African Americans "developed skills which, in some instances, could be applied for their personal benefit."[12] Although technically acknowledging the existence of slavery, these evasions diminish and even mock its gravity.[13] These examples show that within a population individuals may well acknowledge the existence of some past wrongdoing while drawing wholly opposite conclusions about its ethical significance. Many people acknowledge the raw fact that racism, colonialism, and Nazism took place. However, some respond with outrage, which is a form of ethical acknowledgment, while others reply with the sneer of ethical denialism.

Here, too, public officials are not the only culprits. Recall the valiant Ku Klux Klan protecting an honorable white race in D. W. Griffith's film *Birth of a Nation* (1915) or the portrayal of savage Native Americans in John Ford's *Stagecoach* (1939) or the feeble slaves yoked to white melodrama in Victor Fleming's *Gone with the Wind* (1939). Recall the vicious Jews of the film *The Eternal Jew* (1940)—though admittedly that work was linked to the Nazi government, having been commissioned by Adolf Hitler's propaganda minister Joseph Goebbels. Millions viewed these films in a pretelevision age when a night at the cinema promised a feast of education and enchantment.

These two forms of denialism, factual and ethical, might at first seem mutually exclusive. After all, factual denial claims that an event never occurred, while ethical denial admits it only to dismiss it. Yet in practice the distinction remains cryptic because denialists play a shell game that you will never win. Holocaust deniers relish ambiguities, trafficking in both stances, the real message being that it scarcely matters whether the Shoah occurred or not. As Jean-Paul Sartre wrote in 1946, "Don't think that antisemites are completely unaware of the absurdity of their replies." He explained: "They know that their remarks are flimsy and tenuous but they're having fun. It's their adversary's job to use words conscientiously since he believes in words, while antisemites have the *right* to play. They like to play with words because by making ludicrous claims they discredit the seriousness of their interlocutor. They bask in their bad faith because they seek not to persuade through sober arguments but to intimidate and to disconcert."[14]

PIETOSA CRUDELTÀ

In chapter 6, I recalled *The Prince*, published in 1532, in which Niccolò Machiavelli links politics to the self-interest of those who hold power. This son of Florence, at the time a hotbed of political skullduggery, certainly understood the mechanics of purity narratives.[15] Consider chapter 21, which bears the title "How a Prince Should Act to Acquire Esteem." Machiavelli hails Ferdinand II of Aragon, legendary for the Inquisition and for expanding Spanish power and wealth. Ferdinand had begun his career as "a weak ruler" but rose to become "the most famous and most glorious king in Christendom," in part by "using religion for his own purposes."[16] Ferdinand cultivated *pietosa crudeltà*, "pious cruelty," presenting his ruthlessness—for example, in driving all Muslims out of Spain—as the fulfillment of God's will. In other words, Ferdinand mastered the logic of the purity narrative: *if you cannot deny evils committed in your name, then portray them as part of a larger and benign plan.*[17]

The Prince swiftly worked its way through sixteenth-century Europe, sometimes echoed in popular culture—for example, in stock "Machiavel" characters who displaced the earlier stage devils that used to pop up in medieval morality plays.[18] In a famous scene in Shakespeare's *Richard III* (c. 1592), we witness the power monger on the verge of seizing the crown. To propagandize his legitimacy, Richard appears in public "between two clergymen," whom one of his sidekicks lauds to the crowd as "two props of virtue for a Christian prince." When Richard clasps "a book of prayer in his hand," the same toady assures the crowd that such trimmings can be taken as "true ornaments to know a holy man."[19] Here, too, we see that purity narratives emerge not only through words but also through iconography. Recall Donald Trump brandishing a Bible at St. John's Church in Washington, DC, in 2020, after instructing police to use tear gas and hefty riot control to clear a path for him during a Black Lives Matter protest.[20] Or consider the Russian Orthodox patriarch Kirill, one of Putin's pawns and a billionaire oligarch, publicly blessing Russian soldiers who were sent to wage mass murder in Syria and then Ukraine, while praising the bravery of God's own army marching to defend *russky mir*, the "Russian world": whatever harms the soldiers might seem to commit, those wrongs formed part of a greater good.[21]

Although religions still concoct purity narratives, they also come wrapped in secular banners of nationhood, freedom, democracy, equality, and social progress. While millions of young and old were being slaughtered in concentration camps, the Nazi regime propagated images of rosy-cheeked Aryans basking in domesticity.[22] This mood was symbolically captured in Jonathan Glazer's 2023 film *Zone of Interest*, which reconstructed the carefree days enjoyed by the family of Auschwitz commandant Rudolf Höss living directly adjacent to the camp. With hundreds of civilians burning in ovens every day, Höss's wife savored the home as her "little paradise," reveling: "It's so peaceful here. The flowers are blossoming beautifully, the garden is picture perfect." Similarly, millions of Ukrainians, Kazakhs, and Russians died in Stalin's famines, whole peoples were deported from their ancestral homes through operations in which many died, and dissidents perished in labor camps, while Moscow decked the Soviet Union with images of well-fed peasants basking in bounteous wheat fields.[23]

Let me distinguish between *absolute* purity and *whitewashed* purity. We create an absolute purity narrative when we depict a nation, movement, or group in entirely virtuous tones, either omitting atrocities for which it bears responsibility or blaming them on someone else. Again, Gauland could not factually deny Nazi wrongdoing, which would have pushed him too far to the fringes to be useful for his party, so he instead adopted a more hygienic narrative by conceding wrongdoings in one breath only to erase them in the next. Gauland packaged Nazism as an incidental occurrence, a mistake, an aberration in the history of the *real* Germany. This was why his critics insisted that Nazism was not a random error or deviation but emerged from centuries of autocracy, militarism, and antisemitism. Gauland skated around factual denialism by toying with ethical denialism, denying nothing, indeed, confessing everything, while finishing up with a perfectly sanitized German history. Of course, the far right does not need to attain Nazi extremes in order to spin purity narratives. In Britain, after the country's exit from the European Union caused all the predicted hits to the economy and to Britain's global stature, the movement's driving force Nigel Farage by no means took any blame. Instead, he accused the government of failing to achieve the *real* Brexit.[24]

AFTER TRIBALISM

"We all face a choice," Barack Obama declared in his final speech to the United Nations as president in 2016. "We can choose to press forward with a better model of cooperation and integration. Or we can retreat into a world sharply divided, and ultimately in conflict, along age-old lines of nation and tribe and race and religion."[25] Two months later, just days after Donald Trump's election victory, Obama again warned that "we are going to have to guard against a rise in a crude sort of nationalism or ethnic identity or tribalism that is built around an 'us' and a 'them.'"[26]

Also immersed in questions of social and political tribalism, Professor Eli Finkel of Northwestern University describes it as follows: "People on the other side are not just wrong; they're evil."[27] The Yale law professor Amy Chua depicts tribalism as a form of "group identification where your identity is so bound up" with a particular group "that you will basically defend the group and cling to the group no matter what and you start to see everything through that group's lens."[28] In fact, Finkel doubts whether *tribalism* is the best term to describe these tendencies because "tribalism is based on the metaphor of kinship." He instead argues that "a better metaphor may be the near-schismatic divides that have historically separated religious sects such as Sunni from Shia or Protestant from Catholic." Together with his colleague Cynthia S. Wang at Northwestern, Finkel speaks about "political sectarianism," which they describe as "the tendency of political groups to align on the basis of moralized identities rather than shared ideas or policy preferences."[29]

For now, I will stick to the more familiar term *tribalism* and will use it to denote *adherence to a nation, party, movement, group, or belief system irrespective of the injustices that have been committed in its name.* A sad lesson in politics is that all of us are tribal to some degree, since even seemingly apolitical people remain bound to the dominant political order simply to manage from one day to the next. However high our ideals may soar, no political program is ever implemented without harm caused to innocent victims—or, at least, to victims who can be described as innocent from the standpoint of some competing political outlook. For example, aborted fetuses are deplored as victims of murder by religious fundamentalists, who deem the practice to be a supreme injustice, indeed a mortal sin. But these same fetuses are deemed by secular liberals to be by-products of a legitimate exercise of individual autonomy. For the fundamentalists, liberals are tribalists who disregard mass injustice done to prenatal children. For the liberals, it is the fundamentalists who are tribalists in disregarding mass injustices done to women. The fundamentalists view the liberals as tribalists who deny the injustices lurking beneath a liberal purity narrative about the primacy of individual freedom while the liberals see fundamentalists as tribalists who deny the injustices lurking beneath a religious purity narrative about the primacy of fetal life. Of course, these are not the only positions on abortion—nor do these observations lead to the ethically relativist conclusion that all standpoints are equally compelling. The only point of this standoff between fundamentalists and liberals is to illustrate how easily all of us adopt ideals that others see as rife with injustice. They can readily brand us, and we can readily brand them, as tribalist.

Yet the question is not whether we are or are not tribal, but to what degree, and how honest we are about our tribalism. Purportedly universal regimes such as Christianity, Islam, liberalism, capitalism, democracy, or socialism, when translated into institutions, always claim innocent victims from the standpoint of some rival political outlook. In the nineteenth century the German philosopher Georg Wilhelm Friedrich Hegel explained that in human affairs there is no such thing as perfect justice versus perfect injustice but rather struggles between competing views about justice. There is no such thing as complete good versus complete evil but only struggles between competing versions of the good.[30] Again, the tragedy of Auschwitz or plantation slavery was not that they were manifestly evil but that for countless participants and bystanders they became routine, their evil being anything but obvious. They became banal in Hannah Arendt's sense, so that rather than overthrowing such regimes, the rival good of people sticking to the routine of their everyday lives won out, as it does for all of us to greater or lesser degrees.[31]

The closest any of us can come to justice, although we rarely describe our quest in such crudely utilitarian terms, is by comparing competing courses of action and choosing whichever course seems likely to claim the fewest innocent victims overall. We often choose wrongly, with all the human suffering this entails, even running into millions of victims. Yet we delude ourselves and others if we believe that we can choose a political platform that harms only deserving victims, whoever they may be, and no others. In chapter 3, I mentioned a few stalwarts of modern liberalism such as Karl Popper, John Rawls, and Ronald Dworkin. Each of them proposed detailed visions of politics, yet none of them spent much time asking who the innocent victims of their political models would be. Presumably they would have seen such injustice as nothing but errors and accidents, and not the *real* liberalism. This reductionism is what crits have long dissected. The problem, as we have seen, is that it is not only liberals who commit it. By adopting the philosophies of Popper, Rawls, or Dworkin, we commit ourselves to systemic injustice but only because we commit ourselves to *any* political model, however "ideological" or "pragmatic" that model may appear to be.

Consider another example. Members of the Just Stop Oil movement have blocked traffic as a form of protest.[32] They know that by delaying emergency vehicles, they jeopardize vulnerable individuals. To be candid, their calculation here is that the loss of a few lives is a price worth paying to avert calamities that would devastate millions of lives. This is the age-old choice of sacrificing a lesser number of lives to save a greater number, as occurred, for example, in a famous nineteenth-century case where shipwrecked sailors ate a weak crew member to save others.[33] Activists rarely phrase their calculus so bluntly because most of us rarely advance our agendas by confessing that we want to place innocent people in harm's way. Instead, the activists stick to the line that this is one of the few ways of drawing attention to an urgent crisis because docile protests are ignored. Given their belief in the scale and urgency of the problem, they are in effect pleading a defense of necessity: they must act as they are acting because no milder alternative has proved to work. Some critics may counter that these environmentalists undermine their own cause by angering the public, but my only point for now is that, for better or worse, such choices always involve some balancing of goods in principle, regardless of what may be the most effective activist strategies in practice. Far from being outliers, these campaigners dramatize the trade-offs we all make in our daily life choices (for example, when we purchase consumer goods produced by exploited workers or at a high environmental cost), and which inevitably dictate that some people will unfairly lose out so that others may benefit.

In sum, there is no such thing as tribal versus nontribal politics but only degrees of tribalism, degrees of overlooking innocent victims. The best politics is the one that aims for the fewest innocent victims *and* is honest about the innocent victims it claims. That honesty was the original impulse of progressives who, a century ago, started to develop schools of critical theory.[34] Today, crits still claim to elevate social justice as a high ethical value, and yet tribalism always pushes people in the opposite direction, subordinating justice to the goals of a faction, even when they claim to speak in the name of a whole community or society. To state the point simply: on its own terms, when critical theory succumbs excessively to tribalism, it destroys itself. This is what happens when leftists pursue self-criticism only when it brings political gains. When leftists stick to tribalism, demanding collective self-criticism of others that they neglect for themselves, they abandon critical theory and therefore can scarcely expect others to adopt it.[35]

VIVA LOS MARICONES!

Upon the death of the Cuban ruler Fidel Castro in 2016, the *Guardian* journalist Jamie Doward sampled left-wing opinion in Britain. Doward noted, for example, the member of Parliament (MP) George Galloway tweeting a photo of himself with Castro: "You were the greatest man I ever met Comandante Fidel. You were the man of the century."[36] Nowadays many in Britain would view Galloway as an extremist, yet at that time he had many fans and enjoyed regular mainstream-media coverage. Meanwhile, Ken Livingstone—another crank in some eyes yet also a former MP, former London mayor, former radio host, and at the time regular media guest— did sense that a nod to Castro's repression was in order: "Of course, Fidel did things that were wrong," Livingstone conceded. "Initially he wasn't very good on lesbian and gay rights."[37]

Of course, pre-revolutionary histories of American exploitation on the island are germane to Cuban history, and the continuing US blockade has weighed heavily, particularly after the collapse of the Soviet bloc. In the words of the historian Ada Ferrer, "Cuba—its sugar, its slavery, its slave trade—is part of the history of American capitalism."[38] Yet leftists have often viewed repression under Castro not as systemic or structural but as individual errors and accidents. One pro-regime organization known as the Cuba Solidarity Campaign attributed anti-LGBTQ+ persecution on the island to everything *except* the Castro regime: "Spanish colonialism, the influence of the Catholic church, and a culture of machismo."[39] Leftists propagate purity narratives when they fail to apply autocritique to such histories. Writing around the same time for the *Daily Beast*, even the conservative commentator James Kirchick recalled how it "wasn't long after Castro came to power that police began rounding up gay men":

> In 1965, the regime established prison work camps . . . into which it deposited homosexuals, Jehovah's Witnesses, and other "undesirable" elements. . . . Though the Cuban regime closed down the [prison camps] in the late 1960s, it continued to repress gay men as ideologically subversive elements. Openly homosexual people were prevented from joining the Communist Party and fired from their jobs. One of the country's most distinguished writers, Reinaldo Arenas, recounted the prison experience he and countless other gay men endured in his memoir *Before Night Falls* [published in 1992]. "It was a sweltering place without a bathroom," he wrote. "Gays were not treated like human beings, they were treated like beasts. They were the last ones to come out for meals, so we saw them walk by, and the most insignificant incident was an excuse to beat them mercilessly."

Yet what about Fidel's celebrated niece Mariela, daughter to his brother and successor Raul? She was heaped with praise by the West when she urged Fidel to change Cuba's LGBTQ+ policies. But Kirchick was unconvinced: "Mariela Castro has emerged as an LGBT activist, helming an organization called the Cuban National Center for Sex Education," which was founded in 1989. Kirchick noted at the time that "Mariela has been lauded by many in the West as a force for progressive change, and her decision to push for acceptance of LGBTs may be helping on the margins." However, by the late 1980s progressive opinion worldwide was condemning LGBTQ+ persecution, and ongoing reports of anti-LGBTQ+ repression were harming Cuba's international reputation, so the interest-convergence was glaring. Kirkchick added that "no matter how much life for gay Cubans might have improved from the days of forced labor camps, it's all occurring within the context of a totalitarian society whose citizens cannot vote, are denied basic freedoms like the right to speak or protest freely, and cannot form organizations independent of the government. Indeed, it tells you everything you need to know about contemporary Cuba that the country's most visible LGBT activist is the straight daughter of Raul Castro."[40] Kirchick's final sentence here is noteworthy given crits' insistence that marginalized groups must be able to speak in their own voices, not supervised or mediated by overweening power structures. While Castro and Che Guevara had once branded gays as "worms" (*gusanos*) and "faggots" (*maricones*), Cuba admittedly ushered in reversals in the 1980s and, later on, Fidel pronounced a near death-bed apology.[41] Yet the interest-convergence was still too obvious. By the end of the twentieth century, gender and sexual politics were moving to center stage throughout much of the global left, while the Cuban economy was struggling. Any suggestion that rigorous leftist self-scrutiny was at work here would be as cynical as the suggestion that LGBTQ+ people had been liberated by Castro's niece.

How far have leftists' purity narratives extended? Again, sidelining is one of the best means of whitewashing. Lenin's massacre in Kronstadt? Not the real leftism. The Soviet gulags? Not the real leftism. Stalin's mass famines and deportations of whole populations? Not the real leftism. Terror, torture, purges, surveillance, and "reeducation"? Not the real leftism. Mass exterminations during Mao's Cultural Revolution? Not the real leftism. Soviet, Maoist, and other domination of minority ethnic and religious groups? Not the real leftism. China's tyranny over Tibet and Xinjiang? Not the real leftism. The Khmer killing fields? Not the real leftism. The Kim dynasty's North Korea and Enver Hoxha's Albania? Not the real leftism. Nicolae Ceaușescu's orphanages in Romania? Not the real leftism. Erich Honecker's youth-detention systems, mass-surveillance networks, and border shootings in East Germany? Not the real leftism. Hugo Chavez's and Nicolás Maduro's creation of more than seven million refugees fleeing Venezuela, constituting more than 20 percent of the nation's total population? Not the real leftism.[42] No histories of systemic injustice, no dots to link up—let alone to teach to a wider public. I name quite a few individuals in that list, so any downplaying of their roles would be as untenable as the whitewashing of their regimes. No crits could honestly claim that a Lenin, a Stalin, a Mao, a Pol Pot, a Kim, a Ceaușescu, a Hoxha, a Honecker, not to mention the thousands of party hacks without whom their regimes could never have functioned, were not *real* socialists because crits, as in their critiques of liberal democracy, look for the real not in professed ideals but in historical records.

So, no, "initially" Fidel was not "very good" for Cuba's LGBTQ+ citizens. This was Livingstone's *Vogelschiss* claim, his purity narrative, as he reminisced that "the key things that mattered was that people had a good education, good healthcare, and wealth was evenly distributed."[43] Again, the point is not to keep a scorecard of abuses, so my claim here is not that Cuban socialism has been as bad as Nazism, which would be a ridiculous idea, but to note how the logic of Livingstone's cost–benefit calculation echoes Gauland's, generating a purity narrative. Instead of flatly ignoring or denying the persecution of LGBTQ+ Cubans, Livingstone tossed it onto a utilitarian scorecard, in effect declaring: "Yes, some things were bad, but other things were good" or "Perhaps a minority suffered, but others prospered." Decades-long persecution of thousands of gender and sexual minorities under Castro thereby becomes only so many errors and accidents, not the *real* leftism. Jeremy Corbyn, at that time leader of the British Labour Party, also peripheralized systemic repression as "flaws": "For all his flaws," Corbyn winked, Castro the "internationalist" was a "champion of social justice."[44]

Of course, some leftists in the past did oppose the regime's LGBTQ+ persecution—Sartre once called homosexuals "Cuba's Jews"—and in recent years some scholars have acknowledged the persecution. Yet few contemporary leftists have generally described it as systemic or structural, let alone connected dots from past to present patterns of leftist oppression.[45] Rarely outdone in his rhetorical gymnastics, France's Mélenchon coupled sonorous alliteration with sentimental anaphora: "Fidel made mistakes, yes, Fidel made mistakes. Everyone makes mistakes—and yet not everyone is Fidel" (*"Fidel a fait des erreurs, oui, Fidel a fait des erreurs. Tout le monde fait des erreurs. Mais tout le monde n'est pas Fidel."*).[46] Once again we are told that leftist oppression is never embedded within its own longer history, but instead amounts only to mistakes. Critical writers from Hegel to Arendt shifted our study of historical events away from "great men of history" narratives to focus on broad social and political processes. Certainly, Mélenchon rarely mentions his own political rivals without portraying them as marionettes of deep and sinister forces, yet when it came time to acknowledge Cuban repression, Mélenchon's only mention of systemic power was a reference to US policy.[47] Regarding persecution inflicted by Castro's government, suddenly all that mattered was the heart of the man himself, the inner agonies and ecstasies of the cigar-chomping grandee.

Is this logic so wrong? Isn't this the way we often judge nations and institutions, weighing the good against the bad?[48] In his *Guardian* survey, Doward also quoted the more centrist House of Lords member Peter Hain, who composed a similar balance sheet: "Although responsible for indefensible human rights and free speech abuses, Castro created a society of unparalleled access to free health, education and equal opportunity despite an economically throttling US siege. His troops inflicted the first defeat on South Africa's troops in Angola in 1988, a vital turning point in the struggle against apartheid."[49] Soundbites across the political spectrum frequently default to this kind of "pluses versus minuses" formula, often leaning toward the "plus" side upon the death of a prominent personality. We must be seen to weigh up positives and negatives on all sides, so it seems fair for figures such as Livingstone and Hain to take this "some of Castro's policies were bad, but others were good" approach. Yet when confronting Western liberal democracies, crits rightly reject any hint that cost–benefit calculations can be cited to justify systemic oppression.

III HATRED

We simply could not think our way out of our pasts.
—Salman Rushdie, *Midnight's Children*

9 SOCIALISM HATING

By the 1970s, the US Supreme Court had developed strong protections for free speech, yet violence and discrimination against minorities remained widespread. American critical race theorists began to challenge old ideals that free speech could be enjoyed equally for all, as if the only role for government was to butt out of our conversations. These scholars did much to heighten public awareness about what has come to be known as "hate speech." The problem is not that speakers always or even usually harbor conscious feelings of hatred toward traditionally denigrated groups—recall the concepts of unconscious bias and institutional discrimination that I mentioned in chapter 2. The real problem is that racist, sexist, heteronormative, and other such forms of speech readily become normalized, seeping into everyday attitudes. Contrary to clichés about "sticks and stones" and calls that "we all need to toughen up," critical race theorists remind us that hate speech does not fall randomly or equally across all citizens but often threatens groups with the least clout in the public arena.[1]

HATRED AS AN INTERNATIONAL CONCEPT

In 1993, the law professors Mari Matsuda, Charles Lawrence, Richard Delgado, and Kimberlé Williams Crenshaw collected these insights in their landmark book *Words That Wound*. An influential chapter by Matsuda entitled "Public Response to Racist Speech: Considering the Victim's Story," describes episodes not from some past century but in the here and now:

A Black family enters a coffee shop in a small Texas town. A white man places a card on their table. The card reads, "You have just been paid a visit by the Ku Klux Klan." The family stands and leaves.

A law student goes to her dorm and finds an anonymous message posted on the door, a caricature image of her race, with a red line slashed through it.

An African-American worker found himself repeatedly subjected to racist speech when he came to work. A noose was hanging one day in his work area. "KKK" [Ku Klux Klan] references were directed at him, as well as other unfortunately typical racist slurs and death threats. His employer discouraged him from calling the police, attributing the incidents to "horseplay."

In San Francisco, a [Nazi] swastika was placed near the desks of Asian-American and African-American inspectors in the newly integrated fire department. The official explanation for the presence of the swastika at the fire department was that it was presented several years earlier as a "Joke" gift to the battalion chief, and that it was unclear why or how it ended up at the work stations of the minority employees.

An African-American FBI agent was subject to a campaign of racist taunts by white co-workers. A picture of an ape was pasted over his child's photograph, and racial slurs were used. Such incidents were called "healthy" by his supervisor.[2]

These incidents took place out of the public eye, yet Matsuda's claim is that hate speech harms its victims regardless of whether it is open or covert. Strictly speaking, the term *hateful expression* more accurately captures the problem because nonverbal expression, including displays of symbols such as the Nazi swastika, also send messages. However, most of the time the terms *hateful expression* and *hate speech* can be used interchangeably.[3] (Also, just to avoid confusion, Matsuda is talking here about straightforward communication, not contexts where an offensive idea is used in ironic, in-group, or critical contexts. So her concern is not, for example, about ethnic minority comedians satirically using slurs that are often targeted against their own groups. After all, the Black comedian Richard Pryor and the Jewish comedian Mel Brooks were using such slurs and stereotypes long ago, not to bolster prejudice but to lampoon it.) Consider Matsuda's account of the swastika incident. Many crits would argue that in such a situation the swastika can cause harm regardless of whether it is targeted at specified individuals or is randomly unfurled in public. Similarly, another of the book's contributors, the law professor Charles Lawrence, cites examples of hate speech that is not hurled at specified individuals yet is calculated to cause distress:

> Northwest Missouri State University: White Supremacists distribute flyers stating, "The Knights of the Ku Klux Klan are Watching You."
> Kansas University: KKK members speak.
> Temple University: White Student Union formed.
> Stanford University: Aryan Resistance literature distributed.
> A student walks into class and sees this written on the blackboard: "A mind is a terrible thing to waste—especially on a nigger."[4]

Crits have often endorsed hate speech bans, praising the governments that adopt them.[5] At first glance, you might think it would be difficult to generalize across the globe about a problem such as hatred, which seems specific to cultures. Yet the concept of hate speech went global decades ago, and international organizations have increasingly adopted positions similar to those of critical theorists. For example, as far back as 1966 with the International Covenant on Civil and Political Rights, the UN summoned nations to adopt this provision: "Any advocacy of national, racial or religious hatred that constitutes incitement to discrimination, hostility or violence shall be prohibited by law."[6] Many nations now have such laws, which today reach far beyond these three categories of "national, racial or religious" groups.[7]

Again, the single greatest achievement of the left has been to articulate the very concepts we use to discuss justice in the modern world, regardless of the positions any of us may take on a given controversy. The problem of defining hatred shows how conceptions of justice formulated on the left, far from dwelling on the margins of dissent, have gained international dominance, a trend I want to explore in this and the next chapter. In fact, crits have had complex relationships with organizations such as the UN, often reproaching them for being beholden to Western powers, who in turn are driven by big business interests.[8] However, the problem of hate speech illustrates how crits and human rights professionals mutually influence each other's broader philosophies of social justice. When American critical race theorists started to write about hate speech, some of them praised crackdowns pushed in the

UN, objecting that the United States had become an outlier, and in turn international experts have often explained their policies in the language of critical theory.[9]

Advocates of bans claim that hate speech fuels enmities against marginalized groups, which we must combat by regulating such speech.[10] In response, free speech activists object that people should not be punished solely for expressing ideas, even malicious ones.[11] In other words, much of the debate about hate speech has focused on the question, "How much free speech should people have?" I have waded into the debate elsewhere, so I will not do so here.[12] Instead, in this chapter and the next the question I want to ask is: Who is defining "hatred," and how are they doing it? Squabbles about free speech are usually waged with an eye toward the future. The typical questions posed are: Will bans end up stifling too much speech? and Do bans really help in the fight against discrimination? Yet questions about the future always lead back to the past. In asking, Who is defining "hatred"?, my aim is not to propose a fixed meaning but to ask: Whose memories are honored and omitted in the definitions we are using?

I have already noted the importance of memory politics on the left, and one element of that politics goes by the name "memory laws," coined by the historical novelist Françoise Chandernagor in 2005. At that time Holocaust denial had recently been criminalized in France, and Chandernagor used the term in a mocking vein—not to deride the Shoah but to ask whether we can seriously confront it by trying to legislate historical truth and then punishing people who defy it.[13] It helps here to note that memory laws have long existed. They have taken many forms and do not always inflict penalties on offenders. For example, countries throughout the world have long adopted laws to commemorate their war dead or to celebrate a political revolution or to declare an annual holiday to honor a national hero.[14] These are memory laws in the most obvious sense, since commemoration of the past is their main aim. Some citizens may disagree with such laws, yet, unlike with Holocaust denial bans, no one is punished for disobeying them. In fact, it is unclear what disobedience to such purely commemorative enactments would look like. For example, some Americans may disagree with laws to designate holidays like Presidents Day, Labor Day, and Memorial

Day, yet there is no obvious way for them to disobey such laws so as to incur a fine, prison sentence, or some other penalty (except in an atypical sense, for example, if the law required raising of the flag on public buildings and an official refused to comply). In some cases, a law pays homage to the past without mentioning the events that prompted it. For example, according to the Thirteenth Amendment to the US Constitution, slavery is prohibited "within the United States, or any place subject to their jurisdiction" (sec. 1). This law makes no reference to history, and resembles countless other laws that declare a given practice—in this case slavery—to be illegal. Yet as soon as we recall the text's place in history, we see it operating as a memory law by paying homage to a grievous past.

With this concept of memory laws in mind, let's return to the UN. I have just recalled the type of international hate speech ban that was urged in the International Covenant on Civil and Political Rights (ICCPR) in 1966. Similarly, a year earlier, the UN General Assembly had adopted the International Convention on the Elimination of All Forms of Racial Discrimination (ICERD), including a provision that called on governments to penalize "all dissemination of ideas based on racial superiority."[15] Here, too, writers commenting on these types of measures focus mostly on questions about how much free speech we should have, yet ICERD also serves to promote historical memory. In one passage it recalls that the UN condemns "colonialism and all practices of segregation and discrimination associated therewith." With this same eye on history, ICERD declares that "any doctrine of superiority based on racial differentiation is scientifically false, morally condemnable, socially unjust and dangerous, and that there is no justification for racial discrimination, in theory or in practice, anywhere."[16] Later efforts to tackle hate speech have continued to highlight their memorial role. For example, in a General Policy Recommendation on hate speech issued in 2015 by the European Commission against Racism and Intolerance (ECRI), one passage states:

> Europe derives from its history a duty of remembrance, vigilance and combat against the rise of racism, racial discrimination, gender-based discrimination, sexism, homophobia, transphobia, xenophobia, antisemitism, islamophobia, anti-Gypsyism and intolerance, as well as of crimes of genocide, crimes against

humanity or war crimes and the public denial, trivialisation, justification or condonation of such crimes. . . . [T]his duty of remembrance, vigilance and combat is an integral part of the protection and promotion of universal and indivisible human rights, standing for the rights of every human being.[17]

OTHER HISTORIES

I shall have more to say about these international measures, but for a moment I want to pause to remember some other pasts. We have seen that to understand an event such as the Ukraine war, histories of socialist dictatorships widely supported on the left remain as paramount as any actions undertaken by Western governments. Let's briefly consider those histories again, this time bearing in mind our globalized concept of "hatred."

After the Russian Revolution of 1917, one of Vladimir Lenin's first moves was to appoint his ally Felix Dzerzhinsky as head of a secret police force known as the Cheka, an acronym for Vserossiyskaya Chrezvychaynaya Komissiya (All-Russian Extraordinary Commission for Combating Counter-revolution and Sabotage). In one speech, Dzerzhinsky announced the Cheka's task as being "the terrorization, arrest, and extermination of enemies of the revolution on the basis of their class affiliation or their pre-revolutionary roles." The organization proceeded with summary detentions and executions of thousands of civilians. From 1918 to 1922, these campaigns became known as the "Red Terror," or the period of "war communism."[18] Now compare those beginnings to events occurring a century later in Castro's Cuba, where the activist group Ladies in White (Damas de Blanco) was created by wives and other female relatives of jailed and disappeared dissidents. After 2003, when the group first formed, the women were routinely smeared in the state media as "traitors" and "terrorists."[19]

A considerable gap of time and space separates 1917 Russia from today's Cuba, but notice the continuity of terms such as "traitors" and "terrorists." In twentieth-century dictatorships, this lexicon of betrayal included plenty of other smears—"spies," "conspirators," "saboteurs," "decadents," "scroungers," "leeches," "parasites," "foreign agents," "enemies," "enemies of the workers," "enemies of the people," and "enemies of socialism." We find such accusations pervading public discourse in post-1949 China, the Kim dynasty's North Korea, Pol Pot's Cambodia, Nicolae Ceaușescu's Romania, Daniel Ortega's Nicaragua, and other such regimes.[20] They form a lexicon of what I call *disloyalty propaganda*. Today, if a government were to tar any of its country's racial, ethnic, national, religious, or LGBTQ+ minorities with such accusations, crits as well as human rights monitors would rightly condemn officials for spreading hate speech, even if we might disagree about whether or how legal penalties should be imposed. Yet human rights professionals have never designated disloyalty propaganda as hate speech per se—that is, in situations where it is not expressly targeted at a group defined by any such identity-based trait.

Admittedly, international organizations have long condemned practices of discrimination and political persecution in general terms, yet the reason why experts have highlighted hate speech as a special problem for human rights is that they view verbal assaults as forming part of broader patterns of social exclusion.[21] Clearly, socialist dictatorships have at times targeted disloyalty propaganda at identity-based groups, such as members of national, ethnic, or religious minorities or LGBTQ+ persons.[22] When Stalin rounded up Jews, and when Che Guevara imprisoned gays or Black religious leaders, they were obviously perpetrating identity-based persecution.[23] Yet for the most part, the official vocabularies of socialist states have not been directed against Jews for being Jewish, homosexuals for being homosexual, or ethnic minorities as such, but through universalist vocabularies trumpeting the state's heroic protection of its people against "conspirators," "bourgeois decadents," "parasites," and the like. Disloyalty propaganda was articulated in general terms to target whole populations. Even high-ranking officials could be eliminated instantly on these grounds when it suited the moment.

Of course, socialist regimes have not been the only ones to unleash disloyalty purges, which have also abounded on the far right. In Adolf Hitler's *Mein Kampf* (1925), charges of treason (*Verrat, Landesverrat, Vaterlandsverrat*) and against traitors (*Verräter, Landesverräter, Vaterlandsverräter*) crop up compulsively. Yet unlike socialist propaganda, far-right disloyalty accusations have casually blended with identity-based invective, starkly inflecting racist, nationalist, patriarchal, and heteronormative narratives. Famously, although *Mein Kampf* takes aim at "traitors" of all stripes, the arch-antinomy to the Aryan is the Jew. It comes as no surprise, then, that disloyalty accusations hurled at identity-based groups have long nurtured the impression that categories such as race, ethnicity, nationality, religion, gender, and sexuality would suffice for us to identify hate speech. Indeed, human rights experts have long made clear their view that bans on hate speech protect identity groups above all from the far right.[24]

In stark contrast to far-right propaganda, socialist disloyalty accusations represent the purest form: they do not need identity-based traits because they target betrayal as such. Disloyalty propaganda points toward totalitarianism in the strictest sense. The individual and private sphere, which is the final refuge of the dissident, is erased through absorption of an entire people into prescribed trajectories.[25] Consider the following comparison. On the far right, racist discourses not only target certain ethnic minorities but also send messages to other social groups including the dominant one, implicitly deterring them, for example, from marrying into, befriending members of, or openly agitating in support of the stigmatized groups. By contrast in the case of disloyalty propaganda, this very distinction between primary and secondary effects disappears because all remain potential targets from the outset. Admittedly, the people most affected are the ones facing immediate repercussions, with open dissidents being the obvious example, yet no one stands beyond the reach of betrayal accusations. The Nazi jurist Carl Schmitt, a great influence on contemporary critical theory, explained— and celebrated—the tactics whereby a group collectivity defines a real or imagined enemy as menacing its own existence.[26] For Nazis, that collectivity became Jews. For white supremacists, it became nonwhites. For autocracies, it became democracies. For socialists, it became agglomerations of industrial capitalists, bourgeois elites, and rural kulaks because the terror of disloyalty propaganda works precisely through uncertainty about whether or when someone will be slapped with a label such as "capitalist," "bourgeois," or "kulak."

Some may argue that the concept of hate speech was introduced to protect vulnerable groups, meaning that it cannot apply to disloyalty propaganda, which targets entire populations. Yet this objection remembers the solution by forgetting the original problem. As critical race theorists remind us, hate speech poses a problem above all when people who are socially or politically dominant use language to subordinate people who are excluded from that monopoly. In some contexts this dynamic translates into identity groups, yet there is nothing about the sheer existence of power-political differentials that would mean that they can only ever run between groups defined, say, by race, ethnicity, religion, gender, sexuality, or some other identitarian trait.

Even seemingly centrist liberal democracies have witnessed their share of disloyalty propaganda. For more than two decades after its founding in 1938, the US House Un-American Activities Committee damaged thousands of innocent lives by investigating alleged Communist Party operatives, often with threadbare evidence.[27] Or if we look beyond that kind of official government action, we can recall more recently that at the Republican National Convention in 2016, soon-to-be president Donald Trump rallied mass chants of "Lock Her Up" against his rival Hillary Clinton, who had been neither convicted nor even indicted for any crime.[28] Then just a few months later, the UK *Daily Mail* branded as "Enemies of the People" three High Court judges who had ruled that the government needed a parliamentary majority to leave the European Union, a ruling that Brexiters saw as a roadblock.[29] Notwithstanding these incidents, disloyalty propaganda in liberal democracies, particularly via mass state orchestration, has rarely achieved the scope, intensity, or duration witnessed under dictatorial regimes.

DISLOYALTY PROPAGANDA AS HATE SPEECH

The end of the Cold War witnessed a moment of openness but the Kremlin soon renewed its former repressive practices, hurling Soviet-style disloyalty propaganda at dissidents, journalists, and others. Once again, the Ukraine war offers breathtaking examples. After Russia's 2022 invasion, the monitoring organization Human Rights Watch (HRW) found that "high-level officials," including Putin, were labeling "people critical of the war 'national traitors.'" HRW lamented that Moscow "portrays independent journalists and activists as traitors and treats them as a threat to the state."[30]

One news editor whose paper published a comment critical of the war was branded a "foreign agent." Journalists and activists reported that vandals had painted "Don't betray your motherland" and "A traitor lives here" on their apartment doors.[31] In these types of cases, it may at times be unclear whether the perpetrators work for the state, yet even if we assume that some of them act independently, crits have long challenged fixed lines drawn between public and private power, as in the area of hate speech, where Western crits have focused mostly on private speakers.[32] HRW noted that in March 2022 the Russian Parliament authorized a uniform registry of "foreign agents" and "those affiliated with them." In addition, HRW noted that "unidentified assailants repeatedly harassed the Movement for Human Rights, one of the oldest rights organizations in Russia, which the authorities formally shut down in 2019." Authorities designated its founder and leader, Lev Ponomarev, as "foreign agent mass media." In February 2022, Ponomarev had "initiated a petition, calling on the Russian military to withdraw from Ukraine, which gathered more than 1.2 million signatures."[33] According to HRW, several events followed:

- "On March 3, a woman attacked Ponomarev on the street throwing coins at him and then insulting and calling him a foreign agent. Journalists with the pro-Kremlin television channel NTV, known for such provocations, filmed the entire incident."
- "On March 16, four masked men and apparently the same woman went to the organization's door, seemingly trying to enter. Before leaving they glued 'get out traitor' and 'enemy foreign agent' stickers to the nameplate and the walls."
- "On February 28, Russia's Supreme Court [had] rejected the appeal to pause the implementation of the decision to liquidate another prominent human rights organization, International Memorial. On March 22, the court upheld the ruling to shut down Memorial for allegedly violating the draconian 'foreign agent' legislation."

- "On March 4, police raided the offices of Memorial and its partner organization, Civic Assistance Committee, in connection with an 'extremism' case opened against one of Memorial's members. . . . For years, the authorities have been harassing Memorial in retaliation for its human rights work, labeling the group a 'foreign agent' and imposing hefty fines.'"
- In a remarkable act of government-orchestrated historical memory, a statue of the Cheka head Dzerzhinsky was raised in front of Russia's Foreign Intelligence Service in 2023, three decades after crowds had cheered the toppling of his statue at KGB headquarters in Moscow.[34]

It is not only in Russia that disloyalty propaganda has continued. Elsewhere in post-Soviet central and eastern Europe, far-right nationalists have repackaged old antisemitic discourses as references to "liberals" and "capitalists" (both terms long serving as code for "Jews" in the region) whose loyalty to the nation cannot be trusted.[35] Farther afield, according to one China expert, "Pro-Beijing internet trolls have reportedly become more active among overseas Chinese communities." For example, the "US-based democracy advocate and political commentator Chen Pokong 'remarked that YouTube videos of his popular political talk show are now frequently targeted with . . . comments that accuse him of being a traitor.'"[36] In 2023, a "group of Chinese female economists and entrepreneurs who dined with Treasury Secretary Janet Yellen [were] blasted by online nationalists for betraying their country by interacting with the U.S. official."[37] That same year, the Nicaraguan dictatorship stripped 94 prominent dissidents of their citizenship, calling them "traitors to the fatherland."[38] A year earlier, Radio Free Asia reported that "North Koreans whose family members have escaped the country and resettled in South Korea are being banished to rugged rural areas, in the latest punishment for citizens vilified as traitors by the regime."[39] In 2018, the UN Human Rights Committee held Turkmenistan responsible for the torture and death of the human rights activist Ogulsapar Muradova, whom senior officials, including the country's president, publicly branded, along with her colleagues, as "traitors."[40] No one can divorce such incidents from these nations' dictatorial pasts, in which open political discussion was suppressed.

I am challenging our dominant conception of hatred not because the identitarian model is wrong but because it neglects countless histories that have fallen outside its confines. Experts' initial reason for highlighting hate speech as a distinctive problem was to condemn verbal assaults as conduct that is pernicious in itself. This is why Matsuda describes racist words as "weapons to ambush, terrorize, wound, humiliate, and degrade."[41] Yet note that nothing in this criterion requires us to construe such speech only with reference to identity-based groups. The legal theorist Jeremy Waldron depicts hate speech as the "ugliness," the "disfiguring" or "slow-acting poison" that becomes "a disfiguring part of the social environment."[42] The sociologist Anthony Cortese proposes a "cultural transmission theory," whereby broadcast or other popular media "pass hate on to each succeeding generation," making intolerance "normal or conventional."[43] The linguistic philosopher Rae Langton has examined hate speech as "illocutionary," not merely denoting hostility hatred but socially enacting it, and as "perlocutionary," spawning psychological harms regardless of any materially demonstrable impact.[44]

On all these accounts, hate speech functions not merely to justify oppressive policies and practices ad hoc but to brainwash whole populations, often over long stretches of time. Yet none of these descriptions suggests that an identitarian character trait must be present as a prior condition for a speech act to qualify as demeaning. On all these accounts, we should treat disloyalty propaganda, too, as pernicious in itself. We can further add the insights of writers such as Hannah Arendt and Michel Foucault, who showed how the proliferation of objectifying vocabularies fuels the social and political objectification of human beings, reminding us that racism, patriarchy, and heteronormativity do not necessarily—or even typically—involve conscious feelings of "hatred." In the same way, disloyalty propaganda becomes a systemic hatred perpetrated by citizens who may feel no personal animosities toward the targeted individuals or groups. So the problem with defining hatred solely in identitarian terms is not that such a definition is wrong but that it is too narrow, excluding millions of victims, past and present. Some skeptics might respond that accusations such as "traitor" and "enemy" form part of the political rough-and-tumble and cannot be treated on a par with identitarian hate speech.[45] Moreover, as implied by Trump's "Lock Her Up" chants, there are no obvious criteria for deciding what counts as a sufficiently "hateful" disloyalty slur. However, as we will see in the next chapter, these problems of vagueness, line drawing, and ballooning concepts have long haunted definitions of hate speech without prompting leftists to abandon their campaigns against it.

10 IDENTITIES EMERGING

For centuries, when governments wanted to silence unwanted speech, they did so by reciting boilerplate concerns about national security, public safety, and public order, as many nations today continue to do.[1] In the past, when they censored speech on moral grounds, it was mostly to curb offenses such as obscenity or blasphemy, rarely to protect the safety or dignity of identity-based groups.[2] After World War II, this picture changed, but why did professionals and activists come to define hatred in identitarian terms to designate vilification as hateful primarily when it is targeted at identity groups?

THE UNIVERSALIZATION OF WESTERN IDENTITY POLITICS

In 1948, responding to an atrocity on a scale that the world was still only starting to discover, the UN adopted the Convention on the Prevention and Punishment of the Crime of Genocide. This treaty obliged participating states to punish all "direct and public incitement to commit genocide." The delegates, some with fresh memories of fascist propaganda at its ugliest, agreed to define genocide with reference to "national, ethnical, racial or religious" groups.[3] This document, too, stands as a memory law, mentioning no past events yet drawing its meaning and symbolism from history.

In the previous chapter, I cited two treaties from the 1960s that also committed participating nations to ban hateful expression: the International Convention on the Elimination of All Forms of Racial Discrimination and the International Covenant on Civil and Political Rights. Further texts included, for example, a series of resolutions condemning South African apartheid.[4] These documents did not emerge in a void. They echoed vast trends typical of the immediate post–World War II era. Western powers such as Britain and France were losing colonies; the United States and South Africa were gaining civil rights movements; and a Cuban revolution was fêted globally as a rebellion against US hegemony. By contrast, the oppression of ethnic minorities in the Soviet Union and China, although not unknown, garnered less attention because on the international stage their governments often succeeded in projecting a reputation as guarantors of equal citizenship and opportunity.[5] Chronicles of Western colonial and ethnic oppression were relayed to global audiences. Writers such as Aimé Césaire, Frantz Fanon, Albert Memmi, and Kwame Nkrumah were nuancing older leftist ideals of worldwide proletarian emancipation to focus on ethnic and colonial struggles.[6]

Of course, territories first acquired, say, by czarist Russia or imperial China were eventually incorporated into the Soviet and Maoist Empires, yet on the left and often in the UN, references to "colonialism" pointed mostly toward Western pasts. Lenin's *Imperialism: The Highest Form of Capitalism* (1917) and Mao's *Little Red Book* (1964) still circulated widely, expounding purity narratives that hygienically excised imperialism from socialism. According to these narratives, socialism by definition could never be oppressive. By their nature, capitalism sowed divisions while socialism forged unity. Activists around the world cheered official Soviet and Maoist doctrines that socialism was by definition anti-imperial, by definition on the side of decolonization. If leftists hated anyone, it was only the oppressor, only the wealthy and powerful exploiter, but this was a heroic hatred.[7] As I mentioned in chapter 4, Western nations certainly supported autocracies repressive of individual freedom, while the Soviet Union, China, and other socialist regimes entrenched massive inequalities, often borne by national and ethnic minority populations.[8] Still, the drift was that the essential problem in socialist states was with individual liberty while the West's problem was with equality due to legacies of racism, colonialism, and capitalism.[9] While socialist states faced censure for violating individual rights and liberties, these condemnations were connected mostly to political repression without viewing the accompanying state propaganda as requiring separate attention in the way that identitarian hate speech was viewed as a related yet distinct problem alongside wider problems of discrimination.

Certainly, ethnic conflicts had existed long before Western colonialism, yet the model of identitarian discrimination cast in a Western mold allowed socialist nations to applaud the aforementioned UN-sponsored hate speech provisions that were drafted in identity-based language. Throughout the Cold War, the model of identitarian discrimination remained strongly associated with Western rather than socialist forms of oppression. It goes without saying that socialist states would have rejected anything resembling condemnations of disloyalty propaganda, since they were still massively spreading it during the years in which international norms against hate speech were adopted.

The logic was clear: in much of the world today, hatred means identitarian hatred, and identitarian hatred follows patterns of oppression that have been pervasively associated with the West. Certainly, international monitors have criticized incidents of identitarian hate speech where no Western influence was involved, as when the UN Committee on the Elimination of Racial Discrimination condemned China's "negative portrayals and hostile statements in traditional and social media targeting ethnic minorities, in particular South Asians."[10] Nevertheless, by pushing for bans in a progressive spirit of anti-Eurocentrism, experts have ended up entrenching conceptions of hatred that, despite their universalist wording, were modeled on characteristically Western patterns of abuse. Again, the concept of Eurocentrism has always been loosely defined. Insofar as Europe was equated with the West, the Soviet bloc as well as nations such as Cuba, Nicaragua, and other socialist regimes could never tidily be stamped as either "European" or "non-European." Nor did either label fit entirely with liberal democracies in Japan, Taiwan, and South Korea. Still, the concept invariably referred to power manifested through Western military and economic dominance as well as through cultural habits of conceiving of all humans according to Western norms.[11] So while claiming to combat Eurocentrism, experts achieved the opposite, a *Eurocentric anti-Eurocentrism*. Universalized conceptions of hatred came to impose a distinctly Western framework, while experts overlooked millions of victims of disloyalty propaganda.

This triumph of identity-based classifications betrays a Eurocentrism within the very organizations that have claimed to challenge Eurocentric philosophies and policies. Again, we see that what might at first seem like marginally leftist ideas have in fact become dominant ideas about justice. The problem is not that identitarian criteria are wrong, and I believe we should keep them. Yet by universalizing Western identitarian classifications based on histories of Western oppression, we have imposed upon the world a pervasively Eurocentric conception of injustice. After the Cold War, the East–West showdown temporarily eased and human rights professionals promoted multicultural views of law and society. Yet the identitarian paradigm had already taken root, and further classifications continually recapitulated it.[12] For example, in places where blasphemy offenses declined, hatreds targeting religion were often viewed along ethnic lines. Many nations also added categories of gender and sexuality in identitarian terms, often following Western precedents, even though there was never anything exclusively Western about the subordination of women or the marginalization of sexual nonconformities.[13]

Some skeptics may still doubt whether even large-scale disloyalty propaganda should be viewed as a type of hatred. For example, they might think that identitarian hate speech differs from disloyalty propaganda because identity-based traits such as ethnicity or LGBTQ+ status define the very humanity of an individual or group, whereas governments spread disloyalty propaganda merely to achieve political aims.[14] Yet crits could not seriously voice that objection, given that they reject distinctions between one sphere of life that is political and a separate sphere of pure humanity dwelling beyond politics. In the context of hate speech, crits view identity traits as socially constructed to serve political and often oppressive ends, even if the speakers believe they are speaking with no hateful intentions.[15] Disputes still rage globally about which identity groups merit legal protections, yet such disagreements further confirm the culturally constructed aspect of individual and group identities. To take an obvious example, many religiously conservative governments reject classifications based on sexual and gender identity.[16]

Indeed, some of these regimes actively spread anti-LGBTQ+ messages in the guise of religious morality.[17]

No globally recognized definition of hate speech has been adopted, nor would such a definition be easy to achieve given those types of cultural differences.[18] Yet the General Policy Recommendation on hate speech issued by the European Commission against Racism and Intolerance (ECRI) in 2015, although drafted solely for nations that belong to the Council of Europe, reflects much expert opinion even outside Europe. It defines hate speech in broad terms as "the advocacy, promotion or incitement, in *any* form, of the denigration, hatred or vilification of a person or group of persons, as well as *any* harassment, insult, negative stereotyping, stigmatization or threat in respect of such a person or group of persons, and the justification of *all* the preceding types of expression." The recommendation further adds: "[Hate speech may] take the form of the public denial, trivialisation, justification or condonation of crimes of genocide, crimes against humanity or war crimes which have been found by courts to have occurred, and of the glorification of persons convicted for having committed such crimes."[19]

The recommendation then goes on to list upward of fourteen identity traits to which this definition would apply, including "'race,' colour, descent, national or ethnic origin, age, disability, language, religion or belief, sex, gender, gender identity, sexual orientation and other personal characteristics or status."[20] For crits, these traits spur patterns of degradation not because they contain any intrinsic property but through adverse attitudes bred within culture. For example, from a crit perspective even genetically inherited disabilities are socially constructed as "disabling" because what we are or are not deemed able to do depends in part on what we are expected to do within our cultural norms.[21] Similarly, anthropologists have long held that classifications based on race and ethnicity are social constructs reflecting popular opinion at the time they were conceived.[22] Race or ethnicity may manifest through biological traits, but stigmas or other social meanings attached to those traits have never been fixed in nature and have fluctuated according to cultural trends.

The recommendation's authors explain why they put "race" in quotation marks: "all human beings belong to the same species," therefore the "ECRI rejects theories based on the existence of different races." The recommendation adds that it uses the "term 'race' in order to ensure that those persons who are generally and erroneously perceived as belonging to another race are not excluded." Similarly, the authors define gender as "the socially constructed roles, behaviours, activities and attributes that a given society considers appropriate for women and men." "Gender identity" is defined as "each person's deeply felt internal and individual experience of gender." The recommendation notes that these subjective experiences "may or may not correspond with the sex assigned at birth, including the personal sense of the body (which may involve, if freely chosen, modifications of bodily appearance or function by medical, surgical or other means) and other expressions of gender, including dress, speech and mannerism."[23] Similarly, for crits, vilified groups become subordinated not because of any fixed characteristics but because the vilification itself fixes these characteristics into a subordinated role.

Consider also the fate of blasphemy laws. At first glance, the ECRI recommendation seems to point toward similarities between the category of "religion" and disloyalty propaganda. Certainly, both hostility toward religious believers and accusations of political betrayal can lead to persecution based on people's actual or assumed beliefs. In fact, in earlier times and in some places still today, blasphemy laws have worked similarly to disloyalty propaganda. Both methods of shaping people's minds are aimed at entrenching established power by silencing citizens who deride dominant doctrines, symbols, officials, or institutions. Yet in many countries such laws have been repealed or abandoned, which at first seems like a step toward free expression, but in another sense blasphemy laws have been reborn through hate speech laws. For example, in the recommendation religion stands beside race and ethnicity as an identity-group trait. Indeed, in some contexts these categories merge, given that racist assaults may be based on religious affiliation.[24] (Note also that the ECRI's list of traits does include "belief." However, paired as it is with "religion," "belief" has never been interpreted to include disloyalty propaganda.[25])

As controversies around trans identity have shown, disagreements can arise around which human traits are products of nature and which are products of culture, and how nature and culture interact. But for present purposes these debates need not be settled, since the essential point is that within international law and in many democracies, identity-based traits are viewed as socially constructed. Consequently, disloyalty propaganda comes closer to identity-based speech than we might at first think. Disloyalty propaganda constructs outcasts with the same psychological force and the same social detriments as identitarian classifications. Certain groups become targeted by hostile and demeaning language, thereby coupling the immediate effects of personal intimidation with longer-term aims of confirming them as the enemy within—indeed, as subversive and insalubrious to the body politic.

"QUESTIONS OF DIFFERENT NATURE"

Czechoslovakia was founded as an independent democracy in 1918, but after World War II it fell under Kremlin control, which continued until the end of the Cold War. The country's Velvet Revolution, led by the dissident playwright Václav Havel, witnessed the overthrow of dictatorial rule in 1989. In 1992 the country divided into the two independent nations of Czechia, also called the Czech Republic, and Slovakia. Czech lawmakers then introduced a new provision into the country's criminal code banning "the public rejection, questioning, approval or attempt to justify Nazi or Communist genocide or other Nazi or Communist crimes against humanity."[26]

In this context, too, many observers might doubt the wisdom or pragmatics of outlawing such speech, but leaving that question aside, I shall assume that concern about messages of support for mass atrocities is always valid. In a report in 2007, the UN Committee on the Elimination of Racial Discrimination challenged this provision, yet its worry was not that the Czech authorities might crack down too harshly on free speech. Rather, the report accused Czech lawmakers of "mixing up the ideas of hate crimes, racist propaganda and genocide with that of class struggle." The committee continued: "Such confusion not only weakens the objective of fighting racial discrimination, but also politicizes a phenomenon like genocide, which is abhorrent in itself." The committee recommended that Czech officials ought to "ensure that such confusion of questions of different nature" would not arise in the application of the country's criminal laws.[27] To be sure, this law combining communist and Nazi crimes had been supported by right-wing factions eager to smear leftist rivals, given that Nazi atrocities on Czech soil had considerably exceeded Soviet-backed ones.[28] Be that as it may, in its wording the law did not require that the crimes in question be limited solely to acts committed on Czech territory, so even-handed applications of the law remain possible.

Admittedly, few people would have read this specialized report. In fact, it was only advisory and did not strictly require the Czech government to make any changes. Moreover, anyone who did peruse it might have read these comments as little more than quirks. Yet they were no such thing. They embodied a Eurocentric anti-Eurocentrism that runs deep within leftist thought as well as international organizations. As a threshold matter, the committee contradicted a long-settled human rights principle that there must be no hierarchies of rights. Until this time, no major human rights body had ever criticized a country for tackling one human rights problem on grounds that doing so would "weaken" or "politicize" action taken on others. Admittedly, with limited resources, hard choices must at times be made on pragmatic grounds, as in emergency situations. But these situations are inevitably acknowledged as exceptions to the rule that human rights experts do not rank atrocities, and in any event Czechia faced no urgent situations at the time of the report.[29]

Moreover, it is worth recalling that Nazis committed violations against various groups, yet the committee did not urge the Czech authorities to avoid "confusion" by referring distinctly to racist crimes.[30] The reason can only be that other Nazi atrocities (though not all of them) also targeted identity-based groups. Consider the following hypothetical: instead of banning apologetics for "Nazi or Communist genocide or other Nazi or Communist crimes against humanity," suppose that the Czech law had instead banned apologetics for "racist or ableist genocide or other racist or ableist crimes against humanity." Clearly, the committee would never have objected that such legislation enacted to protect disabled persons would cause "confusion" about racism or would "weaken" or "politicize" the struggle against it.

Of course, we can accept that a racial or ethnic genocide is "abhorrent in itself" regardless of political contexts. Yet it hardly follows that Soviet mass murder was somehow distinctly political in a way that racism is not. By calling a racist atrocity "abhorrent in itself," in express contrast to atrocities waged in the name of socialism, the committee assumed that socialist atrocities may or may not be repugnant depending on the context, while racism is repugnant regardless of context. Yet any suggestion that Kremlin hacks engineered mass famines, exterminations, and detention camps to liberate the masses from bourgeois oppression would be hilarious if it were not monstrous. It is similarly difficult to imagine how Moscow's antisemitic purges, along with mass deportations organized along patently ethnic lines and claiming thousands more lives, were distinctly political or based on class struggle, while other crimes along racial or ethnic lines were abhorrent in themselves.[31] By rebranding Soviet atrocities through the heroizing iconography of "class struggle," the committee assumed that these atrocities must be construed according to the perpetrators' own official justifications. In ascribing such credibility to the perpetrators' own version of events, the committee reopened the question about whether Soviet brutalities even counted *as* crimes against humanity. Certainly, when assessing the grossest episodes of racism, the committee has never urged that the perpetrators' own version of events ought to carry such decisive weight. Unsurprisingly, the epilogue to our story reads like a punchline: the Czech authorities ignored the committee's recommendation, which is not a result that a human rights body should view with pride.[32]

HATRED AND POWER

Leftists have certainly acknowledged hate speech within their own ranks. Yet by defining hatred entirely in identitarian terms, they have spun a purity narrative, fashioning as benign and heroic those victims of hate who in turn utter hate speech. For example, although crits focus on the standard situation of hatred expressed by members of dominant groups, Matsuda acknowledges situations where the tables are turned. She concedes that someone from a vulnerable group may unjustly label someone from a privileged group as racist, sexist, homophobic, or transphobic. But she argues that hostilities arising from an excluded group cannot be equated with hostilities spoken by empowered groups:

> Expressions of hatred, revulsion, and anger directed *against* members of historically dominant-groups *by* subordinated-group members are . . . not tied to the perpetuation of racist vertical relationships, [and such an attack] is not the paradigm worst example of hate propaganda. The dominant-group member . . . is more likely to have access to a safe harbor of exclusive dominant-group interactions. Retreat and reaffirmation of personhood are more easily attained for members of groups not historically subjugated. . . . I would interpret an angry, hateful poem by a person from a historically subjugated group as a victim's struggle for self-identity in response to racism. It is not tied to the structural domination of another group. Part of the special harm of racist speech is that it works in concert with other racist tools to keep victim groups in an inferior position.[33]

Matsuda rejects what she sees as a spurious moral equivalence. She denies that the typical targets of leftist critique, privileged whites who punch down, can be equated to speakers with whom the left has long allied: oppressed groups punching up, thereby engaging in acts of understandable and at times justified resistance. There is nothing wrong with this point as far as it goes, but it does not go far enough. Matsuda and others have noticed only identitarian hierarchies while bypassing the types inflicted on millions of victims and spun by regimes often supported on the left. Yet if our primary concern is with expression mobilized by more powerful actors against less powerful, then socialist regimes count among history's main purveyors of hate speech. In Matsuda's defense, it might be argued that she and other American crits are focused on the United States and do not propose to analyze conditions elsewhere, yet, as I have mentioned, she and other crits have frequently cited non-US sources to bolster their advocacy of bans. Indeed, a disappointing feature of Matsuda's analysis is her praise of Soviet support for international norms against hate speech from the 1960s through to the 1980s.[34]

At the time Matsuda wrote her piece in the late 1980s, Soviet despotism had softened, but we have seen that the international guidelines she praises date back to the 1960s and 1970s. During those years, Moscow of course supported international hate speech bans because they reinforced the Kremlin's age-old line of presenting hatred as a Western evil that socialism had overcome. In page after page of *Words That Wound*, the contributors rightly insist that liberal democratic ideals cannot be taken at face value and have to be construed in the light of their actual and often appalling histories. This is critical theory at its best. But then Matsuda, whose chapter explicitly discusses these UN documents, can prop up her US–USSR comparison only by praising the Kremlin's officially declared policies while disregarding socialist states' actual and often appalling histories of deploying speech to vilify dissidents and to achieve mass conformity, which, on her own account, is how hate speech works.[35] Although it might be argued that the contributors to *Words That Wound* are focused mostly on ethnicity and not on all forms of aggressive speech, crits have otherwise freely grouped together and compared other identitarian hatreds, such as speech targeting women, religious minorities, and LGBTQ+ people, which they treat as complementary and not antagonistic concerns.

Overwhelmingly, crits have welcomed expanding lists of identitarian traits in the spirit of inclusion. Intersections of research on racism, colonialism, gender, sexuality, and other areas have been seen as broadening horizons and enriching the possibilities for cross-fertilization. The ECRI's fourteen-plus list of vulnerable identities suggests that problems of sheer pragmatics cannot explain crits' indifference to leftist pasts. Surely it would seem that adding disloyalty to that kind of list would promote rather than inhibit crits' inquiries into the politics of hatred—again, irrespective of our debates about the legitimacy or efficacy of speech bans. Some might call my expansion of the concept of hatred unworkable, yet I can only repeat that whatever positions I have taken elsewhere, my focus at present is not on determining the extent and limits of free speech but on comprehending the genesis, bias, and historical amnesia that have been built into our conceptions of hatred as adopted by governments and international organizations, often in response to critical theory.

11 JEWS WONDERING

In 2015, MP Jeremy Corbyn became leader of the opposition Labour Party in Great Britain, a post he held for five years. Corbyn had first entered the House of Commons in 1983, where he spent years opposing Prime Minister Margaret Thatcher's Conservative Party policies of union busting, economic deregulation, cuts in social services, and increased military spending.

Corbyn persisted in dissent within his own party throughout Tony Blair's "New Labour" years.[1] During the Thatcher era, Blair had drawn the Labour Party from the radical fringe into the mainstream. In the general election of 1997, he led the party to a landslide victory over the Conservatives. In his role as prime minister, Blair took cues from Presidents Bill Clinton, now in his second term of office in the United States, and then George W. Bush in the war against Saddam Hussein. At a dinner party years later, when asked about her greatest achievement, Thatcher smirked: "Tony Blair and New Labour."[2] Following her lead, Blair pushed Britain in pro-business and economically globalizing directions.

These policies outraged "Old" Labourites such as Corbyn, who accused Blair of cozying up to exploitative capitalism with all its vices of class privilege and social inequality.[3] Here again it becomes clear that we cannot use the term *leftist* in any uniform way. Between Blair and Corbyn there was a world of difference and many Corbynites still refuse to describe Blair as leftist. It was against this backdrop that in 2014, a year before Corbyn assumed the Labour leadership, flare-ups between Israel and Gaza were rekindling pro-Palestinian activism. Anti-Jewish incidents among Corbyn supporters spurred charges that antisemitism was rife on the far left of the party. These charges fueled an already fierce dispute: How and when does criticism of Israel spill over into hatred of Jews?[4] That question led to others: Do such criticisms sometimes become a hostile singling out and stigmatizing of Israel? Is Israel held to unfair standards, and, even if it is, should such a standpoint count as antisemitism?[5]

Moderate Labourites reviled what they saw as anti-Jewish tropes circulating among their colleagues on the far left. Corbynites in turn insisted that the moderates had sold out to right-wing Zionism and were conjuring up false accusations of antisemitism to smear the far left of the party.[6] Yet for now my questions are not the usual ones about whether Corbyn "was" or "was not" antisemitic in handling these controversies, nor about whether or in what ways Israel has acted unjustly. These questions, involving precise and detailed probes into the meanings of antisemitism and the relations between Israelis and Palestinians, have filled countless volumes of their own, and lie far beyond the scope of this book.

A CORBYN ALLY

These controversies are hardly confined to Britain. In the United States, some members of the Democratic Party have also been accused of demonizing Israel or trafficking in antisemitic stereotypes.[7] Yet given that party's size and diversity, there has been no evidence of pervasive antisemitism amid the party ranks. Meanwhile, in France similar accusations have been brought against members of Jean-Luc Mélenchon's party La France insoumise, yet despite this party's high profile, it has not formed the primary opposition in a nation where parties and allegiances have frequently shifted and fragmented in recent years.[8] In contrast to these countries, the long-running domination of British politics by the Conservative and Labour Parties meant that accusations of antisemitism under Corbyn climbed to the top of the country's main opposition, making the UK brawls distinctive. So for the purposes of my brief discussions in this chapter and the next—and despite the fact that questions of antisemitism reach beyond the borders of Britain, and beyond the five years of Labour under Corbyn—I will focus only on this set of events to ask what they tell us about leftist self-criticism.

The charges against Corbyn overshadowed much of what he said and did, and sooner or later every pundit in the land weighed in. Most Corbyn supporters rejected the antisemitism charges, while many of those who waged the accusations had harbored suspicions against the party's hard left all along.[9] Yet there were exceptions to this rule, and in this and the next chapter I devote some space to one of them. Owen Jones, one of Britain's most prolific left-wing journalists, cuts a noticeable figure in the antisemitism controversies. He has long marched loyally at Corbyn's side and has avidly echoed the Corbynite left in rebuking Israel.[10] Yet unlike many Corbyn acolytes, Jones has condemned leftist antisemitism in ways seemingly reminiscent of the left's ideals of collective self-scrutiny. I therefore draw on his reports because, as of this writing, he is the last journalist in Britain who could be accused of anti-Corbyn bias, let alone rubber-stamping Israeli policy.

Some onlookers might suspect that Jones's balancing act—joining Corbynites' intense criticisms of Israel while also calling out left-wing antisemitism—was doomed from the start. Instead of reconciling opposed voices, Jones drew scorn from all sides. On the hard right, Douglas Murray charged that Jones had not gone far enough: by failing to condemn leftist antisemitism more forcefully, Jones had whitewashed it.[11] On the hard left, Asa Winstanley charged that Jones had gone too far by kowtowing to the all-powerful Zionist lobby.[12] Meanwhile, a few centrists accused Jones of lacking any coherent narrative.[13] In the next chapter I will briefly mention some crits who have waded into these controversies, such as Alain Badiou and Antony Lerman, asking about essential histories that they and others on the left have silenced. Yet silences are difficult to discuss, and this is where Jones plays a helpful role as one of the few ardent left-wing Israel critics who has probed leftist antisemitism at some length.

So how did Jones tackle this problem? Let's take a step back. Like other figures I have discussed, Jones by no means speaks for all leftists, but neither is he an outlier. His condemnations of poverty, racism, LGBTQ+

persecution, colonial histories, and other injustices have repeatedly echoed today's major crit themes.[14] For example, in 2023 the Black actress Adjoa Andoh triggered outrage when she objected that the coronation ceremony for the newly anointed King Charles III was "terribly white."[15] Borrowing from Robin DiAngelo's bestseller *White Fragility* (2018), Jones leapt to Andoh's defense, blasting "fragile white people—who are so offended by anyone who challenges rampant *systemic* racism that they're obsessed with trying to turn the tables and pretending to be victims."[16]

A few years earlier Jones had lamented: "Twitter reflects hatred that is embedded in the nation's social fabric as much as it incubates it. Racism and other forms of bigotry remain organising principles of British society. . . . [R]acism is not a moral 'problem of "bad" individuals,' as the current debate on Twitter's toxicity encourages us to believe, but a '*systemic* one' rooted in European colonialism, when the subjugation of African and Aboriginal peoples was justified by treating them as biologically inferior."[17] In 2022, as Britain and the world were emerging from COVID lockdowns, Jones observed that the "pandemic disproportionately robbed the poor—who, in turn, disproportionately come from minority communities—of their lives, but it merely heightened the deadly consequences of our entire economic *system*."[18] A few weeks later he wrote: "While women are the principal targets of patriarchy (that is, a society rigged in favour of men), this *system* also punishes those seen to deviate from rigid gender norms. Improving the position of women will probably be accompanied by progress for LGBTQ people; likewise, rolling back women's rights will also mean those of LGBTQ people deteriorate in tandem."[19] Clearly, Jones draws from critical theory, rigorously depicting problems such as racism, poverty, sexism, and heteronormativity as systemic, and not just errors and accidents, within Western societies.

ANTISEMITISM LEFT AND RIGHT

In the summer of 2015, Corbyn headed into the final lap of his leadership campaign.[20] That August, Jones published in the *Guardian* an opinion piece about the antisemitism rows titled "Antisemitism Has No Place on the Left" and attracted 2,645 reader comments. With the leadership contest just weeks away, Jones wanted to nip in the bud one of Corbyn's nagging embarrassments.

Jones began by framing his discussion as a postcard from Berlin, reminding readers of the pan-European train networks that had led directly to Hitler's extermination camps. Of course, the Nazis had also persecuted members of socialist and communist movements, so when we condemn Nazi antisemitism, we ordinarily assume that we are condemning a far-right ideology.[21] Yet this was Jones's first oddity. If he wanted to promote leftist self-reflection, then why was he anchoring his discussion in recollections of Nazi crimes that leftists and the wider public would broadly link to the far right? After all, Jones could hardly think that a leftist condemning history's ultimate far-right movement would amount to leftist self-scrutiny. Still, this seeming misstep can be explained. Presumably, Jones wanted to place these references in a larger timeframe, which was why he rightly explained Nazism as "the culmination of hundreds of years of antisemitism: pogroms, blood libel, scapegoating."[22]

Jones seemed to mean something like this: "Antisemitism has led to horrors, so we on the left need to steer clear of it." I think he also meant something like this: "Antisemitism is fundamentally a far-right ideology that can have no place among leftists and must be driven out whenever it rears its head." Indeed, he concluded by confessing that antisemitism "finds expression not just on the right but on the left." But the next oddity was that his present-day examples, too, belonged to the far right, as he referenced antisemitism in Greece's Golden Dawn party and Hungary's Jobbik party.[23] So this is our first puzzle. Jones seemed willing to reckon with leftist antisemitism but sketched only far-right histories. To be sure, over the past two centuries antisemitism has been worse on the right than on the left.[24] Even Soviet, Polish, East German, and other anti-Jewish persecution under socialism cannot compare in scope to the Holocaust or to the long-standing prejudices that had led to it.[25]

In sum, Jones ended up spinning a purity narrative. Although not factually denying antisemitic incidents on the left, he was treating them as incidental and aberrational. The only conclusion for his readers to draw was that *real* antisemitism dwelled on the right and was therefore, by definition, a deviation from *real* leftism. Certainly, Jones did call out some crude prejudices. He abhorred that "Jewish people are sometimes told that antisemitism is caused by Israel's actions" and that this accusation is leveled by "the same people who would never dream of victim-blaming members of other minorities, or claim that anybody was at fault other than the bigot themselves." He blasted "those who imply that Jewish people are somehow synonymous with the Israeli government" and those who "use terms like 'Jewish lobby,' a classic antisemitic trope suggesting there is an organised Jewish cabal exercising behind-the-scenes influence worldwide." Indeed, a chilling ignorance shrouds suggestions that because Jews are "white," an assumption that elides the Jews of various ethnicities, they have not been targets of racism: "Jews were long excluded from 'whiteness,' but in the post-war period, Jews have often been treated as white."[26]

These were welcome insights, yet the problem lay not with what Jones said but with what he omitted. For example, while mentioning the Jews that Nazis drove into death camps, he ignored those whom the Kremlin had dumped in gulags, sometimes fresh from the Nazi camps, or who long faced other forms of discrimination throughout the Soviet sphere, where periodic blacklistings and purges of Jews recurred over decades. Indeed, leftist antisemitism was paraded in vintage leftist hate speech. Jews were often reviled not *as* Jews but as "enemies of the workers," "foreign agents," and the whole panoply of disloyalty slurs. These pasts made no appearance in Jones's foray into leftist self-critique. Of course, these stories of leftist antisemitism were not specifically British, but then nor were the Nazi train networks or the antisemitism in Greece and Hungary that he mentioned. Jones's casting of antisemitism as fundamentally right-wing allowed him to create a leftist purity narrative—horrified by antisemitism yet downplaying the left-wing versions. The point is not that all antisemitism crisply divides between left-wing and right-wing forms. One reason why we readily overlook leftist antisemitism is because not all forms come stamped with "left-wing" and "right-wing," and history gives us plenty of reasons, when in doubt, to view it as coming from the right.

Hostilities toward Jews trace back over thousands of years, yet many writers date the rise of a distinctly leftist antisemitism to nineteenth-century laissez-faire capitalism and rapid industrialization, along with all the attendant social ills of colossal wealth gaps, mass exploitation, urban misery, and the need for powerful factions to find scapegoats. For two centuries, Judaism has haunted the left as a schizophrenic presence.[27] Secular Jews such as Max Horkheimer, Theodor Adorno, and Hannah Arendt largely invented contemporary critical theory, reevaluating modernity and the Enlightenment through the lens of the Holocaust.[28] Yet after the creation of the Jewish state, the advent of decolonization meant that Palestinian self-determination became increasingly allied to leftist politics, often leaving Jews unwelcome on the left unless they were either staking out vocal anti-Israel positions or keeping silent on the Middle East.[29] A small number of writers who study leftist antisemitism have focused on these pasts, yet, again, my aim is not to rehearse histories already recounted by others but to focus on autocritique as defined by the left itself. Suffice it to say that Jones's focus on the far right flowed from a long-standing schizophrenia in which scrutiny of right-wing antisemitism had triggered volumes of critical theory, while scrutiny of left-wing antisemitism remained largely taboo. And this comes as no surprise. Again, the left has long defined the terms we use to talk about injustice, which means that our conceptions of justice already contain a tacit assumption that left-wing positions challenge injustice while right-wing positions promote it. It follows that right-wing attitudes toward Jews, as toward other groups, would seem presumptively suspect while left-wing attitudes would seem presumptively benevolent.

Today, crits writing about leftist antisemitism work in isolation, enjoying no resonance within any broader community of critical theorists.[30] Some leftists scorn any discussion of leftist antisemitism while others just ignore it, as if bigotry is by definition a right-wing vice.[31] As Martin Luther King Jr. once lamented, "Lukewarm acceptance is much more bewildering than outright rejection."[32] This rift contrasts with other currents in critical theory, which, despite intermittent squabbles, have long pursued dialogue and cross-fertilization among, say, critical race theorists, postcolonial theorists, feminists, LGBTQ+ theorists, social constructionists, deconstructionists, poststructuralists, and a number of others. Some scholars of leftist antisemitism can boast distinguished careers, so in a world of autocritique they would presumably be sought after on the left, yet I know of none who have been invited to discuss this topic at any major crit event. As we saw in chapter 6, leftist self-scrutiny stops at the threshold of interest-convergence.

NEVER-ENDING STORY

How systemic has leftist antisemitism been? Although Nazism inflicted history's most massive crimes against Jews, Germany has by no means been the top purveyor of transnational antisemitism. That distinction goes to Russia, including Soviet Russia, which spread antisemitism widely during periods when Moscow enjoyed much leftist support.[33] So while I am not proposing a general history of leftist antisemitism, one history bears a quick summary to illustrate the failures of leftist autocritique.

Of course, the German and Russian strands of antisemitism cannot be cleanly separated. Nazi rhetoric about Jews' worldwide financial and political control and Jewish bloodlust had deep roots in Europe but received a boost from *The Protocols of the Elders of Zion* (1903), the infamous forgery of a global Jewish plot that originated with the czarist secret police and became, as I explain in a moment, a handy Soviet tool.[34] Yet we cannot compare Russian and German patterns of antisemitism quantitatively without first recalling qualitative differences. Nazi ideology decreed an ontological cleansing: Jews stood as the antinomy and congenital foe of the Aryan race.[35] This contrasted with czarist and then Soviet antisemitism, which took the more prosaic forms of workaday imperial power mongering, meaning that handfuls of Jews could still hold positions of political, economic, and cultural prominence.[36] Early Bolsheviks had condemned czarist pogroms, and after World War II the Kremlin initially supported Israeli statehood, which at the time was socialist in conception and stood as a symbolic rebuke to Western powers.[37] Yet as Israel steadily allied with the West, the Kremlin reverted to its earlier tactics of strategically manipulating antisemitism.[38] Nazi and Soviet antisemitisms also differed in their execution. Nazis achieved unparalleled depth with shocking speed, while the Kremlin's on-and-off tactics spanned a greater geography over longer stretches of time.

As I mentioned in chapter 3, postwar West Germany soon acknowledged Nazi atrocities and then developed public education and independent inquiry with the task of confronting the past, *Vergangenheitsbewältigung*, and promoting a culture of remembrance, *Erinnerungskultur*. By contrast, any seeds of collective self-scrutiny that might have sprouted in central and eastern Europe were extinguished by the 1950s as shifting alliances meant that Israel turned from being a potential Kremlin ally to its new target. Moscow fretted that Jews might want to leave Soviet-ruled lands in which they had faced historical discrimination—indeed, people today forget that the Zionist movement had originally emerged more in response to Russian-imperial antisemitism than to Western antisemitism.[39] Any mass emigration ran the risk of confirming Soviet rule as repressive and of encouraging breakaway movements among other ethnic minorities.[40]

To be sure, Kremlin authorities never officially denied the Holocaust or suppressed facts about raw numbers of deaths. Rather, they crushed any discussion of it *as* antisemitism or, indeed, any open examination of historical antisemitism—which, like all forms of racism and discrimination, was presented as right-wing and Western, having been transcended under socialism.[41] Following Kremlin ideology, it was civilians defined solely in national terms—simply Russian, simply Ukrainian, simply Belarusian, simply Polish, simply Czech, simply Lithuanian, simply Hungarian, simply Romanian— whom the Nazis had deported and exterminated, with no reference to their Jewish identities, despite the vastly greater proportions of deported and exterminated Jews from those places.[42]

In sum, the Holocaust was never only a Nazi story. In the Soviet sphere, World War II was taught through purity narratives of Soviet heroism, not in the sense of being outright lies but in the sense of papering over elements of the Holocaust that raised questions about Russia's long-standing and imperially tactical antisemitism. Well into the 1980s, central and eastern Europe lacked anything like what in the West had come to be known as Holocaust education, which to this day is still sparse in the region. In fact, that designation, long after it became current in the West, never gained any currency in the Soviet sphere. Meanwhile, periodic purges had proceeded in vintage Soviet fashion, with Jews disparaged not *as* Jews, in the manner of the far right, but as "bourgeois capitalists," "enemies of the workers," and the like. Unsurprisingly, nationalists in post-Soviet central and eastern Europe would have no difficulty repackaging antisemitism in coded references to "liberals," "foreign agents," and "capitalists."[43]

After defecting from Ceaușescu's Romania in the 1970s, Ion Pacepa, its senior Securitate official, documented how the Soviet secret police had spotted Muslims' anti-Israel animus as an opportunity. Viewing Muslims as ignorant and impressionable, Yuri Andropov—no second-tier pion but the Kremlin's Secret Police chief and then the ruling party's secretary-general—undertook a program of infusing antisemitic propaganda throughout Muslim populations. In Andropov's view, "We needed to instill a Nazi-style hatred for the Jews throughout the Islamic world, and to turn this weapon of the emotions into a terrorist bloodbath against Israel."[44] Suddenly the *Protocols* were newly minted in Arabic and increasingly displayed for sale in Muslim countries as far away as Malaysia, with passages translated verbatim into the Hamas Charter of 1988.[45]

Despite the attention that the left has long devoted to the Israel–Palestine conflict, indeed presenting it largely as a continuation of Western colonialism with all the attendant racist attitudes, crits have ignored this Kremlin campaign predicated on breathtakingly orientalist assumptions about Muslims as stupid and violent.[46] The Kremlin promoted this late nineteenth-century antisemitism across Muslim nations with few objections from the left. Indeed, the *Protocols* still circulate in Muslim countries with few questions asked on the left about how this came to be or whether they bear any responsibility. To be clear, the Israel–Palestine conflict involves many factors, and certainly none of the observations I make in this book can suffice to resolve that situation. As leftists rightly remind us, pointing out one form of discrimination should not equate with denying another. So this globalization of Soviet-spawned antisemitism by no means implies that racism has been one-sided. Without a doubt, anti-Muslim racism in the West further fueled Middle East enmities.[47]

Still, for decades government-orchestrated antisemitism persisted in regimes that had enjoyed steady and often strong levels of Western left-wing support. On crits' own accounts of how social exclusion works, leftist antisemitism has consisted not of sporadic errors and accidents but of systemic policies with global consequences. Any serious autocritique would document the links to comparable episodes of leftist racism and ethnic cleansing. For example, the mass deportations of Chechens, Tartars, Ingush, Koreans, Turks, and other ethnic groups, which countless victims never survived, were officially justified through purity narratives of Soviet conquest over "class conflict," "counterrevolutionaries," and "enemies of the people." As with leftist antisemitism, these other racisms, although not flatly denied on the left, have never formed any serious part of the left's proactive campaigns of mass public awareness about racism, except in the trivial sense that they occasionally end up tossed into platitudes such as "Of course, the Soviet Union wasn't perfect" or "We condemn all forms of racism."

Imagine a scenario in which a disgruntled white customer in a restaurant speaks angrily to a Black waitress whom he does not know, shouting: "You're just another lazy one." After the waitress complains, the customer insists that he is not racist and did not intend the broadside in a racist vein. For Matsuda, the solution lies in the title of her essay "Public Response to Racist Speech," which requires a presumption in favor of "the victim's story." In other words, in the first instance, it is the target's perception that must take precedence.[48] The same criterion would apply to smears such as "queer pervert," "Arab terrorist," and the like. It would equally apply to a stereotype such as "money-grubbing Jew," which, like these other slurs, has a long history on the far right. By contrast, when the left is asked about equating Jews with Nazis, or using slogans such as "from the river to the sea," which have been prominent on the left but are perceived by many Jews as a call for their elimination from Israel along with the elimination of the state itself, suddenly the analysis reverses as we are told that, in the first instance, the speakers' virtuous intentions must take precedence over their targets' perceptions.[49]

This discrepancy chimes with the UN report on the Czech republic that I discussed in chapter 10, where the concept of "class struggle" served to credit the presumed intentions of perpetrators in ways that human rights monitors would never have accepted for racist atrocities. The point also brings us back to Jones. In the next chapter, I observe that, five years after his *Guardian* op-ed, Jones did acknowledge distinctly leftist forms of antisemitism. However, it was important first to recall this *Guardian* piece to consider the left's tendency to view antisemitism as intrinsically right-wing and therefore only incidental or aberrational on the left.

12 DOTS CONNECTING

After Labour's defeat in 2019, Jeremy Corbyn's successor as party leader, the centrist Keir Starmer, moved to crush antisemitism in the party, suspending Corbyn and various Corbyn allies.[1] In 2020, Owen Jones, although still supporting Corbynite policies, took stock of Corbyn's party leadership in his book *This Land*, which included a lengthy chapter revisiting the antisemitism crisis. This time Jones criticized the Corbyn left more bluntly than he had in his *Guardian* op-ed. During the five intervening years, antisemitic incidents had continued apace, and this time Jones was more willing to situate antisemitism squarely on the left.

THIS LAND

Jones began the antisemitism chapter by recalling Corbyn's endorsement of a street mural appearing in a heavily Muslim immigrant area of London, painted by an American artist going by the name "Mear One." The artwork featured vintage antisemitic imagery and was blasted by the local borough mayor Lutfur Rahman, in stark contrast to Corbyn, who condemned it only several years later. This time Jones more candidly confirmed that "there are distinctive elements to left-wing antisemitism."[2] He conceded that exploitative capitalism had long stood at the heart of the left's concerns about liberal democracy and that these concerns at times spilled over into stereotypes of Jews as manipulators of finance, industry, media, and behind-the-scenes politics.

Jones rightly recalled that these antisemitic stereotypes were not exclusively leftist and had long histories on the right. Yet he conceded that the left-wing manifestations were no anomaly:

> What could be described as "leftism" in its broadest sense understands and analyses capitalism as a series of competing social forces, a system in which classes driven by rational economic self-interest have conflicting needs and aspirations. Then there is "conspiracism," which is quite different: a belief in shadowy individuals wielding sinister unaccountable power and pulling strings behind the scenes. This can—and does—all too easily blend into antisemitism. Rather than talking about the financial sector as a whole, for example, conspiracists often rant about the Rothschilds, a long-vilified family of Jewish financiers, who don't even make the cut of the richest 1,000 people on earth.[3]

Recall my reference in chapter 9 to the Nazi philosopher Carl Schmitt, who described the construction of an enemy as central to unifying a nation, movement, or other collectivity. Jones captured the specificity of a leftist antisemitism that places Jews among the class of the oppressors. He recalled some architects of the modern left who had trafficked in antisemitism, such as Karl Marx, Mikhail Bakunin, and Pierre-Joseph Proudhon. In Britain, the list includes founding fathers of the labor movement, such as Keir Hardie, Sidney Webb, and Ernest Bevin.[4] Of course, as to Marx, in view of his Jewish ancestry and milieu, his antisemitic sideswipes have long been debated, yet whatever Marx's intentions may have been, his remarks thrived in some of his most widely circulated writing.[5] So Jones was willing to cite a few heavyweights, yet the problem was that he drew no visible links to the present.

I return to that problem shortly, but first it is crucial to note that Jones condemned several instances of antisemitism on Corbyn's watch. During the Israel–Palestine clashes of 2014, Naz Shah, who won her seat as a Labour MP the following year, had posted on Facebook an ethnic-cleansing image that had long done the rounds among antisemites. It depicted a map of Israel projected onto a map of the United States and bearing the caption: "Solution for Israel–Palestine conflict—relocate Israel into United States." In 2015 Corbyn attended a Palestinian memorial event organized by the Holocaust denier Paul Eisen. In 2016 the high-profile Corbyn supporter and former

London mayor Ken Livingstone made one of several broadsides against Jews that have littered his career, spouting that Adolf Hitler had supported a Jewish homeland in his early career: "When Hitler won his election in 1932, his policy then was that Jews should be moved to Israel. He was supporting Zionism before he went mad and ended up killing six million Jews."[6]

Jones recalled plenty of other incidents. For example, Jackie Walker, vice president of the pro-Corbyn Momentum movement, boasted both African and Jewish ancestry. In 2016 she described Jews as the "chief financiers" in the African slave trade. At a time of rising attacks on Jews in Britain and Europe, Walker rejected suggestions that Jewish schools needed heightened security and falsely claimed that Holocaust Memorial Day events "commemorated only Jewish victims."[7] Meanwhile, Chris Williamson, another pro-Corbyn MP at the time, "retweeted a Holocaust denier writing about Venezuela; tweeted his pleasure at meeting Miko Peled, an Israeli-American author who said that 'Jews have a reputation for being sleazy thieves,' and that free speech meant Labour members should be able to ask 'the Holocaust: yes or no?' . . . Shortly after the Pittsburgh Synagogue massacre on 27 October 2018, [Williamson] tweeted: 'Wow, well blow me down' as he shared an attack on the president of the Board of Deputies of British Jews, again refusing to delete the tweet when asked."[8] Incidentally, it cannot be repeated often enough that even for the most strident civil libertarians, defending people's free speech rights in no way equates with endorsing their messages.

Jones railed against similar scandals within Labour's rank and file. One party member shared a blog entitled "Timeline of the Jewish Genocide of the British People," accusing Jews of "being behind wars from Oliver Cromwell's time onwards" and perpetuating slurs about Jews hungrily profiting from war and exploitation that prominently figured in the *Protocolos of the Elders of Zion* as well as Nazi propaganda. Jones also quoted Momentum's social media officer, who confirmed: "There was stuff posted in that group like 'Jews are shit, if you want to touch them you have to wash your hands' and sharing Holocaust denial, claims Jews run the world, and claims Jews are behind every war." Jones recalled "at least 170 cases identified as antisemitism meriting investigation" by the Labour Party: "Some of the cases are genuinely disturbing. One [Labour Party] member was found to have posted comments supporting Holocaust denial, called Jews 'cockroaches,' declared 'never trust anything a Jew says' and shared a post which said 'Jews admit organising White Genocide.' . . . The case of another member who had been reported for Holocaust denial was not even logged, let alone investigated."[9] He also cited an internal party report describing twenty-two additional cases:

> [These instances] should have led to suspensions for an assortment of gratu-itous and deeply offensive antisemitic statements and the sharing of antise-mitic material, including explicit Holocaust denial and conspiracy theories. One stated, "speaking for myself I despise Jews I think they are vermin and the scum of the earth"; another explicitly wrote "I am a Holocaust denier" as well as "Israel is a shameful little prostitute of The Big American Bank Rob-bery," combined with talk of the "Zionist owned Western media"; another shared a video entitled "Gentiles will be the slaves of Jews"; yet another shared material form the infamous Holocaust denier David Irving, and promoted an article entitled "The Holocaust™ and the Phony Six Million."[10]

Jones noted a party member who had "shared a picture of the Statue of Liberty's face smothered by an alien tattooed with the Star of David, reca-pitulating the old cliché about Zionist domination of America, along with the comment 'The most accurate photo I've seen all year!'" This case was reported to a Labour councilor, who "opined that the image was 'anti-Israel, not anti-Jewish.'"[11] Again, these are just a few examples, only from Britain and only during the brief period of Corbyn's leadership. And of course they cannot all be viewed in the same light. For example, I have mentioned Jones's account of MP Naz Shah's "relocate Israel" posting, but he rightly added that Shah promptly apologized, describing her previous Facebook comments as "ignorant," "antisemitic," "hurtful," and "offensive." In fact, Shah went on to forge successful links with Britain's Jewish community. Similarly, Corbyn swiftly suspended Livingstone's party membership after the former mayor's public rhapsody on Hitler.[12]

WHEN IS A LEFTIST NOT A LEFTIST?

Yet the disputes dragged on about whether Corbyn "is" or "is not" antise-mitic, as if the decisive question was about some mystery buried deep in the soul of Corbyn the man. This framing resounded endlessly in the headlines: "Jeremy Corbyn Is an Anti-Semite," "Jeremy Corbyn Isn't Antisemitic," "I Still Don't Believe Corbyn Is Antisemitic," and "Jeremy Corbyn's Cynical Anti-Semitism."[13]

What was odd, though, was that leftists who delved into these controversies, including Jones, suddenly abandoned questions that for decades the left had deemed compulsory in matters of social exclusion. In their different ways, stalwarts from Adorno to Arendt, Sartre, De Beauvoir, Fanon, Foucault, Bell, and Crenshaw had taught that incidents of discrimination could be scrutinized as systemic regardless of an individual perpetrator's benign intentions. Recall my mention in chapter 3 of the statue of the eighteenth-century philanthropist Edward Colston, torn down by Black Lives Matter protesters. No critical race theorists have argued that Colston's well-meaning acts of charity nullified the evils that enabled him to acquire his wealth. Again, while critical theory has never flatly denied the salience of individual responsibility, it has long rejected the fetishizing of individual personalities and their high-minded intentions. Critical theory explains discrimination as structural within liberal democracies, even in situations where individuals imagine they are acting on benevolent impulses.

I have paid some attention to Jones's account not because he superficially departs from leftist patterns but because, in fact, he glaringly recapitulates them. In chapter 11 we saw him boldly depict racism, poverty, sexism, and heteronormativity as systemic. Accordingly, given his copious descriptions of past and present leftist antisemitism—not only under Corbyn and not only in Britain—any leftist's obvious next step should have been to explain why and how antisemitism has been *systemic* on the left. Yet we have witnessed nothing of the kind. It is their very aversion to this question that explains why many leftists feel stunned when they are accused of antisemitism and often jump to the conclusion that such charges form part of some covert and tentacular plot.[14] They forget how leftists themselves have taught us to view discrimination not primarily as individual or even conscious but as collective and often unnoticed.

If I have learned anything from critical theory, it is that assertions such as "Corbyn is an antisemite" are not just true or just false. Rather, they are irrelevant to leftists' own accounts of how vilification operates. For any leftists, the question should not be "Is Corbyn an antisemite?" but "Have Corbyn's supporters perpetuated systemic antisemitism regardless of their publicly declared aspirations or their privately felt intentions?" As these controversies raged, I found myself neither agreeing nor disagreeing with accusations about Corbyn's antisemitism because crits had long taught me that what mattered was not the inner stirrings of the private man but the broader social processes in which he and his allies become absorbed. On Jones's own account, antisemitism was rampant regardless of the sentiments of this or that particular leftist, which could always be packaged as benign by virtue of being "really only" a concern for Palestinians. Yet leftists who had always insisted on viewing discrimination as a social and political force, operating regardless of subjective feelings or attitudes, suddenly abandoned that approach through outpourings of character sketches as they scoured Corbyn's CV to prove that deep down his heart was in the right place.

Jones reviled Corbyn's right-wing cavilers, who "were themselves drenched in racism," while hastening to add that their hypocrisy was "not an excuse—or it shouldn't have been. Antisemitism was a genuine problem, and one causing many Jews genuine hurt."[15] Yet Jones, too, lost himself, just as the entire country had lost itself, in the fixation on whether Corbyn "is" antisemitic "deep down"—or, in the words of one party spokesperson, whether Corbyn has "an antisemitic bone in his body"—as if eliminating doubts about the individual would answer pressing questions about the movement. The logic strayed close to Walker's claim that because she as an individual had some Jewish roots, she therefore couldn't be antisemitic. This conjecture about Corbyn the man served not to probe leftist antisemitism but to sideline it through a seamless syllogism: leftists have always opposed all forms of discrimination, and antisemitism is a form of discrimination; therefore, leftists have always opposed antisemitism. Yet a simple analogy illustrates why crits have otherwise shunned this kind of sophistry: liberal democracy has always guaranteed equal citizenship, and equal citizenship includes racial equality; therefore, liberal democracy has always guaranteed racial equality. If this latter formulation amounts to a bogus purity narrative, then so does the former one. By abstracting events from their contexts and histories, these paralogisms merely collapse concrete actions into their actors' own self-proclaimed intentions and ideals.

Jones accepted as an abstract proposition that antisemitism "has always existed on the left."[16] He cited some assorted leftist antisemitism from the past and then some assorted antisemitism in the present, but never connected these dots to the present to explain leftist antisemitism as systemic. As indicated, Jones began his chapter on antisemitism by recalling Corbyn's response to an antisemitic street mural, an incident that Jones described as follows: "It was a classic failing of the Corbyn era: resisting taking an unavoidable step, then suffering self-inflicted damage, and gaining no credit whatsoever for finally bowing to the inevitable. It was also symptomatic of the leadership's inadequate and recalcitrant response to a persistent problem within the Labour Party."[17] "Classic" indeed. Throughout the chapter, Jones observed recurring antisemitic incidents under Corbyn but repeatedly collapsed them into a slapstick of errors and blunders—happenstance deviations from the *real* leftism.

Jones reassured us that Corbyn's CV rendered impossible any conclusion that Corbyn the man could "be" antisemitic.[18] Despite his own chronicle, Jones claimed that only a "small minority" of Labour Party members had engaged in antisemitic conduct—in effect, "a few bad apples," precisely the conclusion that crits rightly scorn for other forms of discrimination.[19] Similarly, in 2024, Jean-Luc Mélenchon referred to leftist antisemitism as purely "residual" in a country where, as we have seen, the far-right Jean-Marie Le Pen had infamously dismissed the Holocaust as a "detail of history" a few decades earlier—the standard denialist technique of acknowledging antisemitism solely with the aim of peripheralizing it.[20] Jones recalled in the aforementioned *Guardian* op-ed that Corbyn had "been a long-term supporter of the Palestinian justice movement," adding, "While the vast majority of people involved in the movement are—like myself—driven by a passionate support for self-determination, there is a minority that indulges antisemitic tropes."[21] Of course, in contexts such as Georgia, Ukraine, Moldova, or Tibet, the "passion" of such support on the left has often seemed lukewarm. Be that as it may, even where evidence suggests that only a minority of whites in some Western countries consciously articulate racist views, such findings have in no way spurred critical theorists to preclude understandings of racism as systemic.[22] It may seem unfair to single out Jones as I have done, yet, again, he illustrates more directly some trends that are widespread yet often less conspicuous. Leftists such as Alain Badiou, Wendy Brown, Judith Butler, Cornel West, and Slavoj Žižek have never hesitated to condemn far-right antisemitism, yet as we have seen this has been easy to do insofar as challenges to the right have always promoted leftists' immediate interests in advancing their political outlooks.[23] These writers have never probed leftist antisemitism even in the deficient ways that Jones at least attempts, let alone analyzed it as systemic within leftist histories.

THE CHAKRABARTI REPORT

It was after Livingstone's comments that pressure grew for an internal party inquiry. Corbyn invited the prominent human rights lawyer and Labour Party member Shami Chakrabarti to head up an investigation, yet far from calming concerns, she ended up fueling them. Many viewed *The Shami Chakrabarti Report* of 2016 as a whitewash, gesturally condemning antisemitism while ultimately letting Corbyn off the hook. Within weeks of the report's publication, Corbyn appointed Chakrabarti to a prestigious government position, sparking questions about whether he was rewarding her for soft-peddling the crisis and whether the two had struck a bargain from the outset.[24]

Some of Chakrabarti's findings were fair and welcome. She echoed the party moderates in condemning the term *Zio*, which had become common among Israel's leftist critics.[25] She drew no final conclusion about whether the insult should be punished in law, though she hinted—rightly in my view—that it should not be. Instead, in this report addressed to party members, she focused not on legal rules but on guidelines of best practice. In her own words: "As a free-speech campaigner, I have always believed in the right to offend. But as a lawyer I know the difference between a [legal] right and a [moral] duty. Self-censorship is a terrible thing when those living under oppressive regimes bite their tongues for fear of persecution or prosecution. It is equally terrible when people restrict their political speech for fear of the lynch mob. But there is another type of restraint that you might call kindness, politeness or good advocacy that is genuinely designed to persuade people and inform debates rather than inflame them."[26]

Of course, prejudice can be articulated in gracious terms, so it is debatable whether Chakrabarti was seriously confronting Labour antisemitism here. In 1994, Harvard professor Henry Louis Gates Jr. doubted how well African Americans fare by agreeing to conditions of polite speech: "The real power commanded by the racist is likely to vary inversely with the vulgarity with which it is expressed."[27] Of course, some would object that pro-Israel groups push equally unbalanced positions and have "weaponized" antisemitism, waging false accusations against leftists to block dialogue about the Palestinian plight.[28] In response, those pro-Israel groups claim that their events, too, have been subject to restrictions, cancellations, and attacks.[29] To be sure, controversies relevant to antisemitism, Islamophobia, and Israel–Palestine cannot be resolved as a full package, and I reject questions about whether "the" left "is" antisemitic, as if the response must be all or nothing.[30] Nevertheless, leftists often draw historical analogies from Israeli policy to South African apartheid, European colonialism, and even Nazism itself, so at the very least they can also bring honest histories of leftist antisemitism and support for murderous and repressive regimes into critical theory without foreclosing discussion on Israel and Palestine.

Proceeding on her default preference for free speech while proposing higher ethical standards for Labour, Chakrabarti again made some further welcome points:

> In day-to-day political debate, it is always incendiary to compare the actions of Jewish people or institutions anywhere in the world to those of Hitler or the Nazis or to the perpetration of the Holocaust. Indeed such remarks can only be intended to be incendiary rather than persuasive. Why? Because the Shoah is still in people's living family experience and because, if every human rights atrocity is described as a Holocaust, Hitler's attempted obliteration of the Jewish people is diminished or de-recognised in our history as is the history of a global minority that has had cause to feel, at worst, persecuted and, at best, vulnerable for thousands of years. Other hideous human rights atrocities from African slavery to the killing fields of Cambodia, the Armenian and

Rwandan genocides are all of course to be remembered and described, but diluting their particularity or comparing degrees of victimhood and evil does no service to anyone.[31]

Chakrabarti concluded her discussion with two recommendations to the Labour Party:

- I recommend that Labour members resist the use of Hitler, Nazi and Holocaust metaphors, distortions and comparisons in debates about Israel-Palestine in particular.
- I further recommend that excuse for, denial, approval or minimisation of the Holocaust and attempts to blur responsibility for it, have no place in the Labour Party.[32]

These insights were legitimate yet phrased in hypothetical terms as if there were no factual record to assess. Like Jones, Chakrabarti found no systemic antisemitism under Corbyn. She condemned nothing more than an "occasionally toxic atmosphere," as if her priority was not antidiscrimination but preserving the Corbyn brand.[33] So Jones and Chakrabarti came to this problem with markedly different biographies and professional mandates, yet their findings followed the same template. Both took leftist antisemitism seriously and provided helpful insights, but then ultimately cast it as accidental and aberrational, not as systemic or as arising from any entrenched or ongoing history.

Support for Corbyn also came from Jewish Voice for Labour (JVL), an organization founded in 2017 amid these crises. As Jones emphasized in *This Land*, JVL must not be confused with the older Jewish Labour Movement, founded more than a century ago, which has supported Israeli statehood while also criticizing aspects of Israeli policy and supporting a two-state solution for Israel-Palestine. Nevertheless, according to Jones, JVL's "membership grew to around 1,200 members, albeit two thirds of whom were not actually Jewish," and JVL's "approach was at odds with where most Jewish people were, including many who had actively supported Corbyn." Jones also cited the Jewish Momentum founder and staunch Corbyn supporter Jon Lansman, who claimed that JVL "is an organization which is not just tiny but has no real connection with the Jewish community at all." Jones faulted

Corbyn for having consulted only with JVL while ignoring other Jews, and added another voice to the mix: "'I spoke to a lot of Jewish people,' explains journalist and author Rachel Shabi, who supported Corbyn in [two] leadership elections and had gone on record as backing him, 'and their frustration with JVL is: "How has this crank group become privileged inside the Labour Party?" They [JVL] became everyone's mascot, anyone's antisemitism alibi: 'They don't think [leftist] antisemitism is so, and so it isn't.'"[34]

Of course, the Jewish community has never spoken with a single voice, and JVL cannot be discounted even if it represents only a small minority. JVL did not categorically deny left-wing antisemitism but insisted that it was "no worse than in the rest of society."[35] Yet by now the problem should be obvious. Leftist autocritique has never meant "We scrutinize ourselves only when no one else is committing the same faults." Feminists have not stopped teaching about Western patriarchy when reminded that other civilizations have also been sexist. Critical race theorists have not stopped teaching about slavery when reminded that other civilizations have also had slavery, and so forth. So the more serious question would be: Which characteristics have been distinctive of leftist antisemitism, and how do they trace back into history? Yet JVL proved even more recalcitrant than Jones and Chakrabarti on this question, not just passively neglecting to call leftist antisemitism systemic but actively opposing any such suggestion.[36] So even if JVL was right to complain that Corbyn had been politically targeted, this targeting did not erase a track record of antisemitic words and deeds on the left.

LEFTISM "BY DEFINITION"

Many on the left have blasted accusations of leftist antisemitism as forming part of a Zionist campaign to combat progressive politics altogether. I won't challenge these allegations here because even if we assume that they are true, we still cannot discount evidence solely on the grounds that we despise the motives of the people who bring it.

For example, in chapter 11, I mentioned the activist Asa Winstanley, who fantasized that even Jones had sold out to Zionism.[37] For argument's sake, we can assume that even this far-fetched charge was valid because what matters is whether the concrete facts recited by Jones had in fact occurred on the left and not whether Jones or anyone else had recited them on the basis of being open or secret Zionists. To draw an analogy, as we have seen, countless millions were brutalized by regimes largely supported on the left, and the truth of this fact does not change solely because it has been opportunistically recited on the far right.[38] Nor, then, can leftists abandon self-scrutiny on the pretext that certain claims have been waged as part of a secret and sinister campaign, even if we assume this claim to be true. No one has shown Jones's factual allegations to be false, so the problem in insisting that they have been propelled by devious motives is not whether that charge is true or false but that it is irrelevant to why and how antisemitism has arisen on the left.

The scholar Antony Lerman took a view similar to JVL's. Interest-convergence meant that he, too, could easily condemn right-wing antisemitism while presenting leftist antisemitism as a history that has come to an end. Lerman did not merely decline to connect the types of historical dots that leftists otherwise connect for other groups but espoused a purity narrative, actively insisting that we *must* not connect those dots given the suspect motives of Corbyn's opponents. He denied antisemitism on the Corbynite left precisely by treating individual incidents *as* individual, in effect not showing but merely stipulating from the outset that they cannot be systemic or ongoing.[39] Lerman denied leftist antisemitism not by applying critical theory but, in effect, by insisting that applying it would be a methodological fault. Lerman did not simply abandon the methods that leftists otherwise apply to other forms of social exclusion but also went a step further by proposing a precise photonegative of critical theory. While crits invoked other forms of discrimination to challenge liberal democracies' proclaimed ideals, Lerman did the reverse, invoking contemporary leftist ideals as proof of the absence of antisemitism. Here, too, leftist antisemitism ended up dissolved into a purity narrative that never flatly denied the problem yet reduced it to errors, accidents, and deviations from the *real* leftism—thus practicing ethical denialism in lieu of factual denialism.

Lerman was no innovator in this respect. In 2005, the prominent French crit Alain Badiou, pursuing his long-standing criticisms of Israel, published an essay to contemplate various meanings of the word *Jewish*. Although others promptly challenged him, these spats might have remained obscure if global politics had taken a different turn. Yet the Israel–Palestine crisis of 2014 witnessed escalated attacks on French Jews, and some of Badiou's critics refused to ignore his views as innocuous reveries from the ivory tower. They argued that Badiou had long pushed a brand of leftism that encouraged antisemitism under the guise of criticizing Israel.[40] The debates raged across leading French publications, including *Le Monde*, *Libération*, and *Les temps modernes*.

As it was with Corbyn, my question is not whether Badiou "is" or "is not" antisemitic in the depths of his soul. Instead, my question is about how this preeminent leftist applied critical theory to the left's own pasts. In response to the charges that his depiction of Jews and Israel had tipped into antisemitism, Badiou summarily—almost comically—concluded that "far-left antisemitism, by definition, cannot exist" and called the very concept an "aberrant oxymoron."[41] His syllogism was plain enough: leftism cannot tolerate any form of discrimination, and antisemitism is a form of discrimination; therefore, leftism cannot tolerate antisemitism. Even if crits such as Butler and Žižek have avoided this particular line of reasoning in writing on Israel and Palestine, they have certainly adopted the same overall approach—gladly assailing right-wing antisemitism and vigorously condemning Israel, yet omitting any serious question about whether antisemitism, or support for Soviet or other dictatorships often deeply involved in Middle East politics, has been systemic on the left and what that would mean for their own ongoing condemnations of the Jewish state.

With Badiou, we again witness not merely the abandonment of critical theory but another photonegative of it. Badiou, too, suddenly forgot the very methods he had so dexterously applied throughout his career. We would be hard-pressed to find any philosopher who has more fastidiously charged liberal democracy with creating realities in opposition to its proclaimed ideals, thus exposing the deceptions that historically have hovered behind liberal democracies' self-proclaimed ideals of equality, citizenship, and the like.[42] From Badiou's own vantage point, nothing could be more ridiculous than to deduce what classical liberalism is and does by hopping and skipping only through its own proclaimed ideals. Yet suddenly he was weaving the purity narrative that leftism does amount to *its* own proclaimed ideals, with even a rather conspicuous deviation counting merely as "aberrant." On Badiou's account, *real* antisemitism cannot exist on the *real* left.

Badiou's remark scarcely differs from Žižek's "time to get serious" tweet, which I described in chapter 7. With Badiou, too, my first response was to imagine a conference organized by crits to explore, say, racist, sexist, or heteronormative histories in the West. I wondered what would happen if someone were to wave around pages of officially promulgated antidiscrimination laws from a country such as the United States or Britain and exclaim, "See? In liberal democracies discrimination, by definition, cannot exist!" Any crit would rightly respond with derision, and yet no crits, in France or elsewhere, voiced any objection to Badiou. In essence, Badiou defined his leftism as ethically perfect: not that it is never implicated in injustice, but that when it is, it can only be through a random deviation that is not *real* leftism.

After the Hamas attack on Israel of October 7, 2023, more than 1,000 attacks on Jews in France in a single month prompted government officials to organize a national and cross-party march against antisemitism on Sunday, November 12. The route passed central locations, including the National Assembly, the Senate, the Quai d'Orsay, and the Luxembourg gardens.[43] Understandably, anger erupted when Marine Le Pen's far-right National Rally party announced its participation. The party had been founded in the 1970s by collaborators and supporters of the former pro-Nazi Vichy regime, including open Holocaust deniers such as her father—again, construing "denial" here in the ethical rather than the factual sense. Le Pen's calculation was that she had long ago and very publicly kicked her father out of the party, firmly breaking away from these earlier origins. Yet antisemites still formed part of the party's rank and file. Mélenchon promptly announced his refusal to attend a march that included Le Pen's party, and some members of La France insoumise organized an alternative at the more symbolically laden site of the Vél d'Hiv arena, which had been used during World War II to round up thousands of Jews for deportation to Nazi Germany, leaving few survivors.[44] As if orchestrated by Badiou, these LFI members visually defined antisemitism as right-wing only, with no leftist history of it worthy of note.

To be clear, nothing I am claiming presupposes any fixed stance on the Israel–Palestine conflict. Nor does the foregoing discussion of leftist antisemitism imply anything about the victims of violence or discrimination who have long been caught up in the hostilities. Rather, the left has rightly thrown down the gauntlet by challenging us to revisit our political homes. To those of us committed to institutions of liberal democracy, the left rightly replies that we must learn about the devastation wrought by centuries of Western colonialism, racism, and neo-imperialism. We must factor these pasts into our assessments of the Middle East and other global crises. Leftists promote this view through widespread public education campaigns, often tying in struggles with minimal ties to the Middle East—for example, by showing how overarching mechanisms of oppression link Palestinian suffering to the Black Lives Matter movement. Their drift is to assimilate Israeli politics into long-standing patterns of apartheid, settler colonialism, and even Nazism.[45]

Israel's defenders respond by disputing such analogies. Yet we have seen that these histories of racism and colonialism, although certainly forming an essential backdrop, tell only half the story. They omit long chronicles of leftist support for brutal and at times antisemitic regimes that were often closely tied to Israel's self-declared enemies. So let's be consistent. Either all these histories are relevant or none of them are. What we cannot accept is crits who insist on seeing centuries of Western oppression recapitulated in Israeli policy while assuring us that the left's own historical support for repressive and antisemitic regimes was only ever incidental, only errors and accidents, never the *real* leftism. In this book I have noted how voices on the left, even when purporting to condemn autocracy in places like Russia, China, Cuba, Nicaragua, or Venezuela, end up falling in line with those governments' policies when they fail to connect the dots to the left's own long-standing support for dictatorial regimes. The same holds true for Israel–Palestine, where activists—insisting that they have no truck with Hamas, Hezbollah, Iranian mullahs, the Organisation of Islamic Cooperation, or other such entities—ultimately recapitulate these entities' stances on Israel, again with little reference to a long history on the left of supporting repressive powers: suddenly leftists see no dots to connect.

Some might argue that antisemitism since the attacks of October 2023, such as harassment individually targeting Jewish students, represents the actions of only a small minority and not the *real* left, yet here too this is not a distinction that leftists ordinarily draw. As we have seen, George Floyd and Stephen Lawrence are seen on the left as victims not of a small minority of racists but of broader, unconscious, and structural biases. This is why my accusations in this book have not been primarily about hypocrisy, which we find throughout politics, but about the promises of autocritique that leftists have long invoked to justify their vocal condemnations of the West. If collective self-scrutiny is ever to become more than a cliché, then leftists will have to push for campaigns that will educate the widest possible public about the left's own histories—histories of the left lending legitimacy to networks of violence, repression, and discrimination that have damaged and destroyed countless millions of lives, with effects that persist in full force today.

13 CONCLUSION

In May 2023, a gang of hooligans pummeled Jean-Baptiste Trogneux, the thirty-year-old manager of a chocolate shop in Amiens in northern France, leaving him with several injuries that required medical attention. As the thugs drubbed Trogneux they shouted, "The President, his wife, and her family!" As it happens, Trogneux is the grandnephew of Brigitte Macron, wife of President Emmanuel Macron, who had begun his second term in office the previous year.[1]

A month earlier, Macron had pushed through the National Assembly a reform of the nation's retirement laws. The change ignited a long-festering anger among low earners who would be expected to stay at work an average of two additional years as a condition for receiving their full pensions. Nationwide protests followed, at times bringing life to a halt. Fierce opposition also came from Jean-Luc Mélenchon's party La France insoumise. A few weeks earlier, the LFI parliamentarian Thomas Portes had posted online a photo of himself standing triumphantly with his foot on an effigy of the decapitated head of Macron's labor minister, Olivier Dussopt.[2] Then just a few days before the attack on Trogneux, Christophe Prudhomme, another LFI parliamentarian, led a street gathering in which supporters chanted: "We beheaded you, Louis XVI! Macron, we can do it again!"[3] The public guillotining of Louis XVI in 1793, after the king had tried to escape with his family, remains an abiding symbol of the French Revolution of 1789.

Did these stunts staged by Mélenchon's LFI colleagues lead to the beating in Amiens? In individual cases, it can be hard to determine whether hostile messages have induced people to turn to violence, but let's stick for a moment with the LFI members' own regicide analogy. In fact, as a thought experiment, let's tinker with the facts by imagining that Louis XVI had successfully escaped while his fourteen-year-old daughter, Marie-Thérèse, had fallen into the hands of angry rebels. The mob might well have executed her instead on what was at the time a widespread view that the entire family was their enemy. The same logic drove the attack on Trogneux. Yes, the beating was instantly condemned across the political spectrum, including LFI. Yet it never occurred to anyone—not even LFI's rivals, who were otherwise scrambling to score points—to inscribe these incidents within any broader chronicle of leftist violence in the way we rightly do for racist, sexist, homophobic, or other identity-based hostilities. It was as if the left had never supported regimes engaged in mass violence—as if leftists merely need to stamp their own preferred violence with the purity narrative of "resistance," which then bestows upon it the veneer of justice.

But am I drawing a far-fetched link here? Do we really need to plough through the exploits of Stalin and Mao to comprehend a scuffle at a chocolate shop tucked away in a French backwater? Leftists have never vacillated in situating violence from outside their ranks within sweeping pasts. When right-wing hoodlums attack members of ethnic, sexual, or other minority groups, the left rightly connects the dots to longer histories. Indeed, a few weeks after Trogneux was beaten, nationwide tensions flared up again when a youth from an ethnic-minority neighborhood resisted a police check. The seventeen-year-old Nahel Merzouk posed no apparent danger to others or to the police, yet the officer shot him, and he died shortly afterward. A video of the incident went viral, sparking rioting, looting, ransacking, and attacks on police and other officials. Mélenchon correctly denounced France's histories of discrimination and ongoing lack of opportunities for socially disadvantaged youth. He also tarred the French police collectively as murderers, inscribing this violent event within a longer history of state violence.[4] Similarly, in the cases of Stephen Lawrence and George Floyd, leftists correctly insisted that these killings needed to be situated within long histories of racist violence.[5] Beyond immediate physical acts, the left has long insisted that we must recognize aggressive messages, too, as acts of violence that in turn lead to physical violence.[6]

As a footnote, I should add that historians have long debated whether beheading Louis XVI was necessary or helpful to install parliamentary government, and yet many on the left have long vaunted the execution as a point of honor. Members of LFI, notably Mélenchon, have paid homage to the revolutionary mastermind Maximilien Robespierre, who assumed dictatorial powers by overseeing the summary detentions and killings, without trial, inflicted on thousands of French citizens.[7] Yes, these histories are complex and easy to denounce in hindsight. Be that as it may, the left has rightly taught us to see brutality not only on the far right but also within the histories of liberal democracy. Yet figures such as Mélenchon, Portes, and Prudhomme breezily proliferate iconographies of leftist violence as if it were nothing more than heart-warming folklore.

Incidentally, did the violence of the French Revolution, at least before the reign of terror, have a justification in principle that no form of colonial or racist violence ever had? Perhaps it did, yet we have seen that crits have not otherwise accepted recitations of high ideals to justify or relativize histories of mass violence committed by Western powers. To be sure, in countries with revolutionary traditions, such as the United States and France, many generations were nurtured on tales of national bravery and valor, yet in recent years those glorifying histories have become ever harder to recite. We are rightly reminded that rose-tinted histories must be tempered by a recognition of racist, colonial, and other oppressive currents. Signally heroic accounts of the founding of American or French democracy are seen at best as naive and antiquated, at worst as nationalist propaganda, scarcely suitable even for children's books. We are reminded that Western armed force generally, far beyond these revolutions, remains steeped in ruthless histories. The Netherlands boasts the overthrow of Spanish monarchical rule and founding of a republic in the sixteenth century, well before the American and French Revolutions. For generations, nothing was more commonplace than to laud the subsequent era of Spinoza, Rembrandt, Huygens, Hals, Grotius, and Vermeer as a "Golden Age" (*Gouden Eeuw*), yet this label has become taboo as progressives have recalled the conditions of poverty, exploitation, and slave trade that sullied the seventeenth century.[8] By contrast, what is remarkable about figures like Mélenchon, Portes, and Prudhomme are their perky celebrations of leftist violence, unburdened by any such self-doubt as long as they can repackage it in the purity narrative of "resistance." Of course, as I noted in chapter 7, resistance is often justified. Yet while willing enough to nod to bleak leftist pasts, too few leftists today are willing to undertake the public and proactive education about these pasts that they demand for the histories of liberal democracies.

In recent years we have heard endless discussions about where leftists have gone wrong. I do not have all the answers but I do have one: Don't tell us. Show us. You rightly insist that defenders of liberal democracy must use mass media and public education campaigns to scrutinize historical injustice in the West. So show us how leftists use mass media and public education campaigns to scrutinize historical injustice on the left. There are plenty of opportunities for promoting critical politics of leftist histories. Universities need to do it, schools need to do it, mass and social media need to do it. They can do it easily and inexpensively. The *New York Times* can do it, the *Washington Post* can do it, NPR can do it, CNN can do it, MSNBC can do it, the *Guardian* can do it, the BBC can do it. Yes, Fox News will relish headlines such as "Leftists Confess to Supporting Brutal and Murderous Regimes," yet coverage aiming to reinforce tribalist finger-pointing will miss the reasons behind a more genuine memory politics. What is crucial for universities and news agencies is not that *they* must take this step but that they can someday boast a leftist *we* who are willing to take it. The longer crits fail to promote a critical memory politics of the left, the more the right will sweep in to do it for them, far more brazenly, further eroding the credibility with which the left rightfully demands self-critical histories of the West. It is time for the left to change course—not to do less critical theory but to do more, not to become less woke but to wager a new wokeness. The left that does this will be a left worth joining.

Acknowledgments

Some of the ideas in this book draw loosely from earlier essays. Chapters 4 through 7 draw in part from "Critical Theory and Memory Politics: Leftist Autocritique after the Ukraine War," *International Journal of Law in Context* 20, no. 2 (2024): 184–203. Chapters 9 and 10 draw from "Identitarian Hatreds and Disloyalty Propaganda," *Human Rights Quarterly* 46 (2024). Chapters 11 and 12 draw from "A Tool to Advance Imperial Interests: Leftist Self-Scrutiny and Israeli Wrongdoing," in *Responses to 7 October: Universities*, edited by Rosa Freedman and David Hirsh (London: Routledge, 2024), 1–11; and "'But Israel Claims to Be a Democracy!'—Hypocrisy, Double Standards, and False Equivalences," in *Responses to 7 October: Universities*, edited by Rosa Freedman and David Hirsh (London: Routledge, 2024), 26–33.

Research for this book arose from my role as project leader for Memory Laws in European and Comparative Perspectives, 2016–2019, generously funded by the European Union Humanities in the European Research Area program. I also extend heartfelt thanks for exchanges with experts who commented on chapters in this book or on related publications, including John Adenitire, Samia Bano, Uladzislau Belavusau, Mohsin Bhat, Muriel Blaive, Matt Bolton, Edmundo Bracho-Polanco, Thomas Brudholm, Gwénaële Calvès, Lori Charlesworth, Roger Cotterrell, Helena Drakakis, John Drakakis, Kristian Skagen Ekeli, Joke Hermes, Steve Heyman, Adrian Howe, Birgitte Schepelern Johansen, Lesley Klaff, Marian Kuna, Nikolay Koposov, David McGrogan, Richard Moon, Les Moran, Jo Murkens, David Nelken, Dina Newman, Milica Pešić, István (Stephen) Pogany, Jiří Přibáň, Elaine

Sharland, Philip Spencer, and István Zöld. Some of these experts were kind enough to join a workshop at Queen Mary University of London in February 2024, graciously facilitated by my colleagues Gulsh Khaltoun and Mujahid Aziz. Many thanks also to Jaime Marshall and Jessica Pellien, and to Gita Manaktala, Ginny Crossman, Anne Barva, Suraiya Jetha, Katie Lewis, and the rest of the staff at the MIT Press, along with various anonymous peer reviewers.

Some of the themes discussed in chapters 3 through 7 were presented at the following seminars and conferences: Memory Laws—International and Cross-Disciplinary Perspectives, St. Antony's College, Oxford, hosted by Gabriele Metzler and Jakob Zollmann, March 13, 2023; Juris North Legal Theory, hosted online by Jorge Núñez, with discussant Ian Turner, February 8, 2023; Capturing the Past, University of Ghent, hosted by Eva Brems and Alina Cherviatsova, January 21, 2022; Negotiating Troubled Pasts, organized online by RePast (Horizon 2020), May 28, 2021; Just Memories, Universidade NOVA Lisbon (online), hosted by Jeremy Sarkin, December 10, 2020; Collaborative Creativity for Digital Memories, Royal Holloway, University of London, hosted by Jill Marshall, June 17, 2019; Memory Laws in Post-transitional Democracies, Polish Academy of Sciences, Warsaw, hosted by Aleksandra Gliszczyńska-Grabias, October 9, 2018; Transgressive Narratives about the Past, Harvard University, August 28–29, 2018; Time, Memory, and Criminal Law, University of Bologna, hosted by Emanuela Fronza and Corrado Caruso, May 16, 2018; Legal Governance of Historical Memory in Comparative Perspective, University of California at Berkeley Law School, hosted by Uladzislau Belavusau, cosponsored by the T.M.C. Asser Institute (The Hague), the Center for the Study of Law and Society (Berkeley), and the Miller Institute for Global Challenges and the Law (Berkeley), April 3, 2018.

Themes discussed in chapters 8 through 12 were presented at "Free Speech," Society of Legal Scholars Annual Seminar, University of Central Lancashire, organized by Ian Turner, June 11–12, 2024; "Cancellare e punire: Discorso pubblico e conflitti identitari" ("Canceling and Punishing: Public Discourse and Identitarian Conflicts"), Law Faculty, University of Bologna, hosted by Emanuela Fronza and Corrado Caruso, November 3,

2023; Cross-party Parliamentary Group on Accountability in Iran with the UN special rapporteur on Iran Javaid Rehman, organized by the Association of Anglo-Iranian Women in the United Kingdom and Justice for the Victims of the 1988 Massacre in Iran, UK Parliament, July 18, 2023; "Are Universities Supposed to Be Democratic?," Internationalisation and Risks to Academic Freedom, Queen Mary University of London, organized by Matthieu Burnay, Global Policy Institute, July 13, 2023; final conference of the first phase of "The Future of Free Speech," Parliament of Denmark, Copenhagen, sponsored by the Justitia Institute, December 15, 2022; "Criminalization of Hate Speech," General Congress, Asunción, Paraguay, October 27, 2022, where I served as general rapporteur for the Académie internationale de droit comparatif (International Academy of Comparative Law); "What Do Judges Need to Know about Hate Speech?," Forum of Legal Actors, T.M.C. Asser Institute, The Hague, hosted by Uladzislau Belavusau, October 4, 2022; "What Would 'Critical Antisemitism Studies' Look Like?," Conference: 21st Century Antisemitism, London Centre for the Study of Contemporary Antisemitism, hosted by David Hirsh and David Seymour, September 13, 2022; "Disloyalty Propaganda as Hate Speech," European International Studies Association's Fifteenth Pan-European Conference on International Relations, Panteion University, Athens, hosted by Paula Rhein-Fischer and Anna Wójcik, September 4, 2022; "The Inconsistency Inherent within Prevailing Conceptions of Human Rights," Consistency in Human Rights, Department of International Development, Oxford University, December 16, 2019; "How Desirable Is Media Regulation as a Tool for Combatting Hate Speech?," Minority Identity in the Digital Age, European Centre for Minority Issues, Flensburg, Germany, December 12–13, 2019; "Heritage and Change," Global Issues—Integrating Different Perspectives (collaboratively hosted by the Wallenberg Foundation, Sweden; Carlsberg Foundation, Denmark; Compagnia di San Paolo, Italy; Volkswagen Foundation, Germany; and Riksbankens Jubileumsfond, Sweden), University of Lund, Sweden, May 2–3, 2019; "Historical Denialism within Speech Act Theory," commenting on Daniel Innerarity, "Democracy as Interpretation: How to Combat Fake News," University of Bologna, hosted by Emanuela Fronza and Corrado Caruso, March 13, 2019.

Notes

Translations from non-English languages in this book are the author's unless otherwise indicated.

CHAPTER 1

1. Quoted in Natanson, "Fairfax Schools."

2. Quoted in Adams, "NAACP Stands by Leader."

3. Quoted in Natanson, "Fairfax Schools."

4. Lang, "President Trump Has Attacked."

5. Quoted in Associated Press, "DeSantis Knocks Critical Race Theory."

6. Quoted in Meyer, Severns, and McGraw, "'The Tea Party to the 10th Power.'"

7. Power, "Fox News' Obsession."

8. Sarah Jones, "Fake Feminists."

9. Abrams, "Is There a Difference between Being Transgender and Transsexual?"

10. Associated Press, "DeSantis Knocks Critical Race Theory."

11. Quoted in Lang, "President Trump Has Attacked." See also, e.g., Fortin, "Critical Race Theory."

12. See, e.g., Crenshaw, "Mapping the Margins."

13. See, e.g., Collins and Bilge, *Intersectionality*.

14. See, e.g., Rehbein, *Critical Theory after the Rise of the Global South*.

15. On the variety of fields where crits can be found, see, e.g., Tyson, *Critical Theory Today*, and Schwandt, *Kritische Theorie*.

16. See, e.g., Belavusau and Gliszczyńska-Grabias, *Law and Memory*; Heinze, "Theorising Law"; Heinze, "Towards a General Theory"; Heinze, "When the Establishment No Longer Calls the Shots"; Koposov, *Memory Laws*; Lebow, Kansteiner, and Fogu, *The Politics of Memory*.

17. Lopez, "State Education Board Members"; Mervosh, "DeSantis Faces Swell of Criticism."

18. Faulkner, *Requiem for a Nun*, 92.

19. See, e.g., Diem and Welton, *Anti-racist Educational Leadership*; Murphy and Ribarsky, *Activities for Teaching Gender*; Morreira et al., *Decolonising Curricula*.

20. "Teach Britain's Colonial Past."

21. Quoted in Merrick, "Schools Minister."

22. "Teach Britain's Colonial Past."

23. Quoted in Merrick, "Schools Minister."

24. See, e.g., Ignatow, *Zwischen "Selbstkritik"*; Morin, *Autocritique*.

25. Quoted in Robinson, "Noam Chomsky."

26. Cf., e.g., Neiman, *Left Is Not Woke*; McWhorter, *Woke Racism*.

27. On today's conservatives and free speech, see, e.g., Carney, "To Liberals"; ACLU, *Repression*; N. Cohen, "Beware Boris's Sinister Crackdown"; Epstein and Mazzei, "G.O.P. Bills Target Protesters"; French, "Free Speech for Me"; Robinson, "The Right Loves Free Speech"; PEN America, PEN America Index; Solochek, "Pinellas Schools Remove Book." Indeed, over several centuries politically conservative establishments have cracked down on free speech. See, e.g., Marx, "Bemerkungen"; Marx, "Das Verbot"; Marx, "Die Verhandlungen"; Rohrßen, *Von der "Anreizung."*

28. See, e.g., "How the Conservative Party."

29. See, e.g., Lopez, "State Education Board Members"; Mervosh, "DeSantis Faces Swell of Criticism."

CHAPTER 2

1. Engels, *Die Lage*, 237 (using "aristocrats" in the more modern sense to denote wealthy interests as opposed to a ruling and landowning class constituted by lineal descent).

2. Engels, *Die Lage*, 237.

3. See, e.g., Marx and Engels, *Manifest der Kommunistischen Partei*. An influential forerunner, often cited by Marx and Engels, was Jean-Jacques Rousseau. On inequalities emerging through property rights, see, e.g., Rousseau, *Discours*, 164. Cf. Rousseau's influential dictum "Man is born free yet is everywhere in chains." Rousseau, *Du contrat social*, I.i., 351.

4. The state that Marx and Engels had immediately in mind was broadly the "post-Westphalian" order that had consolidated in the sixteenth and seventeenth centuries. See, e.g., Engels, *Die Entwicklung des Sozialismus*; Engels, *Herrn Eugen Dühring's Umwälzung*, 239–303; Marx and Engels, *Manifest der Kommunistischen Partei*, 462–482.

5. The opposition between revolutionaries and reformists echoed philosophical oppositions between theories of idealism and theories of materialism. See, e.g., Engels, *Die Entwicklung*

des Sozialismus, 189–201; Marx and Engels, *Die Deutsche Ideologie*; Marx and Engels, *Manifest der Kommunistischen Partei*, 482–492. On revolution versus reform, see also Luxemburg, *Sozialreform*.

6. See, e.g., Russell, *The Practice and Theory of Bolshevism*; Gide, *Retour de l'U.R.S.S.*

7. Horkheimer, *Traditionelle und kritische theorie*.

8. See, e.g., Jay, *Splinters in Your Eye*; Jay, *The Dialectical Imagination*; Schwandt, *Kritische Theorie*.

9. "Erlass Kaiser Wilhelms II zur Reform." This is not to say that societies had achieved full conformity, as uprisings such as slave and peasant rebellions are well known throughout history.

10. Wollschläger, *Weltgeschichte*, 171.

11. For eighteenth- and nineteenth-century examinations of such issues, see, e.g., Equiano, *The Interesting Narrative*; Gouges, *La déclaration*; Anthony, "On Women's Right to Vote"; Douglass, "What to the Slave."

12. The workers' slogan comes from Marx and Engels, *Manifest der Kommunistischen Partei*, 493.

13. For a criticism of these figures, see, e.g., Neiman, *Left Is Not Woke*.

14. See, e.g., Debray, *Révolution*; R. Harris, *Marxism, Socialism*.

15. See, e.g., Fanon, *L'an V de la révolution algérienne*; Memmi, *Portrait du colonisé*.

16. See, e.g., King, "Letter from Birmingham Jail"; Millet, *Sexual Politics*.

17. See, e.g., Andrews, *The New Age of Empire*; Armstrong, *Bury the Corpse of Colonialism*; Césaire, *Discours sur le colonialisme*; Douzinas, *Human Rights and Empire*; Fanon, *Les damnés de la terre*; Fanon, *Peau noir, masques blancs*; Hardt and Negri, *Empire*; Kirkby and Coleborne, *Law, History, Colonialism*; Loomba, *Colonialism/Postcolonialism*; Mehta, *Liberalism and Empire*; Memmi, *Portrait du colonisé*; Nkrumah, *Neo-colonialism*; Said, *Orientalism*; Thomas, *The Slave Trade*; Vergès, *Un féminisme décolonial*; Watson, *Aboriginal Peoples*.

18. On Russia, see, e.g., Papkova, *The Orthodox Church*; on Iran, see, e.g., Ghanoonparvar, "Through Tinted Lenses."

19. Engels, *Grundsätze des Kommunismus*, 363–365; Marx and Engels, *Manifest der Kommunistischen Partei*, 462–474; Douglass, "What to the Slave"; Anthony, "On Women's Right to Vote."

20. Césaire, *Discours sur le colonialisme*, 20, 12, original emphasis.

21. Sartre, preface to Fanon, *Les damnés de la terre*, 44, 37–38.

22. See, e.g., Habermas, *Strukturwandel der Öffentlichkeit*; Habermas, *Theorie*; Mehta, *Liberalism and Empire*; Mouffe and Errejon, *Construire un peuple*; Rancière, *Au bords de la politique*; Rancière, *La haine de la démocratie*; Rancière, *La méthode de l'égalité*; Unger, *False Necessity*.

23. Fanon, *Les damnés de la terre*, 122.

24. See, e.g., Césaire, *Discours sur le colonialisme*; Beauvoir, *Le deuxième sexe*; Fanon, *Peau noir, masques blancs*; Fanon, *Les damnés de la terre*; Memmi, *Portrait du colonisé*.

25. See, e.g., Bell, "*Brown v. Board of Education*"; Crenshaw, "Race, Reform, and Retrenchment"; Kennedy, "Form and Substance"; Kennedy, "The Structure of Blackstone's *Commentaries*."

26. See, e.g., Samuels and Olorunnipa, *His Name Is George Floyd*.

27. See, e.g., M. Alexander, *The New Jim Crow*; Bell, *And We Are Not Saved*; Bell, "*Brown v. Board of Education*"; Bell, *Faces at the Bottom of the Well*; Bell, *Silent Covenants*; Crenshaw, "Race, Reform, and Retrenchment"; Crozier, *Racism and Education in Britain*; Davis, *Policing the Black Man*; P. Mason, *The Economics of Structural Racism*.

28. See, e.g., McKeown, *With Power Comes Responsibility*; Young, *Responsibility for Justice*; Zheng, "What Is My Role in Changing the System?"

29. Mehta, *Liberalism and Empire*, 49.

30. Mehta, *Liberalism and Empire*, 49.

31. See, e.g., M. Alexander, *The New Jim Crow*; Andrews, *The New Age of Empire*; Bell, *And We Are Not Saved*; Bell, "*Brown v. Board of Education*"; Bell, *Faces at the Bottom of the Well*; Bell, *Silent Covenants*; Crenshaw, "Race, Reform, and Retrenchment"; Crozier, *Racism and Education in Britain*; Davis, *Policing the Black Man*; Douglass, "What to the Slave"; P. Mason, *The Economics of Structural Racism*; Hardt and Negri, *Empire*; Mehta, *Liberalism and Empire*; Memmi, *Portrait du colonisé*; Nkrumah, *Neo-colonialism*.

32. See, e.g., Femia, *Gramsci's Political Thought* (on hegemonic power). Cf. critically, Haslanger, "Systemic and Structural Injustice."

33. Beauvoir, *Le deuxième sexe*, 382–383.

34. Memmi, *Portrait du colonisé*, 138.

35. See, e.g., Fineman, Jackson, and Romero, *Feminist and Queer Legal Theory*; Hunter, McGlynn, and Rackley, *Feminist Judgments*; Moran, *The Homosexual(ity) of Law*.

36. Bonilla-Silva, *Racism without Racists*.

37. See, e.g., Evans, "Stephen Lawrence."

38. See, e.g., *The Stephen Lawrence Inquiry*, paras. 6.5–6.7, 6.10–6.17, 6.27, 6.33, 6.45–48, 6.51, 6.52, 14.34, 14.53.

39. On Floyd, see, e.g., Samuels and Olorunnipa, *His Name Is George Floyd*; on "postracial," see, e.g., Tesler, *Post-racial or Most-racial?*

40. Rice and White, *Race, Ethnicity, and Policing*; Hall, Grieve, and Savage, *Policing*.

41. See, e.g., C. Davies, "Ngozi Fulani."

42. See, e.g., Nordmarken, "Microaggressions"; Pulice-Farrow and Gonzalez, "'Wait, What Is That?'"

43. See, e.g., McKeown, *With Power Comes Responsibility*; Young, *Responsibility*; Zheng, "What Is My Role in Changing the System?" For a related usage, see, e.g., Blow, "Privilege."

44. See, e.g., Costa, "How the Restaurant Industry Viciously Exploits."

CHAPTER 3

1. See National Women's History Museum, homepage, n.d., https://www.womenshistory.org/; Queer Britain Museum, homepage, n.d., https://queerbritain.org.uk/; International Slavery Museum, homepage, n.d., https://www.liverpoolmuseums.org.uk/international-slavery -museum/about; and International African American Museum, homepage, n.d., https:// iaamuseum.org/ (accessed July 1, 2024).

2. For public institutions, see, e.g., SUNY, "Creating a More Equitable"; Universidad Complutense Madrid, "Delegación"; University of California, "Diversity"; Freie Universität Berlin, "Diversity an der FUB"; Universiteit Leiden, "Diversiteit"; University of Oxford, "Equality"; McGill University, "Equity, Diversity"; Australian National University, "Equity and Diversity"; Sorbonne Université, "La mission"; Københavns Universitet, "Ligestilling." For private companies, see, e.g., Coca-Cola Company, "Creating a Culture"; Lockheed Martin, "Global Diversity and Inclusion"; Exxon Mobil, "Inclusion and Diversity"; Lufthansa Group, "Mit Vielfalt."

3. See, e.g., Duncombe and Lambert, *The Art of Activism*.

4. Marx, "Thesen über Feuerbach," 7, original emphasis ("Die Philosophen haben die Welt nur verschieden *interpretiert*, es kömmt drauf an sie zu *verändern*").

5. On the first slogan, see, e.g., Levinson, "Silence Is Complicity"; cf., e.g., Butler, "No, It's Not Anti-Semitic." On the second slogan, see Sartre, *L'Existentialisme*, 64.

6. See, e.g., Thumerel, "De Sartre à Bourdieu."

7. See, e.g., Heinze, "When the Establishment No Longer Calls the Shots"; Reichel, *Vergangenheitsbewältigung*.

8. Or, literally, "memory that acts" ("On pourrait presque dire qu'un être vivant est une mémoire qui agit").

9. For the screenplay, see Haley and Lee, *Roots*.

10. See, e.g., Garrard, "Forgiveness and the Holocaust."

11. Quoted in Wilcock, "Suella Braverman."

12. On Russia, see, e.g., Liapin, "Changes of History and Civics Curriculum"; on China, see, e.g., Lem, "'Comic' Chinese History." For a debate on these questions, see Heinze, "Should Governments Butt Out of History?," with a response by Baets, "Self-Inculpatory Laws Do Not Exist"; followed by Heinze, "Self-Inculpatory Laws Exist," and again a response by Baets, "Criminal Regimes."

13. "Virginia Declaration of Rights and Constitution," in *Statutes at Large*, ed. Hening; *Déclaration des droits de l'homme et du citoyen*.

14. See, e.g., Paine, *Rights of Man.*

15. Dred Scott v. Sandford, 60 U.S. (19 How.) 393 (1857).

16. Bradwell v. Illinois, 83 U.S. (16 Wall.) 130 (1873).

17. Plessy v. Ferguson, 163 U.S. 537 (1896).

18. See, e.g., M. Alexander, *The New Jim Crow*; Bell, *And We Are Not Saved*; Bell, "*Brown v. Board of Education*"; Bell, *Faces at the Bottom of the Well*; Bell, *Silent Covenants*; Crenshaw, "Race, Reform, and Retrenchment."

19. See, e.g., Marx, "Bemerkungen"; Marx, "Die Verhandlungen"; Marx, "Das Verbot." Cf. Heinze, "Karl Marx's Theory of Free Speech, Part 1," and "Karl Marx's Theory of Free Speech, Part 2."

20. See, e.g., Marx, "Zur Judenfrage"; Marx, "Kritik des Gothaer Programms."

21. On shifting alignments of Western leftist currents with Soviet and Maoist policies in the twentieth century, see, e.g., Aron, *L'opium des intellectuels*; Furet, *Le passé d'une illusion*; Julliard, *Les gauches françaises*, 703–766; Evan Smith and Worley, *Against the Grain*; Evan Smith and Worley, *Waiting for the Revolution*; A. Thorpe, *A History of the Labour Party*; Walter, *Die SPD*; Wolton, *Le négationnisme de gauche.*

22. See, e.g., Popper, *The Open Society*, 2:182–209 (agreeing with Marx and Engels about brutality and exploitation under laissez-faire capitalism but challenging their analyses); Rawls, *Political Liberalism*, 123–124 (explaining the injustice of slavery from the perspective of liberal democracy); Dworkin, *Law's Empire*, 382–387 (explaining identity-based discrimination as incompatible with the US Constitution).

23. See, e.g., Heinze, "When the Establishment No Longer Calls the Shots."

24. See, e.g., White-Spunner, *Partition.*

25. Malik, "The Colston Four's Critics."

26. See, e.g., Kant, *Grundlegung*, 428; Rawls, *A Theory of Justice*, 19–24.

27. For a brief outline of some of the relevant difficulties in such defenses, see, e.g., Dow, "Removing Statues."

28. See, e.g., Foucault, *Histoire de la folie*; Foucault, *Histoire de la sexualité*; Foucault, *Surveiller et punir.*

CHAPTER 4

1. See, e.g., Belton, *Putin's People*; Galeotti, *Putin's Wars*; Katerji, "How to Lose an Election"; Niculescu, "Russia's War in Eastern Europe."

2. German, "We at Stop the War."

3. German, "Millions of Us."

4. Stop the War Coalition, "About Stop the War."

5. See, e.g., Levy and Thompson, *Causes of War.*

6. See, e.g., Seib, *Information at War.* Cf., e.g., Blum, "Sanktionen oft wirkungslos"; Pamment, "How the Kremlin Circumvented EU Sanctions."

7. See, e.g., Stohl and Yousif, "The Risks of U.S. Military Assistance."

8. See, e.g., Adenitire, *A General Right to Conscientious Exemption.*

9. German, "We at Stop the War."

10. German, "We at Stop the War."

11. Arendt, *Eichmann in Jerusalem*, 371.

12. See Arendt, *Eichmann in Jerusalem*; Arendt, *Elemente und Ursprünge.*

13. Arendt and Fest, *Eichmann war von empörender Dummheit* (reviewing early criticisms of Arendt—for example, by Golo Mann).

14. See, e.g., Duss, "Calling Trump an Anti-imperialist." This is not to say that Arendt or other critical thinkers reduce individual action to social forces so fully as to eliminate individual responsibility. In addition, contemporary crits do often draw on storytelling to enrich our insight into mechanisms of oppression, although they mostly do this within the boundaries of the Radical Critique of Western Liberal Democracy.

15. German, "We at Stop the War."

16. German, "We at Stop the War," emphasis added; cf. a critique of this view in Spalińska, "Why the Political Left Rejects Ukraine."

17. See, e.g., Douzinas, *Human Rights and Empire*; Ghanoonparvar, "Through Tinted Lenses"; Hardt and Negri, *Empire*; B. Jones and O'Donnell, *Alternatives to Neo-liberalism*; Nelken and Levi, "Sir Philip Green"; Papkova, *The Orthodox Church.* But also see, e.g., Chellaney, "The West Is Hastening Its Own Decline."

18. See, e.g., Applebaum, *Iron Curtain*; Figes, *The Story of Russia*; Kenez, *A History of the Soviet Union*; Snyder, *Bloodlands.*

19. See, e.g., Aron, *L'opium de intellectuels*; Furet, *Le passé d'une illusion*; Julliard, *Les gauches françaises*, 703–766; Evan Smith and Worley, *Against the Grain*; Evan Smith and Worley, *Waiting for the Revolution*; A. Thorpe, *A History of the Labour Party*; Walter, *Die SPD*; Wolton, *Le négationnisme de gauche.* On continued leftist support for Moscow after the Cold War, although the left was not alone in this support, see, e.g., Katerji, "How to Lose an Election."

20. On mass obedience and conformity, see Boterbloem, *Life in Stalin's Soviet Union*; Applebaum, *Iron Curtain.* On opportunity and Western oppression, see, e.g., Losavio, "What Racism Costs"; ILO, "The Gender Gap in Employment."

21. See, e.g., Karlsson and Schoenhals, *Crimes against Humanity under Communist Regimes.*

22. See, e.g., Minkenberg and Végh, *Depleting Democracies.*

23. See, e.g., Benjamin, *Zur Kritik der Gewalt und andere Aufsätze*; Bourdieu, *Méditations pascaliennes*; Derrida, *Force de loi.*

24. See, e.g., Minkenberg and Végh, *Depleting Democracies.*

25. See, e.g., Gabrisch, "Elements, Origins and Future of Great Transformations."

26. See, e.g., Minkenberg and Végh, *Depleting Democracies.*

27. See, e.g., Gashaw, "In the Oppression Olympics."

28. See, e.g., Kailitz, *Die Gegenwart der Vergangenheit.*

29. See, e.g., Orvos-Tóth, *Örökölt sors*; Thurston, "Victims of China's Cultural Revolution, Part I"; Thurston, "Victims of China's Cultural Revolution, Part II."

30. By contrast, international lawyers and human rights experts use more determinate criteria for applying terms such as *genocide, crime against humanity,* and *crime of aggression.* See, e.g., UNGA, Convention on the Prevention and Punishment of the Crime of Genocide, December 9, 1948, art. 2; UN, Rome Statute of the International Criminal Court, July 17, 1998 (subsequently corrected and amended), arts. 6–9.

31. See, e.g., D. Schmitz, *Thank God They're on Our Side*; D. Schmitz, *The United States and Right-Wing Dictatorships.*

32. On "the West," see, e.g., N. Davies, *Europe,* 16–25; on "spheres of influence," see, e.g., McGlynn, *Memory Makers.* On these concepts' influence on Kremlin politics, see, e.g., Papkova, *The Orthodox Church*; Elliot Smith, "Russia, Expansion."

33. See, e.g., Abelow, *How the West Brought War to Ukraine*; Chotiner, "Why John Mearsheimer Blames the U.S."

34. Cf., e.g., Hegel, *Grundlinien der Philosophie des Rechts,* §§ 140, 344.

35. See, e.g., Julliard, *Les gauches françaises,* 767–812.

36. See, e.g., Cervera-Marzal, *Le populisme de gauche.*

37. See, e.g., Alemagna and Alliès, *Mélenchon.*

38. "Résultats de l'élection présidentielle 2017"; "Résultats de l'élection présidentielle 2022."

39. "Effectif des groupes: XVIe législature."

40. La France insoumise, "La France insoumise condamne l'invasion militaire de l'Ukraine"; Ferrero, "Guerre en Ukraine" (quote).

41. See, e.g., "Frank-Walter Steinmeier."

42. See, e.g., "Zeitenwende bei der NATO."

43. Partei DIE LINKE, "Stoppt die Eskalation!," emphasis added.

44. Dagdelen, "Völkermord an den Armeniern erinnern"; Sommer, "Offizielle Anerkennung des Völkermords."

45. For such definitions, see note 29 of this chapter. Mohamed Ali, Bartsch, and Korte, "Keine Geschichtsrelativierung." For similar reasoning in the United Nations, see chapter 10.

46. Gysi, "DDR war kein Unrechtsstaat."

47. See note 43 of this chapter.

48. Partei DIE LINKE, "Stoppt die Eskalation!"

49. See, e.g., Hauck, "Was Wagenknecht unterschlägt."

50. For some party members' questioning of such positions, see, e.g., "Linkenabgeordnete teilen."

51. Quoted in Baroud, "'Not a Justification'" (*Counterpunch* version). As of early 2024, dozens of interviews with Chomsky can be located online, including several recorded after Russia's invasion in 2022 and focused on that crisis.

52. Quoted in Baroud, "'Not a Justification'" (*Counterpunch* version), emphasis added, Baroud's insertion of "'(moral)," and second and third ellipses in the indented extract in the original.

53. Quoted in Baroud, "'Not a Justification'" (*Counterpunch* version).

54. Quoted in Baroud, "'Not a Justification'" (*Counterpunch* version), emphasis added. Once again, the fusion of logic with hyperbole is striking. On Chomsky's reasoning here, the fact that, say, many leftists blame the Israeli state for the Palestinians' plight proves that Israel is *not* to blame. That conclusion may well be true, yet it would wholly contradict decades of Chomsky's openly declared opinions about Israel and Palestine.

55. See, e.g., Agence France-Presse, "Czechs Bust Major Russian Propaganda Network"; Blum, "Sanktionen oft wirkungslos"; Pamment, "How the Kremlin Circumvented EU Sanctions"; Pomerantsev, *Nothing Is True and Everything Is Possible*.

56. See, e.g., Femia, *Gramsci's Political Thought*.

57. See, e.g., B. Jones and O'Donnell, *Alternatives to Neo-liberalism*.

58. On soft power and information technologies, see, e.g., Agence France-Presse, "Czechs Bust Major Russian Propaganda Network"; Blum, "Sanktionen oft wirkungslos"; Pamment, "How the Kremlin Circumvented EU Sanctions."

59. Vock, "Noam Chomsky." For Swedes' support for NATO, see "Nato-opinionen" (yearly opinion poll recording less than 20 percent of Swedes supporting NATO membership in 1994, rising higher than 60 percent in 2022); and for Finns' support, see "Poll: Backing" (recording more than 80 percent of Finns supporting NATO membership in 2023).

60. Vock, "Noam Chomsky." On Ukrainians' view of the invasion, see "Poll: 85% of Ukrainians" (recording more than 80 percent of Ukrainians supporting armed resistance against the Russian invasion).

61. On Azerbaijan, see, e.g., Nechepurenko and Abrahamian, "Refugees Flee to Armenia"; on Slovakia, see Henley, "Slovakia's Pro-Russia Former PM"; and on Serbian forces in Kosovo, see, e.g., Chiappa, "Serbian President Turns to Russia."

62. Cf. Derrida, *De la grammatologie*, 149–202 (commenting on Lévi-Strauss, *Tristes tropiques*); Derrida, *L'écriture et la différence*, 51–97 (commenting on Foucault, *Histoire de la folie*). See generally, e.g., Amin, *L'Eurocentrisme*; Césaire, *Discours sur le colonialisme*; Fanon, *Les damnés de la terre*; Fanon, *Peau noire, masques blancs*; Kanth, *The Challenge of Eurocentrism*; Mehta, *Liberalism and Empire*; Memmi, *Portrait du colonisé*.

63. See, e.g., Polite, "The Dangerous Miseducation of Americans." In some contexts, words such as *Americentrism* and *US-centrism* are also used.

64. On Eurocentrism and standard racism, see UNCERD, International Convention on the Elimination of All Forms of Racial Discrimination, concluding observations: Russian Federation, June 1, 2023. On early Soviet ideology, see, e.g., Lenin, *Imperialism*; Lenin, "The Tasks of the Proletariat." As Lenin once quipped elsewhere, "Scratch a Russian Communist and you will find a Russian chauvinist." Quoted in Huttenbach, introduction to *Soviet Nationality Policies*, ed. Huttenbach, 5.

65. See, e.g., Fanon, *Peau noir, masques blancs*; Fanon, *Les damnés de la terre*; Memmi, *Portrait du colonisé*.

66. See, e.g., Aron, *L'opium des intellectuels*; Furet, *Le passé d'une illusion*; Julliard, *Les gauches françaises*, 703–766; Evan Smith and Worley, *Against the Grain*; Evan Smith and Worley, *Waiting for the Revolution*; A. Thorpe, *A History of the Labour Party*; Walter, *Die SPD*; Wolton, *Le négationnisme de gauche*.

67. As mentioned earlier, various overviews are provided in, e.g., Aron, *L'opium des intellectuels*; Furet, *Le passé d'une illusion*; Julliard, *Les gauches françaises*, 703–766; Evan Smith and Worley, *Against the Grain*; Evan Smith and Worley, *Waiting for the Revolution*; A. Thorpe, *A History of the Labour Party*; Walter, *Die SPD*; Wolton, *Le négationnisme de gauche*.

68. Said, *Orientalism*. Cf. Césaire, *Discours sur le colonialisme*; Fanon, *Les damnés de la terre*; Fanon, *Peau noire, masques blancs*; Memmi, *Portrait de du colonisé*.

69. Prakash, "After Colonialism," 3.

70. To some observers, this point had long been clear even before the war erupted in 2022. See, e.g., Bloodworth, "Too Many on the Left Have Swallowed Putin's Propaganda." For polling of Ukrainian public opinion since the Russian invasion, see, e.g., "Ukraine at War"; "Poll: 85% of Ukrainians"; "Nearly 90% of Ukrainians."

71. As described in Kirk, "Why Noam Chomsky's Ukraine Comments Ruffled so Many Feathers."

72. On NATO helping Ukraine, see, e.g., Kaplan, "Where Realpolitik Went Wrong"; Motyl, "America's Leading 'Realist' Keeps Getting Russia Wrong."

73. Robinson, "Noam Chomsky on How to Prevent World War III."

CHAPTER 5

1. "Stenographic record of Rudolf Virchow's speech in the Prussian House of Representatives on January 17, 1873," *Deutsche Digitale Bibliothek* (n.d.), https://ausstellungen.deutsche-digitale-bibliothek.de/preussen-reichsgruendung-1871/items/show/73 (accessed August 1, 2024). The term "cultural war" seems to derive from the German predecessor, which also translates as "cultural struggle."

2. Gitlin, *The Twilight*, 127.

3. See International Memorial, "What Is International Memorial?"

4. Hopkins and Nechepurenko, "As the Kremlin Revises History." On some actions waged against Мемориал (International Memorial) see below, chapter 9.

5. Nobel Foundation, "The Nobel Peace Prize 2022."

6. Rich, "When We Dead Awaken."

7. Solzhenitsyn, *One Day in the Life of Ivan Denisovich*.

8. See, e.g., Khazan, "The Soviet-Era Strategy."

9. Burgis, "Is 'Whataboutism' Always a Bad Thing?" (revisiting Soviet tactics of whataboutery within the context Russia's invasion of Ukraine).

10. See Jadva et al., "Predictors of Self-Harm and Suicide in LGBT Youth."

11. Parental Rights in Education, Florida CS/CS/HB 1557, effective date July 1, 2022.

12. Individual Freedom, Florida CS/HB 7, effective date July 1, 2022.

13. Tolin, "These 176 Books Were Banned"; Ray and Gibbons, "Why Are States Banning Critical Race Theory?"; PEN America, PEN America Index of School Book Bans; Solochek, "Pinellas Schools Remove Book."

14. Russia's Bolshevik uprising in 1917 is commonly called the "October Revolution" following Julian reckoning, with October 25 translating in the Gregorian calendar to November 7.

15. See Karlsson and Schoenhals, *Crimes against Humanity under Communist Regimes*.

16. Victims of Communism Day, Florida CS/HB 395, effective date May 9, 2022.

CHAPTER 6

1. Bell, "*Brown v. Board of Education*."

2. Brown v. Board of Education, 347 US 483 (1954).

3. Bell, "*Brown v. Board of Education*," 524.

4. Quoted in Bell, "*Brown v. Board of Education*," 524.

5. Warren, introduction to "Notre Dame Law School Civil Rights Lectures," 41, quoted in Bell, "Racial Remediation," 12 n. 33.

6. Bell, "*Brown v. Board of Education*," 523.

7. Machiavelli, *Il principe*, 35, translation from Machiavelli, *The Prince*, 21. Notions of self-interest as decisive for politics were already familiar in antiquity. See, e.g., Plato, *Gorgias*; Plato, *Republic*, 1.338d–339c, pp. 983–984. Cf. Heinze, *The Concept of Injustice*, 1–4.

8. Shakespeare, *Antony and Cleopatra*, IV.vi.4, p. 270.

9. Shakespeare, *Henry V*, III.vi.108–112, p. 193. On why Henry issues this order, see, e.g., Pugliatti, *Shakespeare the Historian*, 138.

10. See, e.g., Hsi and Tsu-Ch'ien, *Reflections on Things at Hand*, 218–259.

11. See, e.g., Plato, *Gorgias*; Plato, *Republic*, 1.338d–339c, pp. 983–984.

12. See, e.g., Heinze, *The Concept of Injustice*, 1–4.

13. See, e.g., Kozlov and Gilburd, *The Thaw*; Hale-Dorrell, review of *The Thaw*, 351.

14. See, e.g., Heinze, *The Most Human Right*, 30.

15. See Russell, *The Practice and Theory of Bolshevism*.

16. See Gide, *Retour de l'U.R.S.S.* Gide won the Nobel Prize for Literature in 1947.

17. See, e.g., Horkheimer, *Traditionelle und kritische theorie*; Horkheimer and Adorno, *Dialektik de Aufklärung*; Fischer, *Stalin*; Arendt, *Elemente und Ursprünge*; and Lefort, *L'invention démocratique* (a selection of essays published in earlier decades).

18. See, e.g., Althusser et al., *Lire le capital*; Balibar, *La philosophie de Marx*; Morin, *Pour et contre Marx*.

19. "Excerpts."

20. See, e.g., Halász, "Őszöd—újratöltve"; Lynch, "Orbán Faces Danger"; Pogany, "Through the Looking Glass."

21. King, "Letter from a Birmingham Jail" (recalling William Gladstone's dictum "Justice delayed is justice denied").

22. See, e.g., Mohanty, Russo, and Torres, *Third World Women*.

23. See, e.g., C. Mason, *Routledge Handbook of Queer Development Studies*.

24. See, e.g., Žižek, "Ukraine Is Palestine."

25. See, e.g., Žižek, "Ukraine Is Palestine"; Butler, *Parting Ways*; Butler, "The Compass of Mourning"; N. Chomsky and Pappé, *On Palestine*.

26. See, e.g., Žižek, "We Must Stop Letting Russia Define the Terms"; Žižek, "Pacifism Is the Wrong Response"; Žižek, "The Dark Side of Neutrality"; Žižek, "The Axis of Denial"; and Butler, "I Am Hopeful."

27. See, e.g., Žižek, "Barbarism with a Human Face."

CHAPTER 7

1. German, "We at Stop the War."

2. See, e.g., Heinze, "Victimless Crimes."

3. "GDP per Capita, 1820 to 2018"; Ireland, "Economy Rankings."

4. Visnji, "McDonald's Net Worth 2023"; Muriuki, "Burger King Net Worth 2023."

5. See, e.g., Faulconbridge, "Ukraine War."

6. Aristotle, *Nicomachean Ethics*, III.i.1110^{a}1–1110^{b}18, pp. 1752–1753. Aristotle cannot be classified as liberal or humanist in any contemporary sense, yet his conception of individual responsibility anticipates later liberal and humanist conceptions.

7. Tests of duress typically include factors such as an immediate threat of harm; a reasonable belief that the threat was real and that the harm would be carried out if the actor in question did not comply; no reasonable opportunity to escape or avoid the threat without committing the crime; and proportionality, meaning that the harm the actor sought to avoid by committing the crime must be greater than or equal to the harm caused by the crime. See, e.g., United States v. Contento-Pachon, 723 F.2d 691 (9th Cir. 1984) (US); S v. Goliath, 1972 (3) SA 1 (A) (South Africa); State of Gujarat v. Kishanbhai, AIR 2003 SC 3886 (India); R. v. Ruzic, [2001] 1 S.C.R. 687 (Canada); Huizingarrest, HC 81.611-8/RS, STF, June 23, 2004 (Brazil); R. v. Oladimeji, (1954) 14 WACA 12 (Nigeria); Hoge Raad, 27 juni 1950, NJ 1951/78 (Netherlands); OGH-Urteil vom 19. November 1985, 14 Os 120/85 (Austria); Kanini Muli v. Republic, [2011] eKLR (Kenya). In other cases, courts have confirmed these principles in general even when finding that they did not apply to the particular defendant at issue. See, e.g., R v. Hasan (formerly Z), [2005] UKHL 22 (UK); Arrêt Perdereau, Cour de cassation, chambre criminelle, le June 16, 1988 (France); Bundesgerichtshof, March 22, 1988 (BGHSt 35, 246) (Germany).

8. John Locke famously provided for a right to rebel against tyranny but just as famously failed to sketch the legitimating conditions in any more than broad outline, sparking ongoing debates ever since. Locke, *Second Treatise*, chap. 19, para. 225, p. 111. Cf. the US Declaration of Independence, para. 2.

9. See, e.g., Alger, *Megamedia*.

10. See, e.g., Lynskey, "Countering the Dominant Narrative."

11. See, e.g., Bushwick, "Russia's Information War"; Cook et al., *Beijing's Global Media Influence*; Kelly et al., *Manipulating Social Media*; Kumar, "How China Uses the News Media"; Schia and Gjesvik, "Hacking Democracy."

12. See, e.g., ISC, *Russia*.

13. See critically Heinze, *The Most Human Right*, 11–24.

14. Cf., e.g,. Heinze, "'But Israel Claims to Be a Democracy!'"

15. Constitution of the Russian Federation, 1993, preambular para. and art. 17(2).

16. Constitution of the People's Republic of China, 1982, preambular para. 6.

17. Slavoj Žižek (@Slavojiek), Twitter/X, June 22, 2016, 9:00 p.m., https://twitter.com/Slavojiek/status/745707933149831169?lang=en-GBs.

18. See, e.g., Žižek, *Trouble in Paradise*, 26.

CHAPTER 8

1. "Gauland: NS-Zeit."

2. All quoted in "Empörung wegen 'Vogelschiss.'"

3. See "A Resident of Wuhan."

4. See, e.g., Litzinger and Ni, "Inside the Wuhan Cabin Hospital."

5. See, e.g., Myers, "China Spins Tale."

6. See, e.g., Heather, *North Korean Posters*.

7. For updated reports, see, e.g., China Dissent Monitor, https://chinadissent.net/.

8. See, e.g., Amnesty International, "New History Textbook"; Zygar, "The Man behind Putin's Warped View of History"; R. Schmitz, "Worries Grow in Hong Kong"; N. Thorpe, "Hungary's New Patriotic Education."

9. German sources commonly speak of *Leugnung* (denial), *Verharmlosung* (trivialization or minimalization), *Verzerrung* (distortion), and similar modes of casting doubt on the existence and gravity of the Shoah. See, e.g., "Billigung, Leugnung."

10. "Jean-Marie Le Pen." Cf. Mestre, "'Détail de l'histoire.'" See, generally, Heinze, "Theorising Law and Historical Memory"; Heinze, "Towards a General Theory of Law and Historical Discourse."

11. See, e.g., Hartocollis and Fawcett, "The College Board Strips Down Its A.P. Curriculum" (noting the exclusion of progressive writers such as Kimberlé Williams Crenshaw, Roderick Ferguson, and Ta-Nehisi Coates from secondary-school curricula).

12. Quoted in Atterbury, "Florida and DeSantis Dig In." See also Bouie, "Ron DeSantis."

13. See, e.g., Lopez, "State Education Board Members"; Klein, "The Rightwing US Textbooks"; Greenlee, "How History Textbooks Reflect America's Refusal to Reckon with Slavery."

14. Sartre, *Réflexions sur la question juive*, 23, original emphasis.

15. The adjective *Machiavellian* long ago became a synonym for despotism, although many have argued that Machiavelli empowers his readers by unmasking the mechanics of rule. As far back as Rousseau, Machiavelli's strategy of unmasking power by seeming to flatter it had become evident. Rousseau, *Du contrat social*, 409.

16. Machiavelli, *Il principe*, 146–147.

17. This is my paraphrase, not Machiavelli's words.

18. See Heinze, "Foundations of Sovereign Authority."

19. Shakespeare, *Richard III*, III.vii.90–94, p. 272. Similarly, in his play *Nicomède* (1651), Pierre Corneille portrays a power-mongering noble obsessed with creating a purity narrative: "Can lies be quelled? Or is there one too great / For virtues to return to their pure state? Some ugly memory will always creep / To drag great virtue into the muddy deep." ("Et peut-on voir mensonge assez tôt avorté / Pour rendre à la vertu toute sa pureté? / Il en reste toujours quelque indigne mémoire / Qui porte une souillure à la plus haute gloire.") *Nicomède* VI.i.1133–1136, in Corneille, *Oeuvres complètes*, 686. Cf. Heinze, "Selecting the Memory."

20. See, e.g., Frazier, "Donald Trump and Uses and Misuses of the Bible."

21. Giovanni, "The Real Reason the Russian Orthodox Church's Leader Supports Putin's War" (noting the theme of sexual purity).

22. See, e.g., Reimer, "Winterhilfswerk."

23. See, e.g., "20 Soviet Propaganda Posters."

24. See, e.g., Freedland, "They're openly saying it."

25. Excerpted in Horsley, "Obama at U.N."

26. Quoted in Harris, "Visiting Europe."

27. Quoted in Calvert, "The Political Divide in America."

28. Hayes and Chua, "Debating the Concept of Political Tribalism." Cf. Haidt, *The Righteous Mind*.

29. Quoted in Calvert, "The Political Divide in America."

30. See, eg., Hegel, *Grundlinien der Philosophie des Rechts*, § 302. See also, e.g., Aristotle, *Nicomachean Ethics*, I.i.1094ª1–3 and I.iii.1095ª17–22, pp. 1729, 1730; and generally Heinze, *The Concept of Injustice*; Heinze, "What Is the Opposite of Injustice?"

31. Arendt, *Eichmann in Jerusalem*.

32. See, e.g., Gayle, "Five Just Stop Oil Activists Receive Record Sentences."

33. See R v. Dudley and Stephens, (1884) 14 QBD 273 (DC) (controversially upholding criminal conviction).

34. Some people might object here that in circumstances of national emergency, such honesty is often impossible. However, that objection would only confirm the point that the best politics by definition is contemplated outside of such states of exception.

35. Cf., e.g., Neiman, *Left Is Not Woke*; McWhorter, *Woke Racism*.

36. Doward, "Castro Was 'Champion of Social Justice.'"

37. Quoted in Doward, "Castro Was 'Champion of Social Justice.'"

38. Ferrer, *Cuba*, 56.

39. Cuba Solidarity Campaign, "Facts and Fact Sheets."

40. Kirchick, "Fidel Castro's Horrific Record on Gay Rights."

41. See Kirchick, "Fidel Castro's Horrific Record on Gay Rights"; "Fidel Castro Takes Blame." Cf. Lumsden, *Machos Maricones & Gays*, 81–95.

42. Cf. Wolton, *Le négationnisme de gauche*.

43. Quoted in Doward, "Castro Was 'Champion of Social Justice.'"

44. Quoted in Doward, "Castro Was 'Champion of Social Justice.'"

45. On Sartre, see, e.g., Desmeules, "Un paradis sous les étoiles." On the recent acknowledgments of the persecution (but not the systemic oppression) of LGBTQ+ people in Cuba, see, e.g., the following essays in Chomsky, Carr, and Smorkaloff, *The Cuba Reader*: Randall, "Women in the Swamps"; Guevara, "Man and Socialism"; Obejas, "We Came All the Way from Cuba so You Could Dress Like This?"

46. Quoted in "Mort de Fidel Castro." Cf. Kipping and Riexinger, "Zum Tod von Fidel Castro"; Wagenknecht and Bartsch, "Zum Tod von Fidel Castro."

47. See, e.g., "Jean-Luc Mélenchon dénonce un système capitaliste." Cf., e.g., Galloway, "Let's Unite"; "Mort de Fidel Castro."

48. Cf. Heinze, *The Most Human Right*, 84–89.

49. Doward, "Castro Was 'Champion of Social Justice.'"

CHAPTER 9

1. On the clichés, see L. Alexander, "Banning Hate Speech"; on "toughening up," see, e.g., Fay, "Thin-Skinned Liberals."

2. Matsuda, "Public Response to Racist Speech," in *Words That Wound*, ed. Matsuda et al., 17, 20–21.

3. See, e.g., Heinze, *Hate Speech and Democratic Citizenship*, 18–19.

4. Lawrence, "If He Hollers Let Him Go," 53–55. The last incident mocks a slogan that had become famous in the 1970s as part of a campaign to facilitate higher education for African Americans.

5. Matsuda, "Public Response to Racist Speech," 30; Stefancic and Delgado, "A Shifting Balance."

6. UNGA, International Covenant on Civil and Political Rights (ICCPR), December 19, 1966, art. 20(2). On free-speech concerns raised by this article, see UNGA, ICCPR, Declarations and Reservations, December 16, 1966.

7. See UNTBD, Ratification Status for ICCPR; Heinze, *Criminalising Hate Speech*; Justitia Institute, *Global Handbook on Hate Speech Laws*.

8. On the UN and Western powers, see, e.g., Douzinas, *Human Rights*.

9. On the United States as an outlier, see, e.g., Matsuda, "Public Response to Racist Speech," 26–31; and Stefancic and Delgado, "A Shifting Balance." On the use of critical theory in international law, see chapter 11.

10. See, e.g., Heyman, *Hate Speech*; Delgado and Stefancic, *Must We Defend Nazis?*; Delgado and Stefancic, *Understanding Words That Wound*; Thiel, *Wehrhafte Demokratie*; Waldron, *The Harm in Hate Speech*.

11. See, e.g., Baker, "Hate Speech"; Dworkin, foreword to *Extreme Speech and Democracy*, ed. Hare and Weinstein; Post, "Hate Speech"; Post, "Participatory Democracy and Free Speech"; Post, "Participatory Democracy and Free Speech: A Reply"; Strossen, *HATE*; Weinstein, "Participatory Democracy"; Weinstein, "Participatory Democracy: A Reply."

12. I sketch my views about hate speech in Heinze, *Hate Speech and Democratic Citizenship*; Heinze, "Democracy, Ontology, and the Limits of Deconstruction."

13. Chandernagor, "L'enfer des bonnes intentions."

14. See, e.g., Heinze, "When the Establishment No Longer Calls the Shots."

15. UNGA, International Convention on the Elimination of All Forms of Racial Discrimination (ICERD), December 21, 1965, art. 4(a). Cf. art. 4(b) (enjoining state parties to ban organizations that promote racist ideas). On free-speech concerns arising under article 4, see UNGA, ICERD, Declarations and Reservations, March 7, 1966.

16. UNGA, ICERD, preambular para. 4 (citing UNGA, Declaration on the Granting of Independence to Colonial Countries and Peoples, December 14, 1960) and para. 6. On how much free speech we should have, see, e.g., Thornberry, "International Convention."

17. ECRI, General Policy Recommendation No. 15, December 8, 2015, preambular para. 3. The ECRI is a subsidiary body of the Council of Europe. Although this recommendation does not legally bind member states, it stands as an authoritative statement disposed to evolve in whole or in part as soft law. Cf., e.g., Lagoutte, Gammeltoft-Hansen, and Cerone, *Tracing the Roles of Soft Law.*

18. See, e.g., Leggett, *The Cheka,* 114.

19. See, e.g., Miroff, "In Raul Castro's Cuba"; Jayakumar, "The Ladies in White."

20. See Human Rights Watch, "Russia."

21. For international condemnation of practices of political persecution, see, e.g., UNHRC, General Comment No. 25 (57), August 27, 1996.

22. See, e.g., Sloin, "Theorizing Soviet Antisemitism"; Haitiwaji and Morgat, "'Our Souls Are Dead'"; Lumsden, *Machos, Maricones, & Gays.*

23. See, e.g., Azadovskii and Egorov, "From Anti-Westernism to Anti-Semitism"; Hicklin, "If Bernie Sanders Thinks Cuba Is Worth Defending"; Huttenbach, *Soviet Nationality Policies.*

24. See, e.g., ECRI, General Policy Recommendation No. 15, para. 24, 25, 46, 53, 158.

25. See, e.g., Applebaum, *Iron Curtain*; Arendt, *Elemente und Ursprünge.*

26. See, e.g., Schmitt, *Der Begriff des Politischen.*

27. See, e.g., Morgan, *Reds.*

28. See, e.g., Fallows, "Trump Time Capsule #140."

29. See, e.g., Rone, "'Enemies of the People'?"

30. Human Rights Watch, "Russia."

31. Human Rights Watch, "Russia."

32. Cf., e.g., UNGA, ICERD, art. 4; UN ICCPR, art. 20(2); ECRI, General Policy Recommendation No. 15.

33. Human Rights Watch, "Russia." In a private communication, the former BBC correspondent and Russia expert Dina Newman described the designation "foreign agent mass media [СМИ-иноагент]" as a neologism strange to Russian ears, which could also be rendered "mass media foreign agent." Newman added: "Lev Ponomarev has an official status of mass

media foreign agent. He is an individual who is considered mass media and is not the only one with that status. This absurd status indicates the absurd nature of Putin's regulations" (June 23, 2023, on file with the author).

34. Human Rights Watch, "Russia." On the statue, see "Statue of Founder of Soviet Secret Police." On the organization International Memorial (Мемориал), see this book, chapter 5.

35. See, e.g., Jenne, Bozóki, and Visnovitz, "2 Antisemitic Tropes."

36. Cook et al., *Beijing's Global Media Influence.*

37. "After Lunching with Janet Yellen."

38. Buschschlüter, "Nicaragua Strips 94 Prominent Dissidents of Citizenship."

39. Kim, "30 North Korean 'Defector' Families."

40. UNHRC, General Comment No. 25, para. 2.7, 5.4, 7.10.

41. Matsuda, "Public Response to Racist Speech," 17.

42. See Waldron, *The Harm in Hate Speech,* 4, 30, 31, 33, 37, 39, 45, 59, 65–69, 72, 96–97, 116–117.

43. Cortese, *Opposing Hate Speech,* 3–9, 4.

44. Langton, "Speech Acts."

45. See, e.g., Oliver, "The Cap versus the Pumpkin."

CHAPTER 10

1. On use of this tactic in the past, see, e.g., Rohrßen, *Von der "Anreizung zum Klassenkampf"*; cf. Marx, "Bemerkungen," "Die Verhandlungen," and "Das Verbot." On current use of it, see, e.g., updated reports from Article 19, https://www.article19.org/; and Index on Censorship, https://www.indexoncensorship.org/.

2. At best, such protections accrued as incidental benefits in pursuit of other state interests. See generally, e.g., Bloed, *Protection of Minority Rights.*

3. UNGA, Convention on the Prevention and Punishment of the Crime of Genocide, December 9, 1948, art. 3(c), 2.

4. See, e.g., UNGA, International Convention on the Elimination of All Forms of Racial Discrimination (ICERD), December 21, 1965, art. 3; UNSC, Question Relating to the Situation in the Union of South Africa, Resolution 134, April 1, 1960; UNGA, International Convention on the Suppression and Punishment of the Crime of Apartheid, November 30, 1973; UNSC, Question of South Africa, Resolution 591, November 28, 1986.

5. See, e.g., Huttenbach, introduction to *Soviet Nationality Policies,* 1–8.

6. See Césaire, *Discours sur le colonialisme*; Fanon, *Les damnés de la terre*; Fanon, *Peau noir, masques blancs*; Memmi, *Portrait du colonisé*; Nkrumah, *Neo-colonialism.*

7. Cf., e.g., Huttenbach, *Soviet Nationality Policies*; Martin, "The Origins of Soviet Ethnic Cleansing"; Van Schaik, *Tibet*, 207–269.

8. On Western nations support for repressive autocracies, see chapter 5. On inequalities in social regimes, see, e.g., Campana, Dufaud, and Tournon, *Les déportations en héritage*; Huttenbach, *Soviet Nationality Policies*; Martin, "The Origins of Soviet Ethnic Cleansing"; Van Schaik, *Tibet*, 207–269. Also, to be sure, we should bear in mind that the US was as unwilling as the USSR or China to acknowledge conquests within their established borders. See, e.g., Rÿser, "The 'Blue Water Rule.'"

9. This became a standard way to explain supposed differences between liberal democracies advocating classical civil and political rights, on the one hand, and socialist governments advocating social and economic rights, on the other. See, e.g., Heinze, *The Most Human Right*, 58–59, 64–67.

10. See, e.g., UNGA, ICERD, concluding observations: China, September 19, 2018, para. 15(d). On ethnic conflicts before Western colonialism, see, e.g., Lévi-Strauss, *Race et histoire*.

11. See, e.g., Amin, *L'Eurocentrisme*; Césaire, *Discours sur le colonialisme*; Fanon, *Les damnés de la terre*; Fanon, *Peau noire, masques blancs*; Kanth, *The Challenge of Eurocentrism*; Mehta, *Liberalism and Empire*; Memmi, *Portrait du colonisé*.

12. On the promotion of multicultural views, see generally, e.g., Vienna Declaration and Programme of Action, June 25, 1993.

13. See, e.g., ECRI, General Policy Recommendation No. 15, Explanatory Memorandum, paras. 7(i) and 7(j).

14. Cf. the text accompanying note 27 of this chapter.

15. See, e.g., Butler, *Excitable Speech*; Butler, *Gender Trouble*; Foucault, *Histoire de la folie*; Foucault, *Histoire de la sexualité*; Lévi-Strauss, *Race et histoire*.

16. See, e.g., OIC, "OIC Strongly Rejects."

17. See, e.g., European Parliament, Resolution of 20 April 2023, para. 2, 6, 12, 20, 31. But cf. African Commission on Human and Peoples' Rights, Declaration of Principles, principles 3, 7, and 20(6). Cf. Heinze, "Sexual Orientation and International Law."

18. Cf., e.g., ECRI, General Policy Recommendation No. 15, preambular para. 5 (noting "the differing ways in which hate speech has been defined and is understood at the national and international level").

19. ECRI, General Policy Recommendation No. 15, preambular para. 6 and 7, emphasis added.

20. ECRI, General Policy Recommendation No. 15, preambular para. 6.

21. See, e.g., Susan Jones, "Toward Inclusive Theory"; M. Jones and Marks, "Law and the Social Construction of Disability."

22. See, e.g., Lévi-Strauss, *Race et histoire*.

23. ECRI, General Policy Recommendation No. 15, preambular para. 6 n. 1 and Explanatory Memorandum, para. 7(i) and 7(j). Germane to these points have been debates among American legal scholars around the concept of "immutable characteristics" in antidiscrimination law and policy. See, e.g., Clarke, "Against Immutability"; S. Hoffman, "The Importance of Immutability"; Serafin, "In Defense of Immutability."

24. See, e.g., Hafez and Bakali, *The Rise of Global Islamophobia*; Bhat, "Mob, Murder, Motivation."

25. The recommendation's reference to "religion or belief" departs from the categorization "political or other opinion" that we find in the nondiscrimination passages of the Universal Declaration and subsequent international and regional documents. See, e.g., UNGA, Universal Declaration of Human Rights, December 10, 1948, art. 2; UNGA, International Covenant on Civil and Political Rights, December 19, 1966, arts. 2(1) and 26. Cf. African Commission on Human and Peoples' Rights, Declaration of Principles, principle 3, which includes the categories "political or any other opinion" and "political association" in its standard nondiscrimination passage to reaffirm the basic background free-speech right but then removes both of those categories when defining "marginalised groups" in principle 7. No major international or regional policy statements or legal developments have indicated any inclusion of disloyalty propaganda targeted at groups that are not defined in identitarian terms.

26. UNGA, ICERD, report by Czech Republic, January 11, 2006, para. 47, note 45.

27. UNGA, ICERD, concluding observations: Czech Republic, April 11, 2007, para. 9. Cf. Fryšták, Čep, and Kandová, "The Czech Republic."

28. See, e.g., Behr et al. "An Anti-Communist Consensus."

29. See Vienna Declaration and Programme of Action, para. 5. Admittedly, doubts have been raised about this principle given that, for example, the Universal Declaration's provision for "periodic holidays with pay" (UNGA, Universal Declaration of Human Rights, art. 24) cannot easily equate with the provisions concerning torture or arbitrary detentions. Yet in practice the sheer extremity of that comparison has made it the exception that proves the rule: contrary to the Committee on the Elimination of Racial Discrimination's report in 2007, human rights professionals cannot and will not generally argue that respect paid to some rights "weakens" or "politicizes" respect due to other rights. See, e.g., Nickel, "Rethinking Indivisibility"; Gilabert, "The Importance of Linkage Arguments"; Nickel, "Indivisibility and Linkage Arguments."

30. On Nazi crimes, see, e.g., Noack, *NS-Euthanasie*.

31. On antisemitic purges, see Boim, "Anti-Semitism." On mass deportations along ethnic lines, see, e.g., Campana, Dufaud, and Tournon, *Les déportations en héritage*.

32. Confirmed in a private communication of June 20, 2023, with the Czech legal scholars Marek Fryšták, David Čep, and Katarína Kandová (on file) and with Professor Jiří Přibáň (on file). See also Fryšták, Čep, and Kandová, "The Czech Republic."

33. Matsuda, "Public Response to Racist Speech," 38–39, emphasis added.

34. Matsuda, "Public Response to Racist Speech," 26–31.

35. Matsuda, "Public Response to Racist Speech," 27–28. For a critique, see Heinze, "Truth and Myth in Critical Race Theory and LatCrit," 121–133.

CHAPTER 11

1. See, e.g., R. Seymour, *Corbyn*.

2. Burns, "Margaret Thatcher's Greatest Achievement."

3. See, e.g., Bolton and Pitts, *Corbynism*; O. Jones, *This Land*; Pogrund and Maguire, *Left Out*; R. Seymour, *Corbyn*.

4. On charges of antisemitism in the Labour Party, see, e.g., Labour Party (UK), *The Forde Report* (finding evidence of mutually hostile conduct waged by both Corbyn's supporters and his opponents); EHRC, *Investigation into Antisemitism in the Labour Party*. See also O. Jones, *This Land*, 210–256; Heppell, "The British Labour Party."

5. On distinguishing Israel and Jews, see IHRA, "About the IHRA Non–Legally Binding Working Definition of Antisemitism." Cf. the critique in Gould, "The IHRA Definition of Antisemitism."

6. See, e.g., Bolton and Pitts, *Corbynism*; O. Jones, *This Land*; Pogrund and Maguire, *Left Out*; R. Seymour, *Corbyn*.

7. See, e.g., Demirjian, "In Congress."

8. See, e.g., Birnbaum, "Jean-Luc Mélenchon"; Mathoux, "La France insoumise accusée d'antisémitisme."

9. See, e.g., Lerman, *Whatever Happened to Antisemitism?*; JVL, *How the EHRC Got It so Wrong*; Philo et al., *Bad News for Labour*; Winstanley, *Weaponising Anti-Semitism*.

10. See, e.g., O. Jones, "Israel Is Clear about Its Intentions"; O. Jones, "Starvation May Prove to Be Israel's Deadliest Crime"; O. Jones, "Welcome to Topsy-Turvy Britain"; Ross Hunter, "Owen Jones." Cf. the critique in Solomon, "I Watched Owen Jones."

11. See, e.g., Murray, "The Sly Dishonesty of Owen Jones."

12. Winstanley, "How Owen Jones Learned to Stop Worrying and Love Zionism." The same charge of selling out to Zionism was also leveled from the hard right—against Douglas Murray. See, e.g., Nick Griffin (@NickGriffinBU), "Douglas Murray—upper class, homosexual, no children, highly paid by neocon and Zionist foundations—is cold-bloodedly winding up a 'very brutal' civil war in the UK," Twitter/X, November 8, 2023, 6:51 p.m., https://twitter.com/NickGriffinBU/status/1722401562549534836.

13. See, e.g., Paxton, "The Political Contortions of Owen Jones."

14. See the *Guardian*'s profile of Owen Jones, n.d., https://www.theguardian.com/profile/owen-jones (accessed July 1, 2024).

15. Osborne, "Adjoa Andoh's 'Terribly White' Coronation Remark."

16. Owen Jones (@OwenJones), Twitter/X, May 10, 2023, 12:14 p.m., emphasis added, https://twitter.com/OwenJones84/status/1656331852762738691.

17. O. Jones, "Tackling Racism on Social Media," emphasis added (quoting the cultural theorist Alana Lentin).

18. O. Jones, "Poverty Costs Lives," emphasis added.

19. O. Jones, "This Terrifying Backslide on LGBTQ Rights," emphasis added.

20. See, e.g., O. Jones, "No Wonder."

21. On ambiguities of leftism under the Third Reich see, e.g., Grashoff, *Gefahr*.

22. O. Jones, "Antisemitism Has No Place on the Left"; O. Jones, *This Land*, 212.

23. Jobbik must not be confused with Viktor Orbán's Fidesz party. Jobbik later underwent erratic shifts, but in 2015 Jones accurately identified Jobbik as on the far right. See, e.g., Hutt, "Soul Searching."

24. See, e.g., Dreyfus, *L'antisémitisme à gauche*, 13.

25. On anti-Jewish persecution under the socialist countries named, see, e.g., Gitelman, *A Century of Ambivalence*; Apelt and Hufenreuter, *Antisemitismus in de DDR*; Plocker, *The Expulsion of Jews from Communist Poland*. As of early 2024, the multiauthor and multivolume project entitled *A Comprehensive History of the Jews in the Soviet Union* under the auspices of New York University's Skirball Department of Hebrew and Judaic Studies is still in production, with some volumes already issued.

26. O. Jones, "Antisemitism Has No Place on the Left."

27. See, e.g., Dreyfus, *L'antisémitisme à gauche*; Fine and Spencer, *Antisemitism and the Left*; Nelson, *Israel Denial*; Hanloser, *Linker Antisemitismus?*; Rich, *The Left's Jewish Problem*; Hirsh, *Contemporary Left Antisemitism*; Campbell and Klaff, *Unity and Diversity in Contemporary Antisemitism*; Gidley, McGeever, and Feldman, "Labour and Antisemitism"; D. Seymour, "Continuity and Discontinuity."

28. Horkheimer and Adorno, *Dialektik der Aufklärung*, 151–186; Arendt, *Elemente und Ursprünge*.

29. On Palestinian self-determination, see, e.g., UNGA, Resolution 2443, December 19, 1968; Butler, *Parting Ways*; N. Chomsky, *Fateful Triangle*; N. Chomsky and Pappé, *On Palestine*; Awad and Bean, *Palestine*. On leftist receptions of Jews, see, e.g., Klaff, "The Intersection of Antisemitism and Misogyny"; Stögner, "Intersectionality and Antisemitism."

30. See, e.g., Campbell and Klaff, *Unity and Diversity in Contemporary Antisemitism*; Dreyfus, *L'antisémitisme à gauche*; Fine and Spencer, *Antisemitism and the Left*; Gidley, McGeever, and Feldman, "Labour and Antisemitism"; Hanloser, *Linker Antisemitismus?*; Herf, *Three Faces of Antisemitism*; Hirsh, *Contemporary Left Antisemitism*; Hirsh, *The Rebirth of Antisemitism*; Johnson, *Mapping the New Left Antisemitism*; Nelson, *Israel Denial*; Rich, *The Left's Jewish Problem*.

31. For such rejections, see, e.g., Lerman, *Whatever Happened to Antisemitism?*; JVL, *How the EHRC Got It so Wrong*; Winstanley, *Weaponising Anti-Semitism*; Kuper, "A Reply." On the EHRC report to which these and other critics of Israel responded, see EHRC, *Investigation into Antisemitism in the Labour Party*. See also Labour Party (UK), "Publication of the Equality and Human Rights Commission."

32. King, "Letter from a Birmingham Jail."

33. See Pacepa, "Russian Footprints."

34. See, e.g., Ben-Itto, *The Lie*; Hagemeister, *The Perennial Conspiracy Theory*.

35. See Hitler, *Mein Kampf*, 724 (describing Jews as the "enemy of humanity [Feind der Menschheit]" and the "origin of all suffering [Urheber allen Leides]").

36. See generally, e.g., Gitelman, *A Century of Ambivalence*; Huttenbach, introduction to *Soviet Nationality Policies*, 1–8.

37. See, e.g., Gorni, "Zionist Socialism and the Arab Question."

38. See Pacepa, "Russian Footprints."

39. On the origins of Zionism, see, e.g., Aronson, *Troubled Waters*.

40. See Pacepa, "Russian Footprints."

41. See Huttenbach, *Soviet Nationality Policies*.

42. See Küchler, "DDR-Geschichtsbilder"; Poltorak and Leshchiner, "Teaching the Holocaust in Russia."

43. See, e.g., Azadovskii and Egorov, "From Anti-Westernism to Anti-Semitism"; Jenne, Bozóki, and Visnovitz, "2 Antisemitic Tropes."

44. Pacepa paraphrasing Andropov in "Russian Footprints."

45. See, e.g., Ben-Itto, *The Lie That Will Not Die*; Hagemeister, *The Perennial Conspiracy Theory*; Cohen and Boyd, "The KGB and Anti-Israel Propaganda Operations." The *Elders of Zion* passages were removed from Hamas's charter of 2017. See Hamas, "A Document of General Principles." Cf. critiques in, e.g., Fattal, "Hamas's Attack"; Hoffman, "Understanding Hamas's Genocidal Ideology." But cf. also Bherer, "La philosophe Judith Butler" (noting Butler's designation of Hamas as a legitimate resistance movement).

46. On the Israel–Palestine conflict and Western colonialism, see, e.g., Ayyash, "The Jerusalem Declaration"; Ashcroft, "Representation and Its Discontents."

47. See, e.g., Beydoun, *American Islamophobia*.

48. Matsuda, "Public Response to Racist Speech," 17.

49. On equating Jews with Nazis, see, e.g., Klaff, "Holocaust Inversion." On the slogan and intentions/perceptions, see, e.g., Boffey, "'From the River to the Sea,'" and Nassar, "'From the River to the Sea.'"

CHAPTER 12

1. See, e.g., Siddique, "Who Has the Labour Party Suspended."

2. O. Jones, *This Land*, 210–212, 214.

3. O. Jones, *This Land*, 213–214.

4. O. Jones, *This Land*, 213–214.

5. See, e.g., Grigat, "Antisemitismus im Marxismus"; Haury, "Antisemitismus in Karl Marx' Frühschrift 'Zur Judenfrage'?"

6. These examples come from O. Jones, *This Land*, 222–224. On Corbyn and Eisen, cf. R. Mason, "Jeremy Corbyn." On Livingstone's remarks, cf. Beaumont, "Ken Livingstone," and Schulze, "Hitler and Zionism."

7. O. Jones, *This Land*, 225–226. Cf. Elgot, "Labour Expels Jackie Walker."

8. O. Jones, *This Land*, 252.

9. O. Jones, *This Land*, 227, 245.

10. O. Jones, *This Land*, 245.

11. O. Jones, *This Land*, 249.

12. Milligan, "Naz Shah"; O. Jones, *This Land*, 223–224.

13. "Jeremy Corbyn Is an Anti-Semite"; Lakha, "Jeremy Corbyn Isn't Antisemitic"; Hattenstone, "I Still Don't Believe Corbyn Is Antisemitic"; Abrams, "Jeremy Corbyn's Cynical Anti-Semitism."

14. See, e.g., JVL, *How the EHRC Got It so Wrong*; Winstanley, *Weaponising Anti-Semitism*.

15. O. Jones, *This Land*, 229.

16. O. Jones, *This Land*, 213.

17. O. Jones, *This Land*, 212.

18. Cf., e.g., Lakha, "Jeremy Corbyn Isn't Antisemitic"; Hattenstone, "I Still Don't Believe Corbyn Is Antisemitic."

19. Corbyn, "What I'm Doing to Banish Anti-Semitism." Cf. JVL, *How the EHRC Got It so Wrong*; Winstanley, *Weaponising Anti-Semitism*.

20. Cassini, "Elections législatives." See also Cassini, "Antisémitisme."

21. O. Jones, "Antisemitism Has No Place on the Left."

22. On whites and racist views, see, e.g., *Race and Ethnicity in Britain*.

23. See, e.g., Badiou, *Portées du mot "juif"*; Badiou and Winter, "La gifle de Badiou"; Brown, "Rights and Identity"; Butler, *Parting Ways*; Samuels, "Cornel West"; and Žižek, "There Is No Conflict."

24. R. Mason, "Corbyn's Offer."

25. *The Shami Chakrabarti Report*, 27.

26. *The Shami Chakrabarti Report*, 11. The terms *right* and *duty* can have divergent meanings in broadly moral as opposed to strictly legal contexts, so I have inserted the modifiers "[legal]" and "[moral]" to clarify what I believe to be the distinction Chakrabarti is drawing.

27. Gates, "War of Words," 47. Cf. Benz, *Was ist Antisemitismus?*, 9–11.

28. See, e.g., Lerman, *Whatever Happened to Antisemitism?*; JVL, *How the EHRC Got It so Wrong*; Philo et al., *Bad News for Labour*; Winstanley, *Weaponising Anti-Semitism*. But see EHRC, *Investigation into Antisemitism in the Labour Party* (concluding that comprehensive and generalized accusations against Jews for bringing false accusations of leftist antisemitism counted as a form of antisemitic denial and as antisemitic harassment of Jewish members of the Labour Party).

29. See, e.g., Hirsh, *Contemporary Left Antisemitism*; Nelson, *Israel Denial*.

30. On disputes about defining antisemitism, see., e.g., IHRA, "About the IHRA Non–Legally Binding Working Definition of Antisemitism"; Gould, "The IHRA Definition."

31. *The Shami Chakrabarti Report*, 11.

32. *The Shami Chakrabarti Report*, 11.

33. *The Shami Chakrabarti Report*, 1.

34. O. Jones, *This Land*, 233, 234. I have inserted "[leftist]" here because, in line with the analysis I have developed here, JVL members readily acknowledge right-wing antisemitism.

35. O. Jones, *This Land*, 233. See generally, Lerman, *Whatever Happened to Antisemitism?*; JVL, *How the EHRC Got It so Wrong*; Winstanley, *Weaponising Anti-Semitism*; Kuper, "A Reply."

36. JVL, "The EHRC Has Spoken"; JVL, *How the EHRC Got It so Wrong*.

37. Winstanley, "How Owen Jones Learned to Stop Worrying and Love Zionism."

38. See, e.g., Behr et al., "An Anti-Communist Consensus."

39. Lerman, *Whatever Happened to Antisemitism?*

40. See, e.g., Bensussan, "L'extrême droite."

41. Badiou and Winter, "La gifle de Badiou."

42. See, e.g., Badiou, *L'éthique.*

43. "Marche contre l'antisémitisme."

44. Royer, "Marche contre l'antisémitisme."

45. See, e.g., Klug, "'We Know Occupation.'"

CHAPTER 13

1. See, e.g., "Le petit-neveu de Brigitte Macron."

2. See, e.g., "'Vous voulez ma tête?'"

3. Leroy, "'Louis XVI.'"

4. "Garde à vue du policier prolongée."

5. See, e.g., *The Stephen Lawrence Inquiry*; Samuels and Olorunnipa, *His Name Is George Floyd*.

6. See, e.g., Matsuda et al., *Words That Wound*; Stefancic and Delgado, "A Shifting Balance"; Delgado and Stefancic, *Must We Defend Nazis?*; Delgado and Stefancic, *Understanding Words That Wound*.

7. See, e.g., Desmoulières, "Jean-Luc Mélenchon."

8. See, e.g., "Amsterdam Museum"; Willem-Alexander, "Toespraak."

Bibliography

Abelow, Benjamin. *How the West Brought War to Ukraine: Understanding How U.S. and NATO Policies Led to Crisis, War, and the Risk of Nuclear Catastrophe.* Great Barrington, MA: Siland Press, 2022.

Abrams, Mere. "Is There a Difference between Being Transgender and Transsexual?" *Healthline*, May 22, 2023. https://www.healthline.com/health/transgender/difference-between-transgender-and -transsexual.

Abrams, Elliott. "Jeremy Corbyn's Cynical Anti-Semitism." *Pressure Points* (blog), Council on Foreign Relations, August 23, 2018. https://www.cfr.org/blog/jeremy-corbyns-cynical-anti-semitism.

ACLU (American Civil Liberties Union). "Repression of Peaceful Protest." N.d. https://www .aclu.org/issues/free-speech/rights-protesters/repression-peaceful-protest (accessed August 1, 2024).

Adams, Char. "NAACP Stands by Leader Slammed over Comments at Critical Race Theory Rally." NBC News, July 22, 2021. https://www.nbcnews.com/news/nbcblk/naacp-stands-leader-slammed -comments-critical-race-theory-rally-rcna1492.

Adenitire, John. *A General Right to Conscientious Exemption.* Cambridge: Cambridge University Press, 2020.

African Commission on Human and Peoples' Rights. Declaration of Principles of Freedom of Expression and Access to Information in Africa. Last update November 10, 2019. https://achpr .au.int/en/node/902.

"After Lunching with Janet Yellen, Chinese Women Economists Are Called Traitors Online." *Time*, July 10, 2023. https://time.com/6293259/chinese-women-economists-yellen-traitors/.

Agence France-Presse. "Czechs Bust Major Russian Propaganda Network." *Moscow Times*, March 27, 2024. https://www.themoscowtimes.com/2024/03/27/czechs-bust-major-russian-propaganda -network-a84656.

Alemagna, Lilian, and Stéphane Alliès. *Mélenchon, à la conquête du peuple.* Paris: Robert Lafont, 2018.

Alexander, Larry. "Banning Hate Speech and the Sticks and Stones Defense." *Constitutional Commentary* 13, no. 1 (1996): 71–100.

Alexander, Michelle. *The New Jim Crow: Mass Incarceration in the Age of Colourblindness*. London: Penguin, 2019.

Alger, Dean. *Megamedia: How Giant Corporations Dominate Mass Media, Distort Competition and Endanger Democracy*. Lanham, MD: Rowman & Littlefield, 1998.

Althusser, Louis, Étienne Balibar, Roger Establet, Pierre Macherey, and Jacques Rancière. *Lire le capital*. 1969. Reprint, Paris: Presses Universitaires de France, 2014.

Amin, Samir. *L'Eurocentrisme: Critique d'une idéologie*. Paris: Anthropos, 1988.

Amnesty International. "New History Textbook Is a Blatant Attempt to Unlawfully Indoctrinate School Children in Russia and Russian-Occupied Ukrainian Territories." September 1, 2023. https://www.amnesty.org/en/latest/news/2023/09/ukraine-russia-new-history-textbook-is-a -blatant-attempt-to-unlawfully-indoctrinate-school-children-in-russia-and-russian-occupied -ukrainian-territories/.

"Amsterdam Museum neemt afscheid van 'Gouden Eeuw.'" *NOS Nieuws*, September 12, 2019. https://nos.nl/artikel/2301454-amsterdam-museum-neemt-afscheid-van-gouden-eeuw.

Andrews, Kehinde. *The New Age of Empire: How Racism and Colonialism Still Rule the World*. New York: Bold Type, 2021.

Anthony, Susan B. "On Women's Right to Vote." 1872. The History Place, n.d. https://www .historyplace.com/speeches/anthony.htm (accessed August 1, 2024).

Apelt, Andreas H., and Maria Hufenreuter. *Antisemitismus in der DDR und die Folgen*. Halle, Germany: Mitteldeutscher, 2016.

Applebaum, Anne. *Iron Curtain: The Crushing of Eastern Europe 1944–56*. London: Penguin, 2013.

Arendt, Hannah. *Eichmann in Jerusalem: Ein Bericht von der Banalität des Bösen*. 1964. Reprint, Munich: Piper, 2011.

Arendt, Hannah. *Elemente und Ursprünge totaler Herrschaft*. 1951. Reprint, Munich: Piper, 1986.

Arendt, Hannah, and Joachim Fest. *Eichmann war von empörender Dummheit*. Munich: Piper, 2013.

Aristotle. *Nicomachean Ethics*. Translated by W. D. Ross. Revised by J. O. Urmson. In *The Complete Works of Aristotle: The Revised Oxford Translations*, vol. 2, edited by Jonathan Barnes, 1729–1867. Princeton, NJ: Princeton University Press, 1984.

Armstrong, Elisabeth B. *Bury the Corpse of Colonialism: The Revolutionary Feminist Conference of 1949*. Oakland: University of California Press, 2023.

Aron, Raymond. *L'opium des intellectuels*. 1955. Reprint, Paris: Calmann-Lévy, 2004.

Aronson, I. Michael. *Troubled Waters: Origins of the 1881 Anti-Jewish Pogroms in Russia*. Pittsburgh: University of Pittsburgh Press, 1990.

Ashcroft, Bill. "Representation and Its Discontents." *Religion* 34 (2004): 113–121.

Associated Press. "DeSantis Knocks Critical Race Theory in Civics Curricula." Associated Press, March 17, 2021. https://apnews.com/article/race-and-ethnicity-ron-desantis-florida-coronavirus -pandemic-naples-56d68d06e08105796e87c684f95bf1a7.

Atterbury, Andrew. "Florida and DeSantis Dig in as Criticism of Black History Curriculum Mounts." *Politico*, July 24, 2023. https://www.politico.com/news/2023/07/24/florida-desantis -black-history-education-00107859.

Australian National University. "Equity and Diversity." N.d. https://services.anu.edu.au/business -units/human-resources-division/equity-and-diversity (accessed August 1, 2024).

Awad, Sumaya, and Brian Bean, eds. *Palestine: A Socialist Introduction*. Chicago: Haymarket, 2021.

Ayyash, M. Muhannad. "The Jerusalem Declaration." *Al Jazeera*, April 21, 2021. https://www .aljazeera.com/opinions/2021/4/21/the-jerusalem-declaration-on-antisemitism-is-an-orientalist -text.

Azadovskii, Konstantin, and Boris Egorov. "From Anti-Westernism to Anti-Semitism." *Journal of Cold War Studies* 4 (2002): 66–80.

Badiou, Alain. *L'éthique*. 1993. Reprint, Paris: Hatier, 2000.

Badiou, Alain. *Portées du mot "Juif."* 2005. Reprint, Paris: Léo Scheer, 2015.

Badiou, Alain, and Cécile Winter. "La gifle de Badiou à la rhétorique de Bensussan." *Libération*, August 11, 2014. https://www.liberation.fr/societe/2014/08/11/la-gifle-de-badiou-a-la-rhetorique -de-bensussan_1079119.

Baets, Antoon De. "Criminal Regimes Are Never Soft on History." *Free Speech Debate*, December 23, 2019. https://freespeechdebate.com/2019/12/criminal-regimes-are-never-soft-on-history/.

Baets, Antoon De. "Self-Inculpatory Laws Do Not Exist." *Free Speech Debate*, December 12, 2019. https://freespeechdebate.com/2019/12/self-inculpatory-laws-do-not-exist/.

Baker, C. Edwin. "Hate Speech." In *The Content and Context of Hate Speech*, edited by Michael Herz and Peter Molnar, 37–80. Cambridge: Cambridge University Press, 2012.

Balibar, Étienne. *La philosophie de Marx*. Rev. ed. Paris: La Découverte, 2001.

Baroud, Ramzy. "'Not a Justification but a Provocation': Chomsky on the Root Causes of the Russia Ukraine War." *Common Dreams*, June 25, 2022. https://www.commondreams.org/views /2022/06/25/not-justification-provocation-chomsky-root-causes-russia-ukraine-war. Reprinted (but slightly varied) in *Counterpunch*, June 28, 2022. https://www.counterpunch.org/2022/06/28 /not-a-justification-but-a-provocation-chomsky-on-the-root-causes-of-the-russia-ukraine-war/.

Beaumont, Peter. "Ken Livingstone Muddies History to Support Claims on Hitler and Zion- ism." *Guardian*, May 1, 2016. https://www.theguardian.com/politics/2016/apr/30/livingstone -muddies-history-to-support-hitler-and-zionism-claims.

Beauvoir, Simone de. *Le deuxième sexe*. Paris: Gallimard, 1949.

Behr, Valentin, Muriel Blaive, Anenoma Constantin, Laure Neumayer, and Máté Zombory. "An Anti-Communist Consensus: The Black Book of Communism in Pan-European Perspective." *Revue d'études comparatives Est-Ouest* 2–3 (2020): 55–88.

Belavusau, Uladzislau, and Aleksandra Gliszczyńska-Grabias, eds. *Law and Memory: Towards Legal Governance of History*. Cambridge: Cambridge University Press, 2017.

Bell, Derrick. *And We Are Not Saved: The Elusive Quest for Racial Justice*. 1987. Reprint, New York: Basic, 1989.

Bell, Derrick. "*Brown v. Board of Education* and the Interest-Convergence Dilemma." *Harvard Law Review* 93 (1980): 518–533.

Bell, Derrick. *Faces at the Bottom of the Well: The Permanence of Racism*. 1992. Reprint, New York: Basic, 2018.

Bell, Derrick. "Racial Remediation: An Historical Perspective on Current Conditions." *Notre Dame Law Review* 52 (1976): 5–29.

Bell, Derrick. *Silent Covenants:* Brown v. Board of Education *and the Unfulfilled Hopes for Racial Reform*. Oxford: Oxford University Press, 2004.

Belton, Catherine. *Putin's People: How the KGB Took Back Russia and Then Took On the West*. London: William Collins, 2020.

Ben-Itto, Hadassa. *The Lie That Will Not Die:* The Protocols of the Elders of Zion. 2nd ed. London: Vallentine Mitchell, 2020.

Benjamin, Walter. *Zur Kritik der Gewalt und andere Aufsätze*. 1921. Reprint, Frankfurt: Suhrkamp, 2009.

Bensussan, Gérard. 2014. "L'extrême droite en a rêvé, l'extrême gauche l'a fait." *Libération*, July 22, 2014. https://www.liberation.fr/france/2014/07/22/l-extreme-droite-en-a-reve-l-extreme-gauche-l-a-fait_1068401/.

Benz, Wolfgang. *Was ist Antisemitismus?* 2nd ed. Munich: Beck, 2005.

Beydoun, Khaled A. *American Islamophobia: Understanding the Roots and Rise of Fear*. Oakland: University of California, 2018.

Bhat, Mohsin. "Mob, Murder, Motivation: The Emergence of Hate Crimes Discourse in India." *Socio-Legal Review* 16 (2020): 76–108.

Bherer, Marc-Olivier. "La philosophe Judith Butler ravive la polémique à gauche sur les attaques du Hamas en Israël, qu'elle qualifie d' 'acte de résistance.'" *Le Monde*, March 14, 2024. https://www.lemonde.fr/idees/article/2024/03/14/resistance-du-hamas-judith-butler-ravive-la-polemique-a-gauche_6221909_3232.html.

"Billigung, Leugnung und Verharmlosung von Völkermorden." Deutscher Bundestag, Recht—Ausschuss—hib 572/2022, October 19, 2022. https://www.bundestag.de/presse/hib/kurzmeldungen-916934.

Birnbaum, Pierre. "Jean-Luc Mélenchon instaure explicitement un fossé entre le peuple français et Yaël Braun-Pivet." *Le Monde*, November 2, 2023. https://www.lemonde.fr/idees/article /2023/11/02/jean-luc-melenchon-instaure-explicitement-un-fosse-entre-le-peuple-francais-et -yael-braun-pivet_6197830_3232.html.

Bloed, Arie, ed. *Protection of Minority Rights through Bilateral Treaties*. The Hague: Kluwer, 1999.

Bloodworth, James. "Too Many on the Left Have Swallowed Putin's Propaganda on Ukraine." *New Statesman*, February 8, 2022. https://www.newstatesman.com/international-politics /geopolitics/2022/02/too-many-on-the-left-have-swallowed-putins-propaganda-on-ukraine.

Blow, Charles M. "Privilege of 'Arrest without Incident.'" *New York Times*, January 4, 2015. https:// www.nytimes.com/2015/01/05/opinion/charles-blow-privilege-of-arrest-without-incident.html.

Blum, Petra. "Sanktionen oft wirkungslos." *Tagesschau*, August 24, 2023. https://www.tagesschau .de/investigativ/wdr/russland-propaganda-newsfront-eu-usa-sanktionen-ukraine-100.html.

Boffey, Daniel. "'From the River to the Sea': Where Does the Slogan Come from and What Does It Mean?" *Guardian*, October 31, 2023. https://www.theguardian.com/world/2023/oct/31/from -the-river-to-the-sea-where-does-the-slogan-come-from-and-what-does-it-mean-israel-palestine.

Boim, Leon. "Anti-Semitism, Anti-Judaism and Anti-Zionism in the USSR." *Israel Yearbook on Human Rights* 8 (1978): 240–266.

Bolton, Matt, and Frederick Harry Pitts. *Corbynism: A Critical Approach*. Bingley, UK: Emerald, 2018.

Bonilla-Silva, Eduardo. *Racism without Racists*. 5th ed. Lanham, MD: Rowman & Littlefield, 2017.

Boterbloem, Kees, ed. *Life in Stalin's Soviet Union*. London: Bloomsbury, 2019.

Bouie, Jamelle. "Ron DeSantis and the State Where History Goes to Die." *New York Times*, July 28, 2023. https://www.nytimes.com/2023/07/28/opinion/desantis-slavery-florida-curriculum -history.html.

Bourdieu, Pierre. *Méditations pascaliennes*. Paris: Seuil, 1997.

Brown, Wendy. "Rights and Identity in Late Modernity." In *Identities, Politics, and Rights*, edited by Austin Sarat and Thomas R. Kearns, 85–130. Ann Arbor: University of Michigan Press, 1995.

Burgis, Ben. "Is 'Whataboutism' Always a Bad Thing?" *Current Affairs*, March 17, 2022. https:// www.currentaffairs.org/2022/03/is-whataboutism-always-a-bad-thing.

Burns, Conor. "Margaret Thatcher's Greatest Achievement: New Labour." *Conservative Home*, April 11, 2008. https://conservativehome.blogs.com/centreright/2008/04/making-history.html.

Buschschlüter, Vanessa. "Nicaragua Strips 94 Prominent Dissidents of Citizenship." BBC, February 16, 2023. https://www.bbc.co.uk/news/world-latin-america-64663711.

Bushwick, Sophie. "Russia's Information War Is Being Waged on Social Media Platforms." *Scientific American*, March 8, 2022. https://www.scientificamerican.com/article/russia-is-having -less-success-at-spreading-social-media-disinformation/.

Butler, Judith. "The Compass of Mourning." *London Review of Books*, October 19, 2023. https://www.lrb.co.uk/the-paper/v45/n20/judith-butler/the-compass-of-mourning.

Butler, Judith. *Excitable Speech: A Politics of the Performative*. 1997. Reprint, London: Routledge, 2021.

Butler, Judith. *Gender Trouble: Feminism and the Subversion of Identity*. 1990. Reprint, London: Routledge, 2006.

Butler, Judith. "I Am Hopeful That the Russian Army Will Lay Down Its Arms." *Ara*, April 28, 2022. https://en.ara.cat/culture/am-hopeful-that-the-russian-army-will-lay-down-its-arms_128_4353851.html.

Butler, Judith. "No, It's Not Anti-Semitic." *London Review of Books*, August 21, 2003. https://www.lrb.co.uk/the-paper/v25/n16/judith-butler/no-it-s-not-anti-semitic.

Butler, Judith. *Parting Ways: Jewishness and the Critique of Zionism*. New York: Columbia University Press, 2012.

Calvert, Drew. "The Political Divide in America Goes beyond Polarization and Tribalism." *Kellogg Insight*, October 29, 2020. https://insight.kellogg.northwestern.edu/article/political-divide-america-beyond-polarization-tribalism-secularism.

Campana, Aurélie, Grégory Dufaud, and Sophie Tournon, eds. *Les déportations en héritage: Les peuples réprimés du Caucase et de Crimée, 60 ans après*. Rennes, France: Presses Universitaires de Rennes, 2009.

Campbell, Jonathan G., and Lesley D. Klaff, eds. *Unity and Diversity in Contemporary Antisemitism*. Boston: Academic Studies Press, 2019.

Carney, Timothy P. "To Liberals, 'Free Speech' Means the Right to Indoctrinate. To Conservatives, It Means the Right to Dissent from the Elites." American Enterprise Institute, April 29, 2022. https://www.aei.org/op-eds/to-liberals-free-speech-means-the-right-to-indoctrinate-to-conservatives-it-means-the-right-to-dissent-from-the-elites/.

Cassini, Sandrine. "Antisémitisme: Comment Jean-Luc Mélenchon cultive l'ambiguïté." *Le Monde*, January 5, 2024. https://www.lemonde.fr/politique/article/2024/01/05/antisemitisme-comment-jean-luc-melenchon-cultive-l-ambiguite_6209231_823448.html.

Cassini, Sandrine. "Elections législatives: Les accusations d'antisémitisme contre LFI ont empoisonné la campagne de la gauche." *Le Monde*, June 28, 2024. https://www.lemonde.fr/politique/article/2024/06/28/elections-legislatives-les-accusations-d-antisemitisme-contre-lfi-ont-empoisonne-la-campagne-de-la-gauche_6245007_823448.html.

Cervera-Marzal, Manuel. *Le populisme de gauche*. Paris: La Découverte, 2021.

Césaire, Aimé. *Discours sur le colonialisme*. 1955. Reprint, Paris: Réclame, 2000.

Chandernagor, Françoise. "L'enfer des bonnes intentions." *Le Monde*, December 16, 2005. https://www.lemonde.fr/idees/article/2005/12/16/l-enfer-des-bonnes-intentions-par-francoise-chandernagor_722124_3232.html.

Chellaney, Brahma. "The West Is Hastening Its Own Decline." *Project Syndicate*, April 24, 2024. https://www.project-syndicate.org/commentary/us-and-eu-sanctions-against-russia-will-undermine-western-global-preeminence-by-brahma-chellaney-2024-04.

Chiappa, Claudia. "Serbian President Turns to Russia amid Rising Tensions with Kosovo." *Politico*, September 25, 2023. https://www.politico.eu/article/serbian-president-aleksandar-vucic-turns-to-russia-amid-rising-tensions-with-kosovo/.

Chomsky, Aviva, Barry Carr, and Pamela Maria Smorkaloff, eds. *The Cuba Reader: History, Culture, Politics*. 2nd ed. Durham, NC: Duke University Press, 2019.

Chomsky, Noam. *Fateful Triangle: The United States, Israel, and the Palestinians*. 3rd ed. London: Pluto, 2016.

Chomsky, Noam, and Ilan Pappé. *On Palestine*. London: Penguin, 2015.

Chotiner, Isaac. "Why John Mearsheimer Blames the U.S. for the Crisis in Ukraine." *New Yorker*, March 1, 2022. https://www.newyorker.com/news/q-and-a/why-john-mearsheimer-blames-the-us-for-the-crisis-in-ukraine.

Clarke, Jessica A. "Against Immutability." *Yale Law Journal* 125, no. 1 (2015): 2–102.

Coca-Cola Company. "Creating a Culture of Diversity, Equity and Inclusion." N.d. https://www.coca-colacompany.com/social/diversity-and-inclusion (accessed August 1, 2024).

Cohen, Eli B., and Elizabeth Boyd. "The KGB and Anti-Israel Propaganda Operations." *Informing Science* 22 (2019): 157–182.

Cohen, Nick. "Beware Boris's Sinister Crackdown on Free Speech." *The Spectator*, June 24, 2021. https://www.spectator.co.uk/article/beware-boris-s-sinister-crackdown-on-free-speech/.

Collins, Patricia Hill, and Sirma Bilge. *Intersectionality*. 2nd ed. Cambridge: Polity, 2020.

Cook, Sarah, Angeli Datt, Ellie Young, and B. C. Han. *Beijing's Global Media Influence*. Washington, DC: Freedom House, 2022. https://freedomhouse.org/report/beijing-global-media-influence/2022/authoritarian-expansion-power-democratic-resilience.

Corbyn, Jeremy. "What I'm Doing to Banish Anti-Semitism." *Evening Standard*, April 24, 2018. https://www.standard.co.uk/comment/comment/jeremy-corbyn-what-i-m-doing-to-banish-antisemitism-from-the-labour-party-a3821961.html.

Corneille, Pierre. *Oeuvres complètes*. Vol. 2, edited by Georges Couton. Paris: Gallimard-Pléiade, 1984.

Cortese, Anthony. *Opposing Hate Speech*. Westport, CT: Praeger, 2006.

Costa, Cassie da. "How the Restaurant Industry Viciously Exploits Its Workers, from Wage Theft to Sexual Abuse." *Daily Beast*, May 23, 2020. https://www.thedailybeast.com/how-the-restaurant-industry-viciously-exploits-its-workers-from-wage-theft-to-sexual-abuse.

Crenshaw, Kimberlé Williams. "Mapping the Margins: Intersectionality, Identity Politics, and Violence against Women of Color." *Stanford Law Review* 43 (1991): 1241–1299.

Crenshaw, Kimberlé Williams. "Race, Reform, and Retrenchment: Transformation and Legitimation in Antidiscrimination Law." *Harvard Law Review* 101 (1988): 1331–1387.

Crozier, Gill. *Racism and Education in Britain: Addressing Structural Oppression and the Dominance of Whiteness*. London: Palgrave, 2023.

Cuba Solidarity Campaign. "Facts and Fact Sheets." N.d. https://cuba-solidarity.org.uk/informa tion/facts/ (accessed August 1, 2024).

"Cultivating Diversity, Equity, and Inclusion in Education Environments." *Resilient Educator*, n.d. https://resilienteducator.com/collections/cultivating-diversity-inclusion-equity/ (accessed August 1, 2024).

Dagdelen, Sevim. "Völkermord an den Armeniern erinnern." DIE LINKE Bundestagsfraktion, April 24, 2021. https://www.linksfraktion.de/themen/nachrichten/detail/voelkermord-an-den -armeniern-erinnern-verbrechen-heute-verurteilen/.

Davies, Caroline. "Ngozi Fulani Receives Personal Apology over Buckingham Palace Racism Incident." *Guardian*, December 16, 2022. https://www.theguardian.com/uk-news/2022/dec/16 /lady-hussey-apologises-ngozi-fulani-buckingham-palace-racism-incident.

Davies, Norman. *Europe: A History*. Oxford: Oxford University Press, 1996.

Davis, Angela J., ed. *Policing the Black Man*. New York: Vintage, 2018.

Déclaration des Droits de l'Homme et du Citoyen. 1789. French National Assembly, Con-seil constitutionnel. https://www.conseil-constitutionnel.fr/le-bloc-de-constitutionnalite/declaration-des -droits-de-l-homme-et-du-citoyen-de-1789 (accessed August 1, 2024). Official translation of the Conseil constitutionnel, n.d. https://www.conseil-constitutionnel.fr/en/declaration-of-human -and-civic-rights-of-26-august-1789 (accessed August 1, 2024).

Debray, Régis. *Révolution dans la révolution? Lutte armée et lutte politique en amérique latine*. Paris: Maspero, 1967.

Delgado, Richard, and Jean Stefancic. *Must We Defend Nazis? Why the First Amendment Should Not Protect Hate Speech and White Supremacy*. New York: New York University Press, 1996.

Delgado, Richard, and Jean Stefancic. *Understanding Words That Wound*. New York: Routledge, 2004.

Demirjian, Karoun. "In Congress, Democrats' Rift over Israel." *New York Times*, July 17, 2023. https://www.nytimes.com/2023/07/17/us/congress-israel-democrats.html.

Derrida, Jacques. *De la grammatologie*. Paris: Minuit, 1967.

Derrida, Jacques. *Force de loi*. Paris: Galilée, 2005.

Derrida, Jacques. *L'écriture et la différence*. Paris: Seuil, 1967.

Desmeules, Christian. "Un paradis sous les étoiles." *Le Devoir*, December 6, 2014. https://www .ledevoir.com/lire/425832/litterature-quebecoise-un-paradis-sous-les-etoiles?.

Desmoulières, Raphaëlle Besse. "Jean-Luc Mélenchon avec cocarde et bonnet phrygien." *Le Monde*, April 19, 2012. https://www.lemonde.fr/election-presidentielle-2012/article/2012/04/19/jean -luc-melenchon-avec-cocarde-et-bonnet-phrygien_1687520_1471069.html.

DiAngelo, Robin. *White Fragility: Why It's so Hard for White People to Talk about Racism*. New York: Penguin, 2018.

Diem, Sarah, and Anjalé D. Welton. *Anti-racist Educational Leadership and Policy*. New York: Routledge, 2020.

Douglass, Frederick. "What to the Slave Is the Fourth of July?" 1852. TeachingAmericanHistory .org, n.d. https://teachingamericanhistory.org/library/document/what-to-the-slave-is-the-fourth -of-july/ (accessed August 1, 2024).

Douzinas, Costas. *Human Rights and Empire: The Political Philosophy of Cosmopolitanism*. London: Routledge, 2007.

Dow, Jamie. "Removing Statues: Racism, Values, Anachronism and 'Hiding from History.'" *Medium*, June 16, 2020. https://medium.com/ethics-central/removing-statues-racism-values -anachronism-and-hiding-from-history-c0a880f75e5b.

Doward, Jamie. "Castro Was 'Champion of Social Justice' despite Flaws, Says Corbyn." *Guardian*, November 26, 2016. https://www.theguardian.com/world/2016/nov/26/jeremy-corbyn -left-uk-politics-fidel-castro.

Dreyfus, Michel. *L'antisémitisme à gauche*. Paris: Découverte, 2009.

Duncombe, Stephen, and Steve Lambert. *The Art of Activism*. New York: OR, 2021.

Duss, Matthew. "Calling Trump an Anti-imperialist Is Nonsense." *Foreign Policy*, April 18, 2023. https://foreignpolicy.com/2023/04/18/donald-trump-presidency-anti-imperialist-militarism -war/.

Dworkin, Ronald. Foreword to *Extreme Speech and Democracy*, edited by Ivan Hare and James Weinstein, v–ix. Oxford: Oxford University Press, 2009.

Dworkin, Ronald. *Law's Empire*. Cambridge, MA: Belknap Press of Harvard University Press, 1986.

Dworkin, Ronald. *Taking Rights Seriously*. Cambridge, MA: Harvard University Press, 1977.

Eaton, George. "Noam Chomsky: 'We're Approaching the Most Dangerous Point in Human History.'" *New Statesman*, April 6, 2022. https://www.newstatesman.com/encounter/2022/04 /noam-chomsky-were-approaching-the-most-dangerous-point-in-human-history.

ECRI (European Commission against Racism and Intolerance). General Policy Recommendation No. 15, December 8, 2015. https://www.coe.int/en/web/european-commission-against-racism -and-intolerance/recommendation-no.15.

"Effectif des groupes politiques: XVIe législature." Assemblée nationale, n.d. https://www2.assem blee-nationale.fr/instances/liste/groupes_politiques/effectif (accessed August 1, 2024).

EHRC (Equality and Human Rights Commission, United Kingdom). *Investigation into Antisem-itism in the Labour Party*. London: EHRC, October 29, 2020. https://www.equalityhumanrights .com/sites/default/files/investigation-into-antisemitism-in-the-labour-party.pdf.

Elgot, Jessica. "Labour Expels Jackie Walker for Leaked Antisemitism Remarks." *Guardian*, March 27, 2019. https://www.theguardian.com/politics/2019/mar/27/labour-expels-jackie-walker-for-leaked-antisemitism-comments.

"Empörung wegen 'Vogelschiss.'" *Taz*, June 3, 2018. https://taz.de/Gaulands-Relativierung-der-NS-Zeit/!5510144/.

Engels, Friedrich. *Die Entwicklung des Sozialismus von der Utopie zur Wissenschaft.* 1880. In *Karl Marx—Friedrich Engels: Werke*, vol. 19, edited by Institut für Marxismus-Leninismus beim Zentralkomitee der Sozialistischen Einheitspartei Deutschlands, 177–228. Berlin: Dietz, 1962.

Engels, Friedrich. *Grundsätze des Kommunismus.* 1847. In *Karl Marx—Friedrich Engels: Werke*, vol. 4, edited by Institut für Marxismus-Leninismus beim Zentralkomitee der Sozialistischen Einheitspartei Deutschlands, 361–380. Berlin: Dietz, 1959.

Engels, Friedrich. *Herrn Eugen Dührings Umwälzung der Wissenschaft.* 1878. In *Karl Marx—Friedrich Engels: Werke*, vol. 20, edited by Institut für Marxismus-Leninismus beim Zentralkomitee der Sozialistischen Einheitspartei Deutschlands, 1–303. Berlin: Dietz, 1962.

Engels, Friedrich. *Die Lage der arbeitenden Klasse in England.* 1845. In *Karl Marx—Friedrich Engels: Werke*, vol. 2, edited by Institut für Marxismus-Leninismus beim Zentralkomitee der Sozialistischen Einheitspartei Deutschlands, 225–506. Berlin: Dietz, 1957.

Epstein, Reid J., and Patricia Mazzei. "G.O.P. Bills Target Protesters (and Absolve Motorists Who Hit Them)." *New York Times*, June 23, 2023. https://www.nytimes.com/2021/04/21/us/politics/republican-anti-protest-laws.html.

Equiano, Olaudah. *The Interesting Narrative and Other Writings.* 1789. Rev. ed. Edited by Vincent Carretta. London: Penguin Classics, 2003.

"Erlass Kaiser Wilhelms II. zur Reform des Schulunterrichts als Mittel zum Kampf gegen den Sozialismus." May 1, 1889. In *Deutsche Sozialgeschichte 1870–1914: Dokumente und Skizzen*, 3rd ed., edited by Gerhard A. Ritter und Jürgen Kocka, 333–334. Munich: Beck, 1982.

European Parliament. Resolution of 20 April 2023 on the Universal Decriminalisation of Homosexuality in the Light of Recent Developments in Uganda (2023/2643(RSP)). April 20, 2023, Strasbourg, France. https://www.europarl.europa.eu/doceo/document/TA-9-2023-0120_EN.html.

Evans, Rob. "Stephen Lawrence: Officer Who Allegedly Spied on Family Named." *Guardian*, April 17, 2018. https://www.theguardian.com/uk-news/2018/apr/17/stephen-lawrence-police-officer-allegedly-spied-family-identified-david-hagan.

"Excerpts: Hungarian 'Lies' Speech." BBC News, September 19, 2006. http://news.bbc.co.uk/1/hi/world/europe/5359546.stm.

Exxon Mobil Corporation. "Inclusion and Diversity." N.d. https://corporate.exxonmobil.com/locations/brazil/inclusion-and-diversity#Committees (accessed August 1, 2024).

Fallows, James. "Trump Time Capsule #140: 'Lock Her Up.'" *Atlantic*, October 11, 2016. https://www.theatlantic.com/notes/2016/10/trump-time-capsule-140-lock-her-up/503684/.

Fanon, Frantz. *L'an V de la révolution algérienne.* 1959. Reprint, Paris: La Découverte, 2011.

Fanon, Frantz. *Les damnés de la terre*. 1961. Reprint, Paris: La Découverte, 2004.

Fanon, Frantz. *Peau noire, masques blancs*. 1952. Reprint, Paris: Seuil, 2015.

Fattal, Isabel. "Hamas's Attack Confounds Middle East Experts." *Atlantic*, October 9, 2023. https://www.theatlantic.com/newsletters/archive/2023/10/what-is-hamas/675594/.

Faulconbridge, Guy. "Ukraine War Shows West's Dominance Is Ending as China Rises, Blair Says." Reuters, July 17, 2022. https://www.reuters.com/world/europe/ukraine-war-shows-wests -dominance-is-ending-china-rises-blair-says-2022-07-17/.

Faulkner, William. *Requiem for a Nun*. New York: Random House, 1951.

Fay, Liam. "Thin-Skinned Liberals Need to Toughen Up." *The Times* (London), December 31, 2018. https://www.thetimes.co.uk/article/thin-skinned-liberals-need-to-toughen-up-qdm3gw7gt.

Femia, Joseph V. *Gramsci's Political Thought: Hegemony, Consciousness, and the Revolutionary Process*. Oxford: Clarendon Press, 1981.

Ferrer, Ada. *Cuba: An American History*. New York: Scribner, 2022.

Ferrero, Livio. "Guerre en Ukraine: Jean-Luc Mélenchon juge Poutine 'coupable.'" *Paris Match*, March 11, 2022. https://www.parismatch.com/Actu/Politique/Guerre-en-Ukraine-Jean-Luc -Melenchon-juge-Poutine-coupable-1793262.

"Fidel Castro Takes Blame for Persecution of Cuban Gays." BBC, August 31, 2010. https://www .bbc.co.uk/news/world-latin-america-11147157.

Figes, Orlando. *The Story of Russia*. London: Bloomsbury, 2023.

Fine, Robert, and Philip Spencer. *Antisemitism and the Left*. Manchester, UK: Manchester University Press, 2017.

Fineman, Martha Albertson, Jack E. Jackson, and Adam P. Romero, eds. *Feminist and Queer Legal Theory*. London: Routledge, 2009.

Fischer, Ruth. *Stalin und der deutsche Kommunismus*. 1948–1950. 2 vols. Reprint, Dietz: Berlin, 1991.

Fortin, Jacey. "Critical Race Theory: A Brief History." *New York Times*, November 8, 2021. https:// www.nytimes.com/article/what-is-critical-race-theory.html.

Foucault, Michel. *Histoire de la folie à l'âge classique*. 1961. In *Oeuvres*, vol. 1, gen. ed. Frédéric Gros, 1–659. Paris: Gallimard-Pléiade, 2015.

Foucault, Michel. *Histoire de la sexualité 1: La volonté de savoir*. 1976. In *Oeuvres*, vol. 2, gen. ed. Frédéric Gros, 615–736. Paris: Gallimard-Pléiade, 2015.

Foucault, Michel. *Surveiller et punir: Naissance de la prison*. 1975. In *Oeuvres*, vol. 2, gen. ed. Frédéric Gros, 261–613. Paris: Gallimard-Pléiade, 2015.

"Frank-Walter Steinmeier räumt Fehler in seiner Russland-Politik ein." *Zeit Online*, April 4, 2022. https://www.zeit.de/politik/deutschland/2022-04/frank-walter-steinmeier-fehler-russland -ukraine.

Frazier, Ian. "Donald Trump and Uses and Misuses of the Bible." *New Yorker*, June 15, 2020. https://www.newyorker.com/news/daily-comment/donald-trump-and-uses-and-misuses-of-the-bible.

Freedland, Jonathan. "They're Openly Saying It: Brexit Has Failed." *Guardian*, May 19, 2023. https://www.theguardian.com/commentisfree/2023/may/19/brexit-failed-blame-remoaner-elite-refugees.

Freie Universität Berlin. "Diversity an der Freien Universität Berlin." N.d. https://www.fu-berlin.de/sites/diversity/index.html (accessed August 1, 2024).

French, David. "Free Speech for Me but Not for Thee: The American Right Has Lost the Plot on Free Speech." *Atlantic*, April 11, 2022. https://www.theatlantic.com/ideas/archive/2022/04/republican-dont-say-gay-bill-florida/629516/.

Fryšták, Marek, David Čep, and Dr. Katarína Kandová. "The Czech Republic." In *Criminalising Hate Speech: A Comparative Study*, edited by Eric Heinze. The Hague: Asser/Springer, 2024.

Furet, François. *Le passé d'une illusion*. Paris: Robert Laffont/Calmann-Lévy, 1995.

Gabrisch, Hubert. "Elements, Origins and Future of Great Transformations: Eastern Europe and Global Capitalism." *Economic and Labour Relations Review* 31 (2020): 172–190.

Galeotti, Mark. *Putin's Wars: From Chechnya to Ukraine*. Oxford: Osprey, 2022.

Galloway, George. "Let's Unite to Drive Out the Disaster of Blairism." *Socialist Worker*, May 8, 2007. https://socialistworker.co.uk/features/george-galloway-let-s-unite-to-drive-out-the-disaster-of-blairism/.

"Garde à vue du policier prolongée, début de soirée calme à Nanterre . . . ce qu'il faut retenir au lendemain de la mort de Nahel." *Libération*, June 28, 2023. https://www.liberation.fr/societe/police-justice/en-direct-nael-tue-par-un-policier-a-nanterre-enquete-tensions-reactions-les-dernieres-informations-20230628_RYWHMQNKSJFGTDGPQCEMY732HE/.

Garrard, Eve. "Forgiveness and the Holocaust." *Ethical Theory and Moral Practice* 5 (2002): 147–165.

Gates, Henry Louis, Jr. "War of Words: Critical Race Theory and the First Amendment." In *Speaking of Sex: Hate Speech, Civil Rights, and Civil Liberties*, by Henry Louis Gates Jr., Anthony P. Griffin, Donald E. Lively, and Nadine Strossen, 17–47. New York: New York University Press, 1994.

Gashaw, Amen. "In the Oppression Olympics, Don't Go for the Gold." *Harvard Political Review*, October 24, 2021. https://harvardpolitics.com/in-the-oppression-olympics-dont-go-for-the-gold/.

"Gauland: NS-Zeit nur ein 'Vogelschiss in der Geschichte.'" *Zeit Online*, June 2, 2018. https://www.zeit.de/news/2018-06/02/gauland-ns-zeit-nur-ein-vogelschiss-in-der-geschichte-180601-99-549766?utm_referrer=https%3A%2F%2Fwww.zeit.de%2Fzustimmung%3Furl%3Dhttps%253A%252F%252Fwww.zeit.de%252Fnews%252F2018-06%252F02%252Fgauland-ns-zeit-nur-ein-vogelschiss-in-der-geschichte-180601-99-549766.

Gayle, Damien. "Five Just Stop Oil Activists Receive Record Sentences for Planning to Block M25." *Guardian,* July 18, 2024. https://www.theguardian.com/environment/article/2024/jul/18/five-just-stop-oil-supporters-jailed-over-protest-that-blocked-m25.

"GDP per Capita, 1820 to 2018." Our World in Data, n.d. https://ourworldindata.org/grapher/gdp-per-capita-maddison-2020 (accessed August 1, 2024).

German, Lindsey. "Millions of Us Marched over Iraq." *Guardian,* February 15, 2023. https://www.theguardian.com/commentisfree/2023/feb/15/march-iraq-politics-war-public-opinion.

German, Lindsey. "We at Stop the War Condemn the Invasion of Ukraine, and Warmongers on All Sides." *Guardian,* March 4, 2022. https://www.theguardian.com/commentisfree/2022/mar/04/stop-the-war-condemn-invasion-ukraine-warmongers.

Ghanoonparvar, Mohammad R. "Through Tinted Lenses: Iranian and Western Perceptions and Reconstructions of the Other." In *Re-imagining the Other: Culture, Media, and Western–Muslim Intersections,* edited by Mahmoud Eid, 57–73. New York: Palgrave-Macmillan, 2014.

Gide, André. *Retour de l'U.R.S.S.* 1936. In *Souvenirs et voyages,* 745–802. Paris: Gallimard, 2001.

Gidley, Ben, Brendan McGeever, and David Feldman. "Labour and Antisemitism: A Crisis Misunderstood." *Political Quarterly* 2 (2020): 413–421.

Gilabert, Pablo. "The Importance of Linkage Arguments for the Theory and Practice of Human Rights: A Response to James Nickel." *Human Rights Quarterly* 32, no. 2 (2009–2010): 425–438.

Giovanni, Janine di. "The Real Reason the Russian Orthodox Church's Leader Supports Putin's War." *Foreign Policy,* April 26, 2022. https://foreignpolicy.com/2022/04/26/ukraine-war-russian-orthodox-church-support-patriarch-kirill-homophobia/.

Gitelman, Zvi. *A Century of Ambivalence: The Jews of Russia and the Soviet Union, 1881 to the Present.* 2nd ed. Bloomington: Indiana University Press, 2001.

Gitlin, Todd. *The Twilight of Common Dreams: Why America Is Wracked by Culture Wars.* New York: Metropolitan, 1995.

Gorni, Yosef. "Zionist Socialism and the Arab Question, 1918–1930." *Middle Eastern Studies* 13 (January 1977): 50–70.

Gouges, Olympe de. *La déclaration des droits de la femme et de la citoyenne.* 1791. Gallica, n.d. https://gallica.bnf.fr/essentiels/anthologie/declaration-droits-femme-citoyenne-0 (accessed August 1, 2024).

Gould, Rebecca Ruth. "The IHRA Definition of Antisemitism." *Political Quarterly* 91 (2020): 825–831.

Grashoff, Udo. *Gefahr von innen: Verrat im kommunistischen Widerstand gegen den Nationalsozialismus.* Göttingen, Germany: Wallstein, 2021.

Greenlee, Cynthia. "How History Textbooks Reflect America's Refusal to Reckon with Slavery." *Vox,* August 26, 2019. https://www.vox.com/identities/2019/8/26/20829771/slavery-textbooks-history.

Grigat, Stephan. "Antisemitismus im Marxismus: Warum die Linke mit Marx kritisiert werden muss." In *Der sich selbst entfremdete und wiedergefundene Marx*, edited by Helmut Lethen, Falko Schmieder, and Birte Löschenkohl, 177–190. Paderborn, Germany: Wilhelm Fink, 2010.

Guevara, Ernesto "Che." "Man and Socialism." In *The Cuba Reader: History, Culture, Politics*, 2nd ed., edited by Aviva Chomsky, Barry Carr, and Pamela Maria Smorkaloff, 370–374. Durham, NC: Duke University Press, 2019.

Gysi, Gregor. "DDR war kein Unrechtsstaat." DIE LINKE Bundestagsfraktion, April 19, 2009. https://www.linksfraktion.de/themen/nachrichten/detail/ddr-war-kein-unrechtsstaat/.

Habermas, Jürgen. *Strukturwandel der Öffentlichkeit: Untersuchungen zu einer Kategorie der burgerlichen Gesellschaft*. 1962. Reprint, Frankfurt: Suhrkamp, 1990.

Habermas, Jürgen. *Theorie des kommunikativen Handelns*. Vol. 2. 8th ed. Frankfurt: Suhrkamp, 1981.

Hafez, Farid, and Naved Bakali. *The Rise of Global Islamophobia in the War on Terror: Coloniality, Race, and Islam*. Manchester, UK: Manchester University Press, 2022.

Hagemeister, Michael. *The Perennial Conspiracy Theory*. London: Routledge, 2021.

Haidt, Jonathan. *The Righteous Mind: Why Good People Are Divided by Politics and Religion*. London: Penguin, 2013.

Haitiwaji, Gulbahar, and Rozenn Morgat. "'Our Souls Are Dead': How I Survived a Chinese 'Re-education' Camp for Uyghurs." *Guardian*, January 12, 2021. https://www.theguardian.com /world/2021/jan/12/uighur-xinjiang-re-education-camp-china-gulbahar-haitiwaji.

Halász, László. "Őszöd—újratöltve." *Élet és Irodalom*, August 28, 2009. https://adt.arcanum.com /en/accounts/login/?next=%2Fhu%2Fview%2FEletesIrodalomIrodalmiUjsag_2009_2%2F%3F pg%3D264%26layout%3Ds.

Hale-Dorrell, Aaron. Review of *The Thaw: Soviet Society and Culture during the 1950s and 1960s*, edited by Denis Kozlov and Eleonory Gilburd. *Region* 4 (2015): 351–353.

Haley, Alex, and James Lee. *Roots* (screenplay). Burbank, CA: Wolper, 1977.

Hall, Nathan, John Grieve, and Stephen Savage, eds. *Policing and the Legacy of Lawrence*. Abingdon, UK: Routledge, 2009.

Hamas. "A Document of General Principles & Policies." Hamas Media Office, Palestine, 2017. https://irp.fas.org/world/para/docs/hamas-2017.pdf.

Hanloser, Gerhard, ed. *Linker Antisemitismus?* Vienna: Mandelbaum, 2020.

Hardt, Michael, and Antonio Negri. *Empire*. Rev. ed. Cambridge, MA: Harvard University Press, 2001.

Harris, Gardiner. "Visiting Europe, Obama Warns against Rise of 'Crude Sort of Nationalism.'" *New York Times*, November 15, 2016. https://www.nytimes.com/2016/11/16/world/europe /obama-trump-nationalism-europe.html.

Harris, Richard L. *Marxism, Socialism, and Democracy in Latin America*. 1992. Reprint, London: Routledge, 2018.

Hartocollis, Anemona, and Eliza Fawcett. "The College Board Strips Down Its A.P. Curriculum for African American Studies." *New York Times*, February 9, 2023. https://www.nytimes.com/2023/02/01/us/college-board-advanced-placement-african-american-studies.html.

Haslanger, Sally. "Systemic and Structural Injustice: Is There a Difference?" *Philosophy* 98, no. 1 (2023): 1–27. https://doi.org/10.1017/S0031819122000353.

Hattenstone, Simon. "I Still Don't Believe Corbyn Is Antisemitic." *Guardian*, August 24, 2018. https://www.theguardian.com/commentisfree/2018/aug/24/jeremy-corbyn-antisemitism-labour-zionists-2013-speech.

Hauck, Uli. "Was Wagenknecht unterschlägt." *Tagesschau*, February 25, 2023. https://www.tagesschau.de/faktenfinder/wagenknecht-217.html.

Haury, Thomas. "Antisemitismus in Karl Marx' Frühschrift 'Zur Judenfrage'?" In *Der sich selbst entfremdete und wiedergefundene Marx*, edited by Helmut Lethen, Falko Schmieder, and Birte Löschenkohl, 161–176. Paderborn, Germany: Wilhelm Fink, 2010.

Hayes, Chris, and Amy Chua. "Debating the Concept of Political Tribalism with Amy Chua." *Think* (NBC News), June 12, 2018. https://www.nbcnews.com/think/opinion/debating-concept-political-tribalism-amy-chua-podcast-transcript-ncna882186.

Heather, David. *North Korean Posters*. Munich: Prestel, 2008.

Hegel, Georg Wilhelm Friedrich. *Grundlinien der Philosophie des Rechts*. 1820. Vol. 7 of *Hegel: Werke*. Frankfurt: Suhrkamp, 1970.

Heinze, Eric. "'But Israel Claims to Be a Democracy!'—Hypocrisy, Double Standards, and False Equivalences." In *Responses to 7 October: Universities*, edited by Rosa Freedman and David Hirsh, 26–33. London: Routledge, 2024.

Heinze, Eric. *The Concept of Injustice*. London: Routledge, 2013.

Heinze, Eric, ed. *Criminalising Hate Speech: A Comparative Study*. The Hague: Asser/Springer, 2024.

Heinze, Eric. "Democracy, Ontology, and the Limits of Deconstruction." In *Hate, Politics and Law: Critical Perspectives on Combating Hate*, edited by Thomas Brudholm and Birgitte Schepelern Johanssen, 94–112. New York: Oxford University Press, 2018.

Heinze, Eric. "Foundations of Sovereign Authority: The Example of Shakespearean Political Drama." In *Shakespeare and Authority*, edited by Katie Halsey and Angus Vine, 135–154. London: Palgrave Macmillan, 2018.

Heinze, Eric. *Hate Speech and Democratic Citizenship*. Oxford: Oxford University Press, 2016.

Heinze, Eric. "Karl Marx's Theory of Free Speech, Part 1." *Humanity Journal*, May 31, 2018. https://humanityjournal.org/blog/karl-marxs-theory-of-free-speech-part-1/.

Heinze, Eric. "Karl Marx's Theory of Free Speech, Part 2." *Humanity Journal*, June 1, 2018. https://humanityjournal.org/blog/karl-marxs-theory-of-free-speech-part-2/.

Heinze, Eric. *The Most Human Right: Why Free Speech Is Everything*. Cambridge, MA: MIT Press, 2022.

Heinze, Eric. "Selecting the Memory, Controlling the Myth: The Propaganda of Legal Foundations in Early Modern Drama." In *Injustice, Memory and Faith in Human Rights*, edited by Kalliopi Chainoglou, Barry Collins, Michael Phillips, and John Strawson, 57–75. New York: Routledge, 2018.

Heinze, Eric. "Self-Inculpatory Laws Exist." *Free Speech Debate*, December 17, 2019. https://freespeechdebate.com/2019/12/self-inculpatory-laws-exist/.

Heinze, Eric. "Sexual Orientation and International Law: A Study in the Manufacture of Cross-Cultural 'Sensitivity.'" *Michigan Journal of International Law* 22 (2001): 283–309.

Heinze, Eric. "Should Governments Butt Out of History?" *Free Speech Debate*, March 12, 2019. https://freespeechdebate.com/discuss/should-governments-butt-out-of-history/.

Heinze, Eric. "Theorising Law and Historical Memory: Denialism and the Pre-conditions of Human Rights." *Journal of Comparative Law* 13 (2018): 43–60. Reprinted in *Diritto penale contemporaneo* 4 (2019): 175–191.

Heinze, Eric. "Towards a General Theory of Law and Historical Discourse." In *Law and Memory: Towards Legal Governance of History*, edited by Uladzislau Belavusau and Aleksandra Gliszczyńska-Grabias, 413–433. Cambridge: Cambridge University Press, 2017.

Heinze, Eric. "Truth and Myth in Critical Race Theory and LatCrit: Human Rights and the Ethnocentrism of Anti-ethnocentrism." *National Black Law Journal* (Columbia University) 20 (2008): 107–162.

Heinze, Eric "Victimless Crimes." *Encyclopedia of Applied Ethics*. Vol. 4. 2nd ed. Edited by Ruth Chadwick, 471–482. San Diego: Academic Press, 2012.

Heinze, Eric. "What Is the Opposite of Injustice?" *Ratio Juris* 30, no. 3 (2017): 353–371.

Heinze, Eric. "When the Establishment No Longer Calls the Shots in Writing History." *New Lines*, May 27, 2022. https://newlinesmag.com/essays/when-the-establishment-no-longer-calls-the-shots-in-writing-history/.

Henley, Jon. "Slovakia's Pro-Russia Former PM Reaches Deal to Form Coalition Government." *Guardian*, October 11, 2023. https://www.theguardian.com/world/2023/oct/11/slovakia-pro-russia-former-pm-robert-fico-reaches-deal-to-form-coalition-government.

Heppell, Timothy. "The British Labour Party and the Antisemitism Crisis." *British Journal of Politics and International Relations* 23 (2021): 645–662.

Herf, Jeffrey. *Three Faces of Antisemitism: Right, Left and Islamist*. London: Routledge, 2024.

Heyman, Steven J. "Hate Speech, Public Discourse, and the First Amendment." In *Extreme Speech and Democracy*, edited by Ivan Hare and James Weinstein, 158–181. Oxford: Oxford University Press, 2009.

Hicklin, Aaron. "If Bernie Sanders Thinks Cuba Is Worth Defending, He Should Talk to Gay Dissidents." *Guardian*, February 27, 2020. https://www.theguardian.com/commentisfree/2020/feb/27/bernie-sanders-cuba-gay-dissidents.

Hirsh, David. *Contemporary Left Antisemitism*. London: Routledge, 2018.

Hirsh, David, ed. *The Rebirth of Antisemitism in the 21st Century*. London: Routledge, 2023.

Hitler, Adolf. *Mein Kampf*. Munich: Franz Eher, 1925.

Hoffman, Bruce. "Understanding Hamas's Genocidal Ideology." *Atlantic*, October 10, 2023. https://www.theatlantic.com/international/archive/2023/10/hamas-covenant-israel-attack-war-genocide/675602/.

Hoffman, Sharona. "The Importance of Immutability in Employment Discrimination Law." *William and Mary Law Review* 52 (2011): 1483–1546.

Hopkins, Valerie, and Ivan Nechepurenko. "As the Kremlin Revises History, a Human Rights Champion Becomes a Casualty." *New York Times*, December 31, 2021. https://www.nytimes.com/2021/12/29/world/europe/russia-memorial-human-rights-center.html.

Horkheimer, Max. *Traditionelle und kritische theorie*. 1937. 7th ed. Frankfurt: Suhrkamp, 1992.

Horkheimer, Max, and Theodor Adorno. *Dialektik der Aufklärung*. 1947. Reprint, Frankfurt: Fischer, 1971.

Horsley, Scott. "Obama at U.N.: Reject Tribalism Home and Abroad." NPR, September 20, 2016. https://www.npr.org/2016/09/20/494751020/obama-at-u-n-reject-tribalism-home-and-abroad.

"How the Conservative Party Got Diverse." *The Economist*, January 28, 2021. https://www.economist.com/britain/2021/01/28/how-the-conservative-party-got-diverse.

Hsi, Chu, and Lu Tsu-Ch'ien. *Reflections on Things at Hand* (*Chin-ssu lu*, twelfth century CE). Translated by Wing-tsit Chan. New York: Columbia University Press, 1967.

Human Rights Watch. "Russia: Arrests, Harassment of Ukraine War Dissidents." March 24, 2022. https://www.hrw.org/news/2022/03/24/russia-arrests-harassment-ukraine-war-dissidents.

Hunter, James Davison. *Culture Wars: The Struggle to Define America*. New York: Basic, 1991.

Hunter, Rosemary, Clare McGlynn, and Erika Rackley, eds. *Feminist Judgments: From Theory to Practice*. London: Bloomsbury, 2010.

Hunter, Ross. "Owen Jones Praises Humza Yousaf's Leadership on Israel-Gaza War." *National*, October 25, 2023. https://www.thenational.scot/news/23879479.owen-jones-praises-humza-yousafs-leadership-israel-gaza-war/.

Hutt, David. "Soul Searching for Hungary's Once 'Neo-Nazi' Jobbik Party." *Euronews*, April 12, 2022. https://www.euronews.com/2022/04/12/soul-searching-for-hungary-s-once-neo-nazi-jobbik-party.

Huttenbach, Henry R. Introduction to *Soviet Nationality Policies: Ruling Ethnic Groups in the USSR*, edited by Henry R. Huttenbach, 1–8. London: Mansell, 1990.

Huttenbach, Henry R., ed. *Soviet Nationality Policies: Ruling Ethnic Groups in the USSR*. London: Mansell, 1990.

Ignatow, Assen. *Zwischen "Selbstkritik" und neuer Hoffnung: Die marxistische Theorie-Debatte in Rußland*. Cologne, Germany: Bundesinstitut für Ostwissenschaftliche und Internationale Studien, 1996.

IHRA (International Holocaust Remembrance Alliance). "About the IHRA Non–Legally Binding Working Definition of Antisemitism." N.d. https://www.holocaustremembrance.com/resources /working-definitions-charters/working-definition-antisemitism (accessed August 1, 2024).

ILO (International Labour Organization). "The Gender Gap in Employment." *InfoStories*, December 2017, updated February 2022. https://www.ilo.org/infostories/en-GB/Stories/Employment /barriers-women#intro.

International Memorial. "What Is International Memorial?" N.d. https://www.memo.ru/en-us/ (accessed August 1, 2024).

Ireland, Sophie. "Economy Rankings: Largest Countries by GDP, 2023." *CEO World*, August 25, 2023. https://ceoworld.biz/2023/08/25/economy-rankings-largest-countries-by-gdp-2023/.

ISC (Intelligence and Security Committee of Parliament). *Russia* (HC 632). London: UK Parliament, July 21, 2020.

Jadva, V., A. Guasp, J. H. Bradlow, S. Bower-Brown, and S. Foley. "Predictors of Self-Harm and Suicide in LGBT Youth: The Role of Gender, Socio-Economic Status, Bullying and School Experience." *Journal of Public Health* 45, no. 1 (2023) 102–108. doi: 10.1093/pubmed/fdab383.

Jay, Martin. *The Dialectical Imagination: A History of the Frankfurt School and the Institute of Social Research, 1923–1950*. Berkeley: University of California Press, 1996.

Jay, Martin. *Splinters in Your Eye: Frankfurt School Provocations*. London: Version, 2020.

Jayakumar, Kirthi. "The Ladies in White." Gender Security Project, December 9, 2020. https:// www.gendersecurityproject.com/post/the-ladies-in-white.

"Jean-Luc Mélenchon dénonce un système capitaliste." *Le Monde*, February 14, 2022. https:// www.lemonde.fr/election-presidentielle-2022/article/2022/02/13/jean-luc-melenchon-denonce -un-systeme-capitaliste-parasitaire-qui-se-nourrit-des-desastres-qu-il-provoque_6113523 _6059010.html.

"Jean-Marie Le Pen définitivement condamné pour ses propos sur les chambres à gaz." *Le Monde*, March 27, 2018. https://www.lemonde.fr/police-justice/article/2018/03/27/jean-marie-le-pen -definitivement-condamne-pour-ses-propos-sur-les-chambres-a-gaz_5277072_1653578.html.

Jenne, Erin K., András Bozóki, and Péter Visnovitz. "2 Antisemitic Tropes, Fifth-Columnism, and 'Soros-Bashing.'" In *Enemies Within: The Global Politics of Fifth Columns*, edited by Harris Mylonas and Scott Radnitz, 45–72. Oxford: Oxford University Press, 2022.

"Jeremy Corbyn Is an Anti-Semite." *Telegraph*, December 5, 2019. https://www.telegraph.co.uk /opinion/2019/12/05/jeremy-corbyn-anti-semite/.

Johnson, Alan. *Mapping the New Left Antisemitism*. London: Routledge, 2023.

Jones, Bryn, and Mike O'Donnell. *Alternatives to Neo-liberalism*. Bristol, UK: Policy, 2017.

Jones, Melinda, and Lee Ann Basser Marks. "Law and the Social Construction of Disability." In *Disability, Divers-Ability and Legal Change*, edited by Melinda Jones and Lee Ann Basser Marks, 3–24. The Hague: Martinus Nijhoff, 1999.

Jones, Owen. "Antisemitism Has No Place on the Left." *Guardian*, August 26, 2015. https://www .theguardian.com/commentisfree/2015/aug/26/antisemitism-left-racism-israel.

Jones, Owen. "Israel Is Clear about Its Intentions in Gaza." *Guardian*, October 24, 2023. https:// www.theguardian.com/commentisfree/2023/oct/24/israel-gaza-world-leaders-un-genocide -palestinians.

Jones, Owen. "No Wonder Jeremy Corbyn's Rivals for the Labour Leadership Are Rattled." *Guardian*, July 8, 2015. https://www.theguardian.com/commentisfree/2015/jul/08/jeremy-corbyn -labour-leadership-humble-demonised-dinosaur-modern-message.

Jones, Owen. "Poverty Costs Lives—and the Left Should Not Be Afraid to Say It." *Guardian*, March 31, 2022. https://www.theguardian.com/commentisfree/2022/mar/31/poverty-uk-cost-of -living-rishi-sunak.

Jones, Owen. "Starvation May Prove to Be Israel's Deadliest Crime." *National*, March 30, 2024. https://www.thenational.scot/politics/24221431.owen-jones-starvation-may-prove-israels-dead liest-crime/.

Jones, Owen. "Tackling Racism on Social Media Is Just the Tip of the Iceberg." *Guardian*, July 29, 2020. https://www.theguardian.com/commentisfree/2020/jul/29/twitter-boycott-racism-social -media-wiley-newspapers.

Jones, Owen. *This Land: The Story of a Movement*. London: Penguin-Allen Lane, 2021.

Jones, Owen. "This Terrifying Backslide on LGBTQ Rights Is a Threat to Women's Rights Too." *Guardian*, July 5, 2022. https://www.theguardian.com/commentisfree/2022/jul/05/lgbtq -womens-rights-abortion-unite.

Jones, Owen. "Welcome to Topsy-Turvy Britain, Where It's Opponents of Israel's War Who Are the Extremist 'Mob.'" *Guardian*, February 29, 2024. https://www.theguardian.com/commentis free/2024/feb/29/britain-israel-war-palestinians-gaza.

Jones, Sarah. "Fake Feminists Fight the Equality Act." *Intelligencer*, March 19, 2021. https:// nymag.com/inteslligencer/2021/03/the-fake-feminists-fighting-the-equality-act.html.

Jones, Susan R. "Toward Inclusive Theory: Disability as Social Construction." *NASPA Journal* 33 (1996): 347–354.

Julliard, Jacques. *Les gauches françaises 1762–2012*. Paris: Flammarion, 2013.

Justitia Institute. *Global Handbook on Hate Speech Laws*. Report. Copenhagen: Justitia Institute, November 20, 2020. https://futurefreespeech.com/global-handbook-on-hate-speech-laws/#post -1391-Toc56591836.

JVL (Jewish Voice for Labour). "The EHRC Has Spoken—Labour Is No Place for Left Wing Jews." February 15, 2023. https://www.jewishvoiceforlabour.org.uk/statement/the-ehrc-has-spoken-labour-is-no-place-for-left-wing-jews/.

JVL (Jewish Voice for Labour). *How the EHRC Got It so Wrong: Antisemitism and the Labour Party*. London: Verso, 2021.

Kailitz, Steffen, ed. *Die Gegenwart der Vergangenheit: Der "Historikerstreit" und die deutsche Geschichtspolitik*. Wiesbaden, Germany: Verlag für Sozialwissenschaften, 2008.

Kant, Immanuel. *Grundlegung zur Metaphysik der Sitten*. 1785. Vol. 4 of *Gesammelte Schriften*. Berlin: Akademie Ausgabe, 1903.

Kanth, Rajani Kannepalli, ed. *The Challenge of Eurocentrism: Global Perspectives, Policy, and Prospects*. London: Palgrave, 2009.

Kaplan, Fred. "Where Realpolitik Went Wrong." *Slate*, November 21, 2022. https://slate.com/news-and-politics/2022/11/putin-mearsheimer-realpolitik-ukraine-political-science.html.

Karlsson, Klas-Göran, and Michael Schoenhals. *Crimes against Humanity under Communist Regimes*. Stockholm: Forum för Levande Historia, 2008.

Katerji, Oz. "How to Lose an Election on Foreign Policy." *Foreign Policy*, August 31, 2020. https://foreignpolicy.com/2020/08/31/election-foreign-policy-russia-corbyn-labour-skripal/.

Kelly, Sanja, Mai Truong, Adrian Shahbaz, Madeline Earp, and Jessica White. *Manipulating Social Media to Undermine Democracy*. Washington, DC: Freedom House, 2017.

Kenez, Peter. *A History of the Soviet Union from the Beginning to Its Legacy*. 3rd ed. Cambridge: Cambridge University Press, 2016.

Kennedy, Duncan. "Form and Substance in Private Law Adjudication." *Harvard Law Review* 88 (1976): 1685–1778.

Kennedy, Duncan. "The Structure of Blackstone's *Commentaries*." *Buffalo Law Review* 28 (1979): 211–382.

Khazan, Olga. "The Soviet-Era Strategy That Explains What Russia Is Doing with Snowden." *Atlantic*, August 2, 2013. https://www.theatlantic.com/international/archive/2013/08/the-soviet-era-strategy-that-explains-what-russia-is-doing-with-snowden/278314/.

Kim, Jieun. "30 North Korean 'Defector' Families Forced to Relocate to Hardscrabble Hinterland." Radio Free Asia, July 20, 2022. https://www.rfa.org/english/news/korea/forced-relocation-07202022182032.html.

King, Martin Luther, Jr. "Letter from a Birmingham Jail." 1963. University of Pennsylvania African Studies Center. https://www.africa.upenn.edu/Articles_Gen/Letter_Birmingham.html (accessed August 1, 2024).

Kipping, Katja, and Bernd Riexinger. "Zum Tod von Fidel Castro." *Die Linke*, November 26, 2016. https://www.die-linke.de/start/presse/detail/zum-tod-von-fidel-castro-1/.

Kirchick, James. "Fidel Castro's Horrific Record on Gay Rights." *Daily Beast*, November 27, 2016. https://www.thedailybeast.com/fidel-castros-horrific-record-on-gay-rights.

Kirk, D. A. "Why Noam Chomsky's Ukraine Comments Ruffled so Many Feathers." *Medium*, April 18, 2022. https://dakirk.medium.com/why-noam-chomskys-ukraine-comments-ruffled-so -many-feathers-4b80b02ccf8c.

Kirkby, Diane, and Catharine Coleborne, eds. *Law, History, Colonialism: The Reach of Empire*. Manchester, UK: Manchester University Press, 2009.

Klaff, Lesley. "Holocaust Inversion and Contemporary Antisemitism." *Fathom*, Winter 2014. https://fathomjournal.org/holocaust-inversion-and-contemporary-antisemitism/.

Klaff, Lesley. "The Intersection of Antisemitism and Misogyny." In *Misogyny as Hate Crime*, edited by Irene Zempi and Jo Smith, 155–177. London: Routledge, 2021.

Klein, Rebecca. "The Rightwing US Textbooks That Teach Slavery as 'Black Immigration.'" *Guardian*, August 12, 2021. https://www.theguardian.com/education/2021/aug/12/right-wing -textbooks-teach-slavery-black-immigration.

Klug, Sam. "'We Know Occupation': The Long History of Black Americans' Solidarity with Palestinians." *Politico*, May 30, 2021. https://www.politico.com/news/magazine/2021/05/30 /black-lives-matter-palestine-history-491234.

Københavns Universitet. "Ligestilling og diversitet." N.d. https://om.ku.dk/profil/mangfoldighed/ (accessed August 1, 2024).

Koposov, Nikolay. *Memory Laws, Memory Wars: The Politics of the Past in Europe and Russia*. Cambridge: Cambridge University Press, 2018.

Kozlov, Denis, and Eleonory Gilburd, eds. *The Thaw: Soviet Society and Culture during the 1950s and 1960s*. Toronto: University of Toronto Press, 2012.

Küchler, Stefan. "DDR-Geschichtsbilder." *Internationale Schulbuchforschung* 22 (2000): 31–48.

Kumar, Raksha. "How China Uses the News Media as a Weapon in Its Propaganda War against the West." Reuters Institute for the Study of Journalism, November 2, 2021. https://reutersinstitute .politics.ox.ac.uk/news/how-china-uses-news-media-weapon-its-propaganda-war-against-west.

Kuper, Richard. "A Reply to 'Labour and Antisemitism: A Crisis Misunderstood.'" *Political Quarterly* 9 (2020): 832–838.

Labour Party (UK). *The Forde Report*. London: Labour Party, 2022.

Labour Party (UK). "Publication of the Equality and Human Rights Commission (EHRC) Report into Allegations of Antisemitism in the Labour Party." October 29, 2020. https://labour.org.uk /wp-content/uploads/2020/10/Publication-of-the-Equality-and-Human-Rights-Commission -final.pdf.

La France insoumise. "La France insoumise condamne l'invasion militaire de l'Ukraine avec la plus grande fermeté." February 24, 2022. https://lafranceinsoumise.fr/2022/02/24/la-france -insoumise-condamne-linvasion-militaire-de-lukraine-avec-la-plus-grande-fermete/.

Lagoutte, Stéphanie, Thomas Gammeltoft-Hansen, and John Cerone. *Tracing the Roles of Soft Law in Human Rights*. Oxford: Oxford University Press, 2016.

Lakha, Shabbir. "Jeremy Corbyn Isn't Antisemitic." *Counterfire*, March 27, 2018. https://www.counterfire.org/article/jeremy-corbyn-the-left-and-antisemitism/.

Lang, Cady. "President Trump Has Attacked Critical Race Theory." *Time*, September 29, 2020. https://time.com/5891138/critical-race-theory-explained/.

Langton, Rae. "Speech Acts and Unspeakable Acts." *Philosophy and Public Affairs* 22 (1993): 305–330.

Lawrence, Charles R., III. "If He Hollers Let Him Go: Regulating Racist Speech on Campus." In *Words That Wound: Critical Race Theory, Assaultive Speech, and the First Amendment*, edited by Mari Matsuda, Charles Lawrence III, Richard Delgado, and Kimberlé Williams Crenshaw, 53–88. Boulder, CO: Westview Press, 1993.

Lebow, Richard Ned, Wulf Kansteiner, and Claudio Fogu, eds. *The Politics of Memory in Postwar Europe*. Durham, NC: Duke University Press, 2006.

Lefort, Claude. *L'invention démocratique*. Paris: Fayard, 1994.

Leggett, George. *The Cheka*. Oxford: Oxford University Press, 1987.

Lem, Pola. "'Comic' Chinese History Teaching 'Breeds Cynics and Opportunists.'" *Times Higher Education*, July 7, 2022. https://www.timeshighereducation.com/news/comic-chinese-history-teaching-breeds-cynics-and-opportunists.

Lenin, Vladimir. *Imperialism: The Highest Stage of Capitalism*. London: Penguin, 2010. Orig. pub. in Russian in 1917.

Lenin, Vladimir. "The Tasks of the Proletariat in Our Revolution." Translated by Isaacs Bernard. In *Lenin Collected Works*, vol. 24, 55–92. Moscow: Progress, 1964. Orig. pub. in Russian in 1917.

"Le petit-neveu de Brigitte Macron agressé à Amiens, le chef de l'Etat dénonce un acte 'inacceptable' et 'inqualifiable.'" *Le Monde*, May 17, 2023. https://www.lemonde.fr/societe/article/2023/05/16/le-petit-neveu-de-brigitte-macron-agresse-a-amiens-lors-d-une-casserolade-contre-la-reforme-des-retraites_6173593_3224.html.

Lerman, Antony. *Whatever Happened to Antisemitism?* London: Pluto, 2022.

Leroy, Benoît. "'Louis XVI, on t'a décapité, Macron, on peut recommencer': Un élu LFI crée un tollé." *Le point*, May 8, 2023. https://www.lepoint.fr/politique/louis-xvi-on-t-a-decapite-macron-on-peut-recommencer-un-elu-lfi-cree-un-tolle-08-05-2023-2519344_20.php#11.

Levinson, K. Riva. "Silence Is Complicity—Whether It's #BlackLivesMatter or #Zimbabwean LivesMatter." *The Hill*, December 8, 2020. https://thehill.com/opinion/international/511623-silence-is-complicity-whether-its-blacklivesmatter-or/.

Lévi-Strauss, Claude. *Race et histoire*. 1952. Reprint, Paris: Gallimard, 1987.

Lévi-Strauss, Claude. *Tristes tropiques*. Paris: Terre humaine, 1955.

Levy, Jack S., and William R. Thompson. *Causes of War*. Oxford: Wiley-Blackwell, 2010.

Liapin, Ilia. "Changes of History and Civics Curriculum and Textbooks in Russia in the Context of the War in Ukraine." *EuroClio*, March 28, 2023. https://euroclio.eu/2023/03/28/changes -of-history-and-civics-curriculum-and-textbook-in-russia-in-the-context-of-the-war-in-ukraine/.

"Linkenabgeordnete teilen nach 'Krieg gegen Russland'-Tweet gegen Wagenknecht aus." *Spiegel Politik*, August 2, 2022. https://www.spiegel.de/politik/deutschland/die-linke-sahra-wagenknecht -empoert-mit-ukraine-russland-tweet-fraktion-distanziert-sich-a-ba4cb5cf-9abf-4b66-baf2 -410d7af6115b.

Litzinger, Ralph, and Yanping Ni. "Inside the Wuhan Cabin Hospital: Contending Narratives during the COVID-19 Pandemic." *China Information* 35 (2021): 346–365.

Locke, John. *Second Treatise of Civil Government*. 1689. In *Two Treatises of Government*, edited by Mark Goldie, 1–120. Oxford: Oxford University Press, 2016.

Lockheed Martin Corporation. "Global Diversity and Inclusion." N.d. https://www.lockheed martin.com/en-us/who-we-are/global-diversity-inclusion.html (accessed August 1, 2024).

Loomba, Ania. *Colonialism/Postcolonialism*. 3rd ed. Abingdon, UK: Routledge, 2015.

Lopez, Brian. "State Education Board Members Push Back on Proposal to Use 'Involuntary Reloca- tion' to Describe Slavery." *Texas Tribune*, June 30, 2022. https://www.texastribune.org/2022/06/30 /texas-slavery-involuntary-relocation/.

Losavio, Joseph. "What Racism Costs Us All." International Monetary Fund, September 2020. https://www.imf.org/en/Publications/fandd/issues/2020/09/the-economic-cost-of-racism-losavio.

Lufthansa Group. "Mit Vielfalt die Zukunft gestalten." N.d. https://www.lufthansagroup.com /de/verantwortung/soziale-verantwortung/vielfalt-und-chancengleichheit.html (accessed August 1, 2024).

Lumsden, Ian. *Machos, Maricones & Gays: Cuba and Homosexuality*. Philadelphia: Temple Uni- versity Press, 1996.

Luxemburg, Rosa. *Sozialreform oder Revolution?* 1899. In *Gesammelte Werke*, vol. 1, 367–466. Berlin: Dietz, 1982.

Lynch, Suzanne. "Orbán Faces Danger from New Enemy Brandishing a Leaked Tape." *Politico*, March 26, 2024. https://www.politico.eu/article/viktor-orban-peter-magyar-judit-varga-new -headache-leaked-tape/.

Lynskey, Angela Cartwright. "Countering the Dominant Narrative: In Defense of Critical Course- work." *Educational Foundations* 28 (2015): 73–86.

Machiavelli, Niccolò. *The Prince*. Translated by Peter Bondanella and Mark Musa. 1979. Reprint, Oxford: Oxford University Press, 1984.

Machiavelli, Niccolò. *Il principe*. 1532. Edited by Giorgio Inglese. Turin: Einaudi, 1995.

Malik, Nesrine. "The Colston Four's Critics Are Deluded to Think Britain Owes No Apology for Its Past." *Guardian*, January 10, 2022. https://www.theguardian.com/commentisfree/2022/jan/10 /colston-four-britain-apology-for-past.

"Marche contre l'antisémitisme: Plus de 182 000 personnes ont défilé en France, dont 105 000 à Paris." *Le Monde*, November 13, 2023.

Martin, Terry. "The Origins of Soviet Ethnic Cleansing." *Journal of Modern History* 70 (1998): 813–861.

Marx, Karl. "Bemerkungen über die neueste preußische Zensurinstruktion." 1843. In *Karl Marx— Friedrich Engels: Werke*, vol. 1, edited by Institut für Marxismus-Leninismus beim Zentralkomitee der Sozialistischen Einheitspartei Deutschlands, 3–25. Berlin: Dietz, 1956.

Marx, Karl. *Das Kapital.* Books 1–3. 1867, 1886, 1894. Vols. 23–25 of *Karl Marx—Friedrich Engels: Werke*, edited by Institut für Marxismus-Leninismus beim Zentralkomitee der Sozialistischen Einheitspartei Deutschlands. Berlin: Dietz, 1962–1964.

Marx, Karl. "Kritik des Gothaer Programms." 1875. In *Karl Marx—Friedrich Engels: Werke*, vol. 19, edited by Institut für Marxismus-Leninismus beim Zentralkomitee der Sozialistischen Einheitspartei Deutschlands, 11–34. Berlin: Dietz, 1962.

Marx, Karl. "Thesen über Feuerbach." 1845. In *Karl Marx—Friedrich Engels: Werke*, vol. 3, edited by Institut für Marxismus-Leninismus beim Zentralkomitee der Sozialistischen Einheitspartei Deutschlands, 5–7. Berlin: Deitz, 1958.

Marx, Karl. "Das Verbot der 'Leipziger Allgemeinen Zeitung.'" 1843. In *Karl Marx—Friedrich Engels: Werke*, vol. 1, edited by Institut für Marxismus-Leninismus beim Zentralkomitee der Sozialistischen Einheitspartei Deutschlands, 152–171. Berlin: Dietz, 1956.

Marx, Karl. "Die Verhandlungen des 6. rheinischen Landtags [Debatten über Preßfreiheit]." 1842. In *Karl Marx—Friedrich Engels: Werke*, vol. 1, edited by Institut für Marxismus-Leninismus beim Zentralkomitee der Sozialistischen Einheitspartei Deutschlands, 28–88. Berlin: Dietz, 1956.

Marx, Karl. "Zur Judenfrage." In *Karl Marx—Friedrich Engels: Werke*, vol. 1, edited by Institut für Marxismus-Leninismus beim Zentralkomitee der Sozialistischen Einheitspartei Deutschlands, 347–377. Berlin: Dietz, 1956.

Marx, Karl, and Friedrich Engels. *Die Deutsche Ideologie.* 1846. In *Karl Marx—Friedrich Engels: Werke*, vol. 3, edited by Institut für Marxismus-Leninismus beim Zentralkomitee der Sozialistischen Einheitspartei Deutschlands, 9–530. Berlin: Dietz, 1958.

Marx, Karl, and Friedrich Engels. *Manifest der Kommunistischen Partei.* 1848. In *Karl Marx— Friedrich Engels: Werke*, vol. 4, edited by Institut für Marxismus-Leninismus beim Zentralkomitee der Sozialistischen Einheitspartei Deutschlands, 459–493. Berlin: Dietz, 1959.

Mason, Corinne L., ed. *Routledge Handbook of Queer Development Studies.* London: Routledge, 2018.

Mason, Patrick L. *The Economics of Structural Racism.* Cambridge: Cambridge University Press, 2023.

Mason, Rowena. "Corbyn's Offer of Peerage to Shami Chakrabarti Causes Labour Tensions." *Guardian*, August 4, 2016. https://www.theguardian.com/uk-news/2016/aug/04/shami -chakrabarti-peerage-labour-tensions-corbyn.

Mason, Rowena. "Jeremy Corbyn Says Antisemitism Claims 'Ludicrous and Wrong.'" *Guardian*, August 18, 2015. https://www.theguardian.com/politics/2015/aug/18/jeremy-corbyn-antisemitism -claims-ludicrous-and-wrong.

Mathoux, Hadrien. "La France insoumise accusée d'antisémitisme." *Marianne*, August 5, 2022. https://www.marianne.net/politique/melenchon/la-france-insoumise-accusee-dantisemitisme -entre-faux-proces-et-vrais-problemes.

Matsuda, Mari. "Public Response to Racist Speech: Considering the Victim's Story." *Michigan Law Review* 87 (1989): 2320–2381. Reprinted in *Words That Wound: Critical Race Theory, Assaultive Speech, and the First Amendment*, edited by Mari Matsuda, Charles Lawrence III, Richard Delgado, and Kimberlé Williams Crenshaw, 17–51. Boulder, CO: Westview Press, 1993.

Matsuda, Mari, Charles Lawrence III, Richard Delgado, and Kimberlé Williams Crenshaw, eds. *Words That Wound: Critical Race Theory, Assaultive Speech, and the First Amendment*. Boulder, CO: Westview Press, 1993.

McGill University. "Equity, Diversity & Inclusion." N.d. https://www.mcgill.ca/studentservices /equity-diversity-inclusion (accessed August 1, 2024).

McGlynn, Jade. *Memory Makers: The Politics of the Past in Putin's Russia*. London: Bloomsbury, 2023.

McKeown, Maeve. *With Power Comes Responsibility: The Politics of Structural Injustice*. London: Bloomsbury Academic, 2024.

McWhorter, John. *Woke Racism: How a New Religion Has Betrayed Black America*. New York: Portfolio-Penguin, 2021.

Mehta, Uday Singh. *Liberalism and Empire*. 2nd ed. Chicago: University of Chicago Press, 1999.

Memmi, Albert. *Portrait du colonisé / Portrait du colonisateur*. Paris: Gallimard, 2002.

Merrick, Rob. "Schools Minister Rejects Lessons about Colonialism and Slave Trade in Case They 'Lower Standards.'" *Independent*, February 25, 2021. https://www.independent.co.uk/news/uk /politics/school-compulsory-lessons-colony-slave-trade-b1807571.html.

Mervosh, Sarah. "DeSantis Faces Swell of Criticism over Florida's New Standards for Black History." *New York Times*, July 21, 2023. https://www.nytimes.com/2023/07/21/us/desantis-florida -black-history-standards.html.

Mestre, Abel. "'Détail de l'histoire': Marine Le Pen en 'désaccord profond' avec son père." *Le Monde*, April 3, 2015, updated August 19, 2019. https://www.lemonde.fr/politique/article/2015/04/03 /detail-de-l-histoire-marine-le-pen-en-desaccord-profond-avec-son-pere_4609050_823448.html.

Meyer, Theodoric, Maggie Severns, and Meridith McGraw. "'The Tea Party to the 10th Power': Trumpworld Bets Big on Critical Race Theory." *Politico*, June 23, 2021. https://www.politico.com /news/2021/06/23/trumpworld-critical-race-theory-495712.

Millet, Kate. *Sexual Politics*. 1969. Reprint, Urbana: University of Illinois Press, 2000.

Milligan, Becky. "Naz Shah: My Words Were Anti-Semitic." BBC, July 18, 2016. https://www
.bbc.co.uk/news/uk-england-leeds-36802075.

Minkenberg, Michael, and Zsuzsanna Végh. *Depleting Democracies: Radical Right Impact on Parties, Policies, and Polities in Eastern Europe*. Manchester, UK: Manchester University Press, 2023.

Miroff, Nick. "In Raul Castro's Cuba, a Limit on New Freedoms." NPR, April 30, 2010. https://www.npr.org/2010/04/30/126415318/in-raul-castros-cuba-a-limit-on-new-freedoms.

Mohamed Ali, Amira, Dietmar Bartsch, and Jan Korte. "Keine Geschichtsrelativierung und Instrumentalisierung von NS-Vergangenheit und Stalinismus." DIE LINKE Bundestagsfraktion, November 30, 2022. https://www.linksfraktion.de/themen/nachrichten/detail/keine-geschichtsrelativierung-und-instrumentalisierung-von-ns-vergangenheit-und-stalinismus/.

Mohanty, Chandra Talpade, Ann Russo, and Lourdes Torres, eds. *Third World Women and the Politics of Feminism*. Bloomington: Indiana University Press, 1991.

Moran, Leslie. *The Homosexual(ity) of Law*. London: Routledge, 1996.

Morgan, Ted. *Reds: McCarthyism in Twentieth-Century America*. New York: Random House, 2003.

Morin, Edgar. *Autocritique*. 1959. Reprint, Paris: Seuil, 1994.

Morin, Edgar. *Pour et contre Marx*. Paris: Flammarion, 2012.

Morreira, Shannon, Kathy Luckett, Siseko H. Kumalo, and Manjeet Ramgotra, eds. *Decolonising Curricula and Pedagogy in Higher Education: Bringing Decolonial Theory into Contact with Teaching Practice*. Abingdon, UK: Routledge, 2021.

"Mort de Fidel Castro: L'hommage de Jean-Luc Mélenchon rassemble 200 personnes à Paris." *BFMTV*, November 26, 2016. https://www.bfmtv.com/politique/mort-de-fidel-castro-l-hommage-de-jean-luc-melenchon-rassemble-200-personnes-a-paris_AV-201611260034.html.

Motyl, Alexander J. "America's Leading 'Realist' Keeps Getting Russia Wrong." *The Hill*, July 4, 2023. https://thehill.com/opinion/international/4079666-americas-leading-realist-keeps-getting-russia-wrong/.

Mouffe, Chantal, and Inigo Errejon. *Construire un peuple*. Paris: Éditions du Cerf, 2017.

Muriuki, Winnie. "Burger King Net Worth 2023." *Wealthy Persons*, February 2, 2022. https://www.wealthypersons.com/burger-king-net-worth-2020-2021/.

Murphy, Michael, and Elizabeth Ribarsky, eds. *Activities for Teaching Gender and Sexuality in the University Classroom*. Plymouth, UK: Rowman & Littlefield, 2013.

Murray, Douglas. "The Sly Dishonesty of Owen Jones." *UnHerd*, October 2, 2020. https://unherd.com/2020/10/oh-dear-jeremy-corbyn/.

Myers, Steven Lee. "China Spins Tale That the U.S. Army Started the Coronavirus Epidemic." *New York Times*, July 7, 2021. https://www.nytimes.com/2020/03/13/world/asia/coronavirus-china-conspiracy-theory.html.

Nassar, Maha. "'From the River to the Sea': Palestinian Historian on the Meaning and Intent of Scrutinized Slogan." *Salon*, November 16, 2023. https://www.salon.com/2023/11/16/from-the-river-to-the-sea-palestinian-historian-on-the-meaning-and-intent-of-scrutinized-slogan_partner/.

Natanson, Hannah. "Fairfax Schools Adopt Updated Guidelines to Protect Transgender Students at Meeting That Drew Dueling Protests." *Washington Post*, July 16, 2021. https://www.washingtonpost.com/local/education/fairfax-schools-transgender-protections/2021/07/16/d2b6c59a-e656-11eb-8aa5-5662858b696e_story.html.

"Nato-opinionen: Rekordstor svängning mellan 2021 och 2022." Göteborgs Universitet, March 7, 2024. https://www.gu.se/nyheter/nato-opinionen-rekordstor-svangning-mellan-2021-och-2022.

"Nearly 90% of Ukrainians Oppose Territorial Concessions to Russia." Reuters, September 15, 2022. https://www.reuters.com/world/europe/nearly-90-ukrainians-oppose-territorial-concessions-russia-poll-2022-09-15/.

Nechepurenko, Ivan, and Nyree Abrahamian. "Refugees Flee to Armenia as Breakaway Enclave Comes under Azerbaijan's Control." *New York Times*, October 2, 2023. https://www.nytimes.com/2023/09/24/world/europe/armenians-nagorno-karabakh-azerbaijan.html.

Neiman, Susan. *Left Is Not Woke*. Cambridge: Polity, 2023.

Nelken, David, and Michael Levi. "Sir Philip Green and the Unacceptable Face of Capitalism." *King's Law Journal* 29 (2018): 36–57.

Nelson, Cary. *Israel Denial: Anti-Zionism, Anti-Semitism, & the Faculty Campaign against the Jewish State*. Bloomington: Indiana University Press, 2019.

Nickel, James W. "Indivisibility and Linkage Arguments: A Reply to Gilabert." *Human Rights Quarterly* 32, no. 2 (2009–2010): 439–446.

Nickel, James W. "Rethinking Indivisibility: Towards a Theory of Supporting Relations between Human Rights." *Human Rights Quarterly* 30, no. 4 (2008): 984–1001.

Niculescu, Luca. "Russia's War in Eastern Europe Is a Central Threat to the International Architecture." Robert Schuman Foundation, June 7, 2022. https://www.robert-schuman.eu/en/european-interviews/0115-russia-%20s-war-in-eastern-europe-is-a-central-threat-to-the-international-architecture.

Nkrumah, Kwame. *Neo-colonialism: The Last Stage of Imperialism*. New York: International, 1965.

Noack, Thorsten. *NS-Euthanasie und internationale Öffentlichkeit*. Frankfurt: Campus, 2017.

Nobel Foundation. "The Nobel Peace Prize 2022." October 7, 2022. https://www.nobelprize.org/prizes/peace/2022/press-release/.

Nordmarken, Sonny. "Microaggressions." *Transgender Studies Quarterly* 1 (2014): 129–134.

Obejas, Achy. "We Came All the Way from Cuba so You Could Dress Like This?" In *The Cuba Reader: History, Culture, Politics*, 2nd ed., edited by Aviva Chomsky, Barry Carr, and Pamela Maria Smorkaloff, 568–580. Durham, NC: Duke University Press, 2019.

OIC (Organisation of Islamic Cooperation). "OIC Strongly Rejects HRC Resolution on Sexual Orientation and Gender Identity." July 2, 2016. https://www.oic-oci.org/topic/?t_id =11338&ref=4456&lan=en.

Oliver, Christian. "The Cap versus the Pumpkin: Bulgaria's Mafia State Reaches Breaking Point." *Politico*, May 17, 2023. https://www.politico.eu/article/the-cap-versus-the-pumpkin-bulgarias -mafia-state-reaches-breaking-point/.

Orvos-Tóth, Noémi. *Egy nárcisztikus hálójában—Felépülés egy érzelmileg bántalmazó kapcsolatból.* Budapest: HVG Könyvek, 2018.

Orvos-Tóth, Noémi. *Örökölt sors—Családi sebek és a gyógyulás útjai.* Budapest: Kulcslyuk, 2018.

Osborne, Samuel. "Adjoa Andoh's 'Terribly White' Coronation Remark Becomes Most Complained about Moment of 2023." *Sky News,* May 10, 2023. https://news.sky.com/story/adjoa -andohs-terribly-white-coronation-remark-becomes-most-complained-about-moment-of-2023 -ofcom-says-12877889.

Pacepa, Ion. "Russian Footprints." *National Review*, August 24, 2006. https://www.nationalreview .com/2006/08/russian-footprints-ion-mihai-pacepa/.

Paine, Thomas. *Rights of Man, Common Sense, and Other Political Writings.* Edited by Mark Philp. Oxford: Oxford University Press, 1995.

Pamment, James. "How the Kremlin Circumvented EU Sanctions on Russian State Media in the First Weeks of the Illegal Invasion of Ukraine." *Place Branding and Public Diplomacy* 19 (2023): 200–205.

Papkova, Irina. *The Orthodox Church and Russian Politics.* New York: Oxford University Press, 2011.

Partei DIE LINKE. "Stoppt die Eskalation!" N.d. https://www.die-linke.de/themen/frieden /ukraine-krieg/ (accessed August 1, 2024).

Paxton, David. "The Political Contortions of Owen Jones." *New European*, August 10, 2018. https://www.theneweuropean.co.uk/brexit-news-political-contortions-owen-jones-jeremy -corbyn-s-fan-labour-guardian-30226/.

PEN America. PEN America Index of School Book Bans—2021–2022. N.d. https://pen.org /banned-book-list-2021-2022/ (accessed August 1, 2024).

Philo, Greg, Mike Berry, Justin Schlosberg, Antony Lerman, and David Miller. *Bad News for Labour: Antisemitism, the Party and Public Belief.* London: Pluto Press, 2019.

Plato. *Gorgias.* Translated by Donald J. Zeyl. In *Complete Works*, edited by John M. Cooper, 791– 869. Indianapolis, IN: Hackett, 1997.

Plato. *Republic.* Translated by G. M. A. Grube. In *Complete Works*, edited by John M. Cooper, 971–1223. Indianapolis, IN: Hackett, 1997.

Plocker, Anat. *The Expulsion of Jews from Communist Poland.* Bloomington: Indiana University Press, 2022.

Pogany, Stephen I. "Through the Looking Glass: The Subversion of Democracy, Human Rights and the Rule of Law in Hungary." In *Public Law in a Troubled Era*, edited by Katarzyna Gromek-Broc, 33–44. Alphen aan den Rijn, Netherlands: Wolters Kluwer, 2023.

Pogrund, Gabriel, and Patrick Maguire. *Left Out: The Inside Story of Labour under Corbyn*. London: Bodley Head, 2020.

Polite, Adira. "The Dangerous Miseducation of Americans through Eurocentric Curricula." *Bowdoin Orient*, February 11, 2016. http://bowdoinorient.com/bonus/article/10888/.

"Poll: Backing for NATO Remains High in Finland." Yle, December 21, 2023. https://yle.fi/a/74-20066206.

"Poll: 85% of Ukrainians Believe Victory in War with Russia Requires Liberating All Territories, Including Crimea and Donbas." *Kyiv Independent*, February 1, 2023. https://kyivindependent.com/news-feed/poll-85-of-ukrainians-believe-victory-in-war-with-russia-requires-liberating-all-territories-including-crimea-and-donbas.

Poltorak, David, and Viatcheslav Leshchiner. "Teaching the Holocaust in Russia." *Internationale Schulbuchforschung* 22 (2000): 127–134.

Pomerantsev, Peter. *Nothing Is True and Everything Is Possible: The Surreal Heart of the New Russia*. New York: Public Affairs, 2014.

Popper, Karl. *The Open Society and Its Enemies*. Vols. 1 and 2. 1945. Reprint, London: Routledge, 2002.

Post, Robert. "Hate Speech." In *Extreme Speech and Democracy*, edited by Ivan Hare and James Weinstein, 123–138. Oxford: Oxford University Press, 2009.

Post, Robert. "Participatory Democracy and Free Speech." *Virginia Law Review* 97, no. 3 (2011): 477–490.

Post, Robert. "Participatory Democracy and Free Speech: A Reply." *Virginia Law Review* 97, no. 3 (2011): 617–632.

Power, Lis. "Fox News' Obsession with Critical Race Theory." Media Matters for America, June 5, 2021. https://www.mediamatters.org/fox-news/fox-news-obsession-critical-race-theory-numbers.

Prakash, Gyan. "After Colonialism." In *After Colonialism: Imperial Histories and Postcolonial Displacements*, edited by Gyan Prakash, 1–23. Princeton, NJ: Princeton University Press, 1995.

Pugliatti, Paula. *Shakespeare the Historian*. Basingstoke, UK: Palgrave Macmillan, 1996.

Pulice-Farrow, Louis Lex, and Kirsten A. Gonzalez. "'Wait, What Is That? A Man or Woman or What?' Trans Microaggressions from Gynecological Healthcare Providers." *Sexuality Research and Social Policy* 19 (2022): 1549–1560.

Race and Ethnicity in Britain. London: Ipsos MORI, 2020. https://www.ipsos.com/en-uk/attitudes-race-and-inequality-great-britain.

Rackin, Phyllis. *Stages of History: Shakespeare's English Chronicles*. Ithaca, NY: Cornell University Press, 1990.

Rancière, Jacques. *Au bords de la politique*. Paris: Gallimard, 1998.

Rancière, Jacques. *La haine de la démocratie*. Paris: La Fabrique, 2005.

Rancière, Jacques. *La méthode de l'égalité*. Montrouge, France: Bayard Culture, 2012.

Randall, Margaret. "Women in the Swamps." In *The Cuba Reader: History, Culture, Politics*, 2nd ed., edited by Aviva Chomsky, Barry Carr, and Pamela Maria Smorkaloff, 363–369. Durham, NC: Duke University Press, 2019.

Rawls, John. *Political Liberalism*. 1993. Rev. ed. New York: Columbia University Press, 1996.

Rawls, John. *A Theory of Justice*. 1971. 2nd ed. Oxford: Oxford University Press, 1999.

Ray, Rashawn, and Alexandra Gibbons. "Why Are States Banning Critical Race Theory?" Brookings Institution, November 2021. https://www.brookings.edu/articles/why-are-states-banning
-critical-race-theory/.

Rehbein, Boike. *Critical Theory after the Rise of the Global South: Kaleidoscopic Dialectic*. Translated by Michael Kinville. Abingdon, UK: Routlede, 2015.

Reichel, Peter. *Vergangenheitsbewältigung in Deutschland*. 2nd ed. Munich: Beck, 2007.

Reimer, Max. "Winterhilfswerk." Ca. 1938. Lebendiges Museum Online, n.d. https://www.dhm
.de/lemo/bestand/objekt/plakat-des-winterhilswerkes-um-1938.html (accessed August 1, 2024).

"A Resident of Wuhan, China." NBC News, February 4, 2020. https://www.nbcnews.com/video
/wuhan-resident-films-inside-coronavirus-hospital-later-confronted-by-police-78092357644.

"Résultats de l'élection présidentielle 2017." Ministère de l'Interieur, France, n.d. https://www
.interieur.gouv.fr/Elections/Les-resultats/Presidentielles/elecresult__presidentielle-2017/(path)
/presidentielle-2017/FE.html (accessed August 1, 2024).

"Résultats de l'élection présidentielle 2022." Ministère de l'Interieur, France, n.d. https://www
.interieur.gouv.fr/Elections/Les-resultats/Presidentielles/elecresult__presidentielle-2022/(path)
/presidentielle-2022/index.html (accessed August 1, 2024).

Rice, Stephen, and Michael White, eds. *Race, Ethnicity, and Policing: New and Essentialist Readings*. New York: New York University Press, 2010.

Rich, Adrienne. "When We Dead Awaken: Writing as Re-Vision." *College English* 34 (1971): 18–30.

Rich, Dave. *The Left's Jewish Problem: Jeremy Corbyn, Israel and Anti-Semitism*. London: Biteback, 2016.

Robinson, Nathan J. "Noam Chomsky on How to Prevent World War III." *Current Affairs*, April 13, 2022. https://www.currentaffairs.org/2022/04/noam-chomsky-on-how-to-prevent-world-war-iii.

Robinson, Nathan J. "The Right Loves Free Speech—Unless They Disagree with What You Say." *Current Affairs*, April 25, 2022.

Rohrßen, Benedikt. *Von der "Anreizung zum Klassenkampf" zur "Volksverhetzung."* Berlin: De Gruyter, 2009.

Rone, Julia. "'Enemies of the People'? Diverging Discourses on Sovereignty in Media Coverage of Brexit." *British Politics* 18 (2023): 519–537.

Rousseau, Jean-Jacques. *Discours sur l'origine et les fondements de l'inégalité parmi les hommes.* 1755. In *Oeuvres complètes*, vol. 3, edited by Berrnard Gagnebin and Marcel Raymond, 109–223. Paris: Gallimard, 1964.

Rousseau, Jean-Jacques. *Du contrat social.* 1762. In *Oeuvres complètes*, vol. 3, edited by Berrnard Gagnebin and Marcel Raymond, 347–470. Paris: Gallimard, 1964.

Royer, Solenn de. "Marche contre l'antisémitisme: Les leçons politiques d'une manifestation apolitique." *Le Monde*, November 13, 2023. https://www.lemonde.fr/politique/article/2023/11/13/marches-contre-l-antisemitisme-l-absence-d-emmanuel-macron-n-a-pas-ete-comprise-notamment-en-macronie-ou-certains-evoquent-une-occasion-manquee_6199810_823448.html.

Russell, Bertrand. *The Practice and Theory of Bolshevism.* London: Allen & Unwin, 1920.

Rÿser, Rudolph C. "The 'Blue Water Rule' and the Self-Determination of Nations." Center for World Indigenous Studies, October 3, 2017. https://www.cwis.org/2017/10/the-blue-water-rule-and-the-selft-determination-of-nations/.

Said, Edward W. *Orientalism.* 1978. Reprint, London: Penguin, 2003.

Samuels, Ben. "Cornel West." *Haaretz*, March 14, 2021. https://www.haaretz.com/us-news/2021-03-14/ty-article/.highlight/cornel-west-explains-why-hes-convinced-his-views-on-israel-led-him-out-of-harvard/0000017f-f51d-ddde-abff-fd7d9d880000.

Samuels, Robert, and Toluse Olorunnipa. *His Name Is George Floyd: One Man's Life and the Struggle for Racial Justice.* New York: Bantam, 2022.

Sartre, Jean-Paul. *L'existentialisme est un humanisme.* 1945. Reprint, Paris: Gallimard, 1996.

Sartre, Jean-Paul. Preface to Frantz Fanon, *Les damnés de la terre* (1961), 37–61. Reprint, Paris: La Découverte, 2004.

Sartre, Jean-Paul. *Réflexions sur la question juive.* 1954. Reprint, Paris: Gallimard, 2004.

Schia, Niels Nagelhus, and Lars Gjesvik. "Hacking Democracy: Managing Influence Campaigns and Disinformation in the Digital Age." *Journal of Cyber Policy* 5 (2020): 413–428.

Schmitt, Carl. *Der Begriff des Politischen.* 1932. 6th ed. Berlin: Duncker & Humblot, 1996.

Schmitz, David F. *Thank God They're on Our Side: The United States and Right-Wing Dictatorships, 1921–1965.* Chapel Hill: University of North Carolina Press, 1999.

Schmitz, David F. *The United States and Right-Wing Dictatorships, 1965–1989.* New York: Cambridge University Press, 2006.

Schmitz, Rob. "Worries Grow in Hong Kong as China Pushes Its Official Version of History in Schools." NPR, December 11, 2017. https://www.npr.org/sections/parallels/2017/12/11/566909240/worries-grow-in-hong-kong-as-china-pushes-its-official-version-of-history-in-sch.

Schulze, Rainer. "Hitler and Zionism: Why the Haavara Agreement Does Not Mean the Nazis Were Zionists." *Independent*, May 3, 2016. https://www.independent.co.uk/news/world/world

-history/adolf-hitler-zionism-zionist-nazis-haavara-agreement-ken-livingstone-labour-antisemitism
-row-a7009981.html.

Schwandt, Michael. *Kritische Theorie: Eine Einführung*. 4th ed. Stuttgart: Schmetterling, 2010.

Seib, Philip. *Information at War: Journalism, Disinformation, and Modern Warfare*. Cambridge: Polity, 2021.

Serafin, Nicholas. "In Defense of Immutability." *Boston University Law Review*, no. 2 (2020): 275–331.

Seymour, David. "Continuity and Discontinuity: From Antisemitism to Antizionism and the Reconfiguration of the Jewish Question." *Journal of Contemporary Antisemitism* 2 (2019): 11–24.

Seymour, Richard. *Corbyn: The Strange Rebirth of Radical Politics*. 2nd ed. London: Verso, 2017.

Shakespeare, William. *Antony and Cleopatra*. Ca. 1607. Edited by Michael Neill. Oxford: Oxford University Press, 1994.

Shakespeare, William. *Henry V*. Ca. 1599. Edited by Gary Taylor. Oxford: Oxford University Press, 1982.

Shakespeare, William. *Richard III*. Ca. 1592. Edited by John Jowett. Oxford: Oxford University Press, 2000.

The Shami Chakrabarti Report. June 30, 2016. https://labour.org.uk/wp-content/uploads/2017/10/Chakrabarti-Inquiry-Report-30June16.pdf.

Siddique, Haroon. "Who Has the Labour Party Suspended in Recent Years?" *Guardian*, July 6, 2021. https://www.theguardian.com/politics/2021/jul/06/who-has-the-labour-party-suspended-in-recent-years.

Sloin, Andrew. "Theorizing Soviet Antisemitism." *Critical Historical Studies* 3 (2016): 249–281.

Smith, Elliot. "Russia, Expansion and Western Relations in the Spotlight as Leaders Gather for Pivotal BRICS Summit." CNBC, August 22, 2023. https://www.cnbc.com/2023/08/22/expansion-russia-and-the-west-in-spotlight-as-brics-leaders-gather.html.

Smith, Evan, and Matthew Worley, eds. *Against the Grain: The British Far Left from 1956*. Manchester, UK: Manchester University Press, 2014.

Smith, Evan, and Matthew Worley, eds. *Waiting for the Revolution: The British Far Left from 1956*. Manchester, UK: Manchester University Press, 2017.

Snyder, Timothy. *Bloodlands: Europe between Hitler and Stalin*. New York: Vintage, 2011.

Solochek, Jeffrey S. "Pinellas Schools Remove Book by Prize-Winning Author Toni Morrison." *Tampa Bay Times*, January 25, 2023.

Solomon, Marlon. "I Watched Owen Jones Watch the Hamas Massacre Video." *Medium*, December 2, 2023. https://marlonsolomon.medium.com/i-watched-owen-jones-watch-the-hamas-massacre-video-my-response-7cdb3e19b105.

Solzhenitsyn, Alexandr. *One Day in the Life of Ivan Denisovich.* Translated by H. T. Willetts. New York: Farrar, Straus and Giroux, 2005. Orig. pub. in Russian in 1962.

Sommer, Helin Evrim. "Offizielle Anerkennung des Völkermords in Namibia kann nur der Anfang eines Versöhnungsprozesses sein." DIE LINKE Bundestagsfraktion, May 28, 2021. https://www.linksfraktion.de/presse/pressemitteilungen/detail/offizielle-anerkennung-des-voelkermords-in-namibia-kann-nur-der-anfang-eines-versoehnungsprozesses-sei/.

Sorbonne Université. "La mission Lutte contre le racisme, l'antisémitisme, la haine anti-LGBT." November 22, 2021. https://www.sorbonne-universite.fr/university/egalite-et-inclusivite/la-mission-lutte-contre-le-racisme-lantisemitisme-la-haine-anti.

Spalińska, Aleksandra. "Why the Political Left Rejects Ukraine, and How to Change It." *The Loop*, n.d. https://theloop.ecpr.eu/why-the-political-left-rejects-ukraine-and-how-to-change-it/ (accessed August 1, 2024).

"Statue of Founder of Soviet Secret Police Unveiled in Moscow." *Guardian*, September 11, 2023. https://www.theguardian.com/world/2023/sep/11/monument-to-founder-of-soviet-secret-police-unveiled-in-moscow.

The Stephen Lawrence Inquiry. Cm 4262-I. Report of an inquiry by Sir William Macpherson of CLUNY, advised by Tom Cook, the Right Reverend Dr John Sentamu, Dr Richard Stone. Presented to Parliament by the Secretary of State for the Home Department by Command of Her Majesty, February 1999. https://assets.publishing.service.gov.uk/media/5a7c2af540f0b645ba3c7202/4262.pdf.

Stefancic, Jean, and Richard Delgado. "A Shifting Balance: Freedom of Expression and Hate-Speech." *Iowa Law Review* 78 (1992): 737–778.

Stögner, Karin. "Intersectionality and Antisemitism—a New Approach." *Fathom,* May 2020. https://fathomjournal.org/intersectionality-and-antisemitism-a-new-approach/.

Stohl, Rachel, and Elias Yousif. "The Risks of U.S. Military Assistance to Ukraine." Henry L. Stimson Center, July 13, 2022. https://www.stimson.org/2022/the-risks-of-u-s-military-assistance-to-ukraine/.

Stop the War Coalition. "About Stop the War." N.d. https://www.stopwar.org.uk/about/ (accessed August 1, 2024).

Strossen, Nadine. *HATE: Why We Should Resist It with Free Speech, Not Censorship.* New York: Oxford University Press, 2018.

SUNY (State University of New York). "Creating a More Equitable SUNY." N.d. https://www.suny.edu/diversity/ (accessed August 1, 2024).

"Teach Britain's Colonial Past as Part of the UK's Compulsory Curriculum." Petitions: UK Government and Parliament. Petition closed on December 10, 2020. https://petition.parliament.uk/petitions/324092.

Tesler, Michael. *Post-racial or Most-racial? Race and Politics in the Obama Era.* Chicago: University of Chicago Press, 2016.

Thiel, Markus, ed. *Wehrhafte Demokratie: Beiträge über die Regelungen zum Schutze der freiheitlichen demokratischen Grundordnung*. Tübingen, Germany: Mohr Siebeck, 2003.

Thomas, Hugh. *The Slave Trade: The Story of the Atlantic Slave Trade, 1440–1870*. New York: Simon & Schuster, 2013.

Thornberry, Patrick. "International Convention on the Elimination of All Forms of Racial Discrimination: The Prohibition of 'Racist Hate Speech.'" In *The United Nations and Freedom of Expression and Information*, edited by Tarlach McGonagle and Yvonne Donders, 121–144. Cambridge: Cambridge University Press, 2015.

Thorpe, Andrew. *A History of the Labour Party*. 4th ed. London: Palgrave, 2015.

Thorpe, Nick. "Hungary's New Patriotic Education Meets Resistance." BBC News, February 25, 2020. https://www.bbc.co.uk/news/world-europe-51612549.

Thumerel, Fabrice. "De Sartre à Bourdieu: La fin de 'l'intellectuel classique'?" *Études sartriennes* 8 (2001): 131–163.

Thurston, Anne F. "Victims of China's Cultural Revolution: The Invisible Wounds. Part I." *Pacific Affairs* 57 (1984–1985): 599–620.

Thurston, Anne F. "Victims of China's Cultural Revolution: The Invisible Wounds. Part II." *Pacific Affairs* 58 (1985): 5–27.

Tolin, Lisa. "These 176 Books Were Banned in Duval County, Florida." PEN America, December 6, 2022. https://pen.org/banned-books-florida/.

"20 Soviet Propaganda Posters Romanticizing Agriculture." *Russia Beyond*, May 26, 2022. https://www.rbth.com/history/335064-soviet-propaganda-posters-agriculture.

Tyson, Lois. *Critical Theory Today*. 4th ed. London: Routledge, 2023.

"Ukraine at War." Gallup, October 18, 2022. https://news.gallup.com/opinion/gallup/403280/ukraine-war-ukrainians-lives-changed.aspx.

UN (United Nations). Rome Statute of the International Criminal Court, July 17, 1998, entered into force July 1, 2002. 2187 U.N.T.S. 90.

UNCERD (United Nations Committee on the Elimination of Racial Discrimination). International Convention on the Elimination of All Forms of Racial Discrimination, concluding observations: China, September 19, 2018. CERD/C/CHN/CO/14–17.

UNCERD (United Nations Committee on the Elimination of Racial Discrimination). International Convention on the Elimination of All Forms of Racial Discrimination, concluding observations: Czech Republic, April 11, 2007. CERD/C/CZE/CO/7.

UNCERD (United Nations Committee on the Elimination of Racial Discrimination). International Convention on the Elimination of All Forms of Racial Discrimination, concluding observations: Russian Federation, June 1, 2023. CERD/C/RUS/25–26.

UNCERD (United Nations Committee on the Elimination of Racial Discrimination). International Convention on the Elimination of All Forms of Racial Discrimination, report by Czech Republic, January 11, 2006. CERD/C/CZE/7.

UNGA (United Nations General Assembly). Convention on the Prevention and Punishment of the Crime of Genocide), December 9, 1948, entered into force January 12, 1951. 78 U.N.T.S. 1021.

UNGA (United Nations General Assembly). Declaration on the Granting of Independence to Colonial Countries and Peoples. Resolution 1514 (XV), December 14, 1960.

UNGA (United Nations General Assembly). International Convention on the Elimination of All Forms of Racial Discrimination. Resolution 2106 (XX), December 21, 1965, entered into force April 1, 1969. 660 U.N.T.S. 195.

UNGA (United Nations General Assembly). International Convention on the Elimination of All Forms of Racial Discrimination, Declarations and Reservations, March 7, 1966. United Nations Treaty Series: Multilateral Treaties Deposited with the Secretary-General, chap. 4, doc. 2.

UNGA (United Nations General Assembly) International Convention on the Suppression and Punishment of the Crime of Apartheid. Resolution 3068 (XXVIII). November 30, 1973, entered into force July 18, 1976. 28 U.N. GAOR Supp. (No. 30) at 75, U.N. Doc. A/9030 (1974). 1015 U.N.T.S. 243.

UNGA (United Nations General Assembly). International Covenant on Civil and Political Rights. Resolution 2200A (XXI), December 19, 1966, entered into force March 23, 1976. 999 U.N.T.S. 171.

UNGA (United Nations General Assembly). International Covenant on Civil and Political Rights, Declarations and Reservations, December 16, 1966. United Nations Treaty Series: Multilateral Treaties Deposited with the Secretary-General, chap. 4, doc. 4.

UNGA (United Nations General Assembly). Resolution 2443, December 19, 1968 (on Israel and Palestinians).

UNGA (United Nations General Assembly). Universal Declaration of Human Rights. Resolution 217A (III), December 10, 1948. UN Doc A/810 at 71 (1948).

Unger, Roberto Mangabeira. *False Necessity: Anti-necessitarian Social Theory in the Service of Radical Democracy.* 2nd ed. London: Verso, 2002.

UNHRC (United Nations Human Rights Committee). General Comment No. 25 (57) on International Covenant on Civil and Political Rights, art. 25, Participation in Public Affairs and the Right to Vote, the Right to Participate in Public Affairs, Voting Rights, and the Right of Equal Access to Public Service. August 27, 1996, CCPR/C/21/Rev.1/Add.7.

Universidad Complutense Madrid. "Delegación del rector para la igualdad." N.d. https://www.ucm.es/unidaddeigualdad/ (accessed August 1, 2024).

Universiteit Leiden. "Diversiteit en inclusie." N.d. https://www.universiteitleiden.nl/dossiers/diversiteit (accessed August 1, 2024).

University of California. "Diversity." N.d. https://diversity.universityofcalifornia.edu/index.html (accessed August 1, 2024).

University of Oxford. "Equality, Diversity & Inclusion." N.d. https://www.oii.ox.ac.uk/people/equality-diversity-inclusion/ (accessed August 1, 2024).

UNSC (United Nations Security Council). Question Relating to the Situation in the Union of South Africa. Resolution 134, April 1, 1960.

UNSC (United Nations Security Council). The Question of South Africa. Resolution 591, November 28, 1986.

UNTBD (United Nations Treaty Body Database). Ratification Status for ICCPR—International Covenant on Civil and Political Rights. N.d. https://tbinternet.ohchr.org/_layouts/15/Treaty BodyExternal/Treaty.aspx?Treaty=CCPR&Lang=en (accessed August 1, 2024).

Van Schaik, Sam. *Tibet: A History*. New Haven, CT: Yale University Press, 2013.

Vergès, Françoise. *Un féminisme décolonial*. Paris: La Fabrique, 2019.

Vienna Declaration and Programme of Action. Adopted by the World Conference on Human Rights, Vienna, June 25, 1993. https://www.ohchr.org/en/instruments-mechanisms/instruments /vienna-declaration-and-programme-action.

"Virginia Declaration of Rights and Constitution." 1776. In *Statutes at Large: Being a Collection of All the Laws of Virginia*, edited by W. W. Hening, vol. 9, 109–119. Richmond, VA: George Cochran, 1823.

Visnji, Margaret. "McDonald's Net Worth 2023." *Revenues and Profits*, April 6, 2020 (updated). https://revenuesandprofits.com/mcdonalds-net-worth-2019/.

Vock, Ido. "Noam Chomsky: Russia Is Fighting More Humanely Than the US Did in Iraq." *New Statesman*, April 29, 2023. https://www.newstatesman.com/the-weekend-interview/2023/04 /noam-chomsky-interview-ukraine-free-actor-united-states-determines.

"'Vous voulez ma tête?' Un député LFI pose le pied sur un ballon à l'effigie d'Olivier Dussopt." *L'Obs*, February 7, 2023. https://www.nouvelobs.com/politique/20230210.OBS69409/vous -voulez-ma-tete-un-depute-lfi-pose-le-pied-sur-un-ballon-a-l-effigie-d-olivier-dussopt-tolle-dans -la-majorite.html.

Wagenknecht, Sahra, and Dietmar Bartsch. "Zum Tod von Fidel Castro." *Die Linke*, November 26, 2016. https://www.die-linke.de/start/nachrichten/detail/zum-tod-von-fidel-castro/.

Waldron, Jeremy. *The Harm in Hate Speech*. Cambridge, MA: Harvard University Press, 2012.

Walter, Franz. *Die SPD: Biographie einer Partei von Ferdinand Lassalle bis Andrea Nahles*. Rev. ed. Munich: Rowohlt, 2018.

Warren, Earl. Introduction to "Notre Dame Law School Civil Rights Lectures." Special issue, *Notre Dame Law Review* 14 (1972): 14–48.

Watson, Irene. *Aboriginal Peoples, Colonialism and International Law*. Abingdon, UK: Routledge, 2015.

Weinstein, James. "Participatory Democracy as the Central Value of American Free Speech Doctrine." *Virginia Law Review* 97, no. 3 (2011): 491–514.

Weinstein, James. "Participatory Democracy as the Central Value of American Free Speech Doctrine: A Reply." *Virginia Law Review* 97, no. 3 (2011): 633–679.

White-Spunner, Barney. *Partition: The Story of Indian Independence and the Creation of Pakistan in 1947.* London: Simon & Schuster, 2018.

Wilcock, David. "Suella Braverman Says White People Should Not Feel 'Collective Guilt' over Slavery." *Mail Online,* May 16, 2023. https://www.dailymail.co.uk/news/article-12085621/Suella -Braverman-says-white-people-not-feel-collective-guilt-slavery.html.

Willem-Alexander of the Netherlands. "Toespraak van Koning Willem-Alexander tijdens de Natio- nale Herdenking Slavernijverleden in het Oosterpark." Amsterdam, July 1, 2023. https://www .koninklijkhuis.nl/documenten/toespraken/2023/07/01/toespraak-van-koning-willem-alexander -tijdens-de-nationale-herdenking-slavernijverleden-2023.

Winstanley, Asa. "How Owen Jones Learned to Stop Worrying and Love Zionism." *Electronic Intifada,* March 21, 2022. https://electronicintifada.net/content/how-owen-jones-learned-stop -worrying-and-love-zionism/34986.

Winstanley, Asa. *Weaponising Anti-Semitism: How the Israel Lobby Brought Down Jeremy Corbyn.* London: OR, 2023.

Wollschläger, W. *Weltgeschichte in Lebensbildern für Mittelschulen.* Leipzig: Julius Baedeker, 1897.

Wolton, Thierry. *Le négationnisme de gauche.* Paris: Grasset, 2019.

Young, Iris Marion. *Responsibility for Justice.* Oxford: Oxford University Press, 2011.

"Zeitenwende bei der NATO." Bundestagsfraktion Bündnis 90/Die Grünen, June 30, 2022. https://www.gruene-bundestag.de/presse/pressemitteilungen/zeitenwende-bei-der-nato.

Zheng, Robin. "What Is My Role in Changing the System? A New Model of Responsibility for Structural Injustice." *Ethical Theory and Moral Practice* 21 (2018): 869–885.

Žižek, Slavoj. "The Axis of Denial." Project Syndicate, June 29, 2023. https://www .project-syndicate.org/commentary/left-right-populist-alliance-against-ukraine-by-slavoj-zizek -2023-06.

Žižek, Slavoj. "Barbarism with a Human Face." *London Review of Books,* May 8, 2014. https:// www.lrb.co.uk/the-paper/v36/n09/slavoj-zizek/barbarism-with-a-human-face.

Žižek, Slavoj. "The Dark Side of Neutrality." Project Syndicate, February 17, 2023. https:// www.project-syndicate.org/commentary/neutrality-functions-as-support-for-russian-aggression -by-slavoj-zizek-2023-02.

Žižek, Slavoj. "Pacifism Is the Wrong Response to the War in Ukraine." *Guardian,* June 21, 2022. https://www.theguardian.com/commentisfree/2022/jun/21/pacificsm-is-the-wrong-response -to-the-war-in-ukraine.

Žižek, Slavoj. "There Is No Conflict." *Independent,* December 5, 2019. https://www.independent .co.uk/voices/labour-jeremy-corbyn-antisemitism-zionism-israel-slavoj-zizek-a9231006.html.

Žižek, Slavoj. *Trouble in Paradise: From the End of History to the End of Capitalism.* London: Allen Lane, 2014.

Žižek, Slavoj. "Ukraine Is Palestine, Not Israel." Project Syndicate, September 14, 2022. https://www.project-syndicate.org/commentary/ukraine-like-palestine-not-israel-by-slavoj-zizek-2022-09?barrier=accesspaylog.

Žižek, Slavoj. "We Must Stop Letting Russia Define the Terms of the Ukraine Crisis." *Guardian*, May 23, 2022. https://www.theguardian.com/commentisfree/2022/may/23/we-must-stop-letting-russia-define-the-terms-of-the-ukraine-crisis.

Zygar, Mikhail. "The Man behind Putin's Warped View of History." *New York Times*, September 19, 2023. https://www.nytimes.com/2023/09/19/opinion/putin-russia-medinsky.html.

Index

Western-centrism. *See* Eurocentrism
Western identity politics, universalization of, 119–125
Western injustices, 37–41, 45, 66. *See also* Mass injustices; *specific topics*
   critical theorists ("crits") and, 41, 43, 62–63, 73–74, 76, 157, 161
   leftists and, 9, 37–39, 66, 157 (*see also* Memory politics: of the left; Radical Critique of Western Liberal Democracy)
Western liberal democracies. *See* Liberal democracy
Western world/the West, 16–18, 43, 73. *See also specific topics*
   antisemitism and, 139–141
   concept of, 43
   critical theorists ("crits") and, 52, 161
   and the East, 43, 53, 54, 122
   ethical standards, values, and, 51, 83–84
   hatred and, 121–122, 129
   leftists and, 52, 54, 73, 83, 141
   orientalism and, 53
   terminology, 52
West Germany, 42, 139
White supremacy, 62, 105–107, 112. *See also* Ku Klux Klan
Wilhelm II, 15
Williamson, Chris, 145
Winstanley, Asa, 133, 153
Wokeness, 8, 64

Xi Zinping, 26

Zeitenwende ("change of the times"), 45–46
Zionism
   antisemitism and, 132, 139, 145, 146, 153
   leftism and, 153–154
   Owen Jones and, 133, 146, 153–154
Žižek, Slavoj, 33, 75, 84–85
   antisemitism and, 150, 155
   and the left, 33, 74–75, 84–85
   life history and overview, 75

Noam Chomsky and, 74, 75, 85
"time to get serious" tweet, 84, 156
on Ukraine war, 33, 73–75
and the West, 74, 84, 85